For my parents – Jenny and Oliver –
who believe in having adventures

Contents

Prologue

Chris and I went to Asia for a lot of reasons. For the challenge. For the adventure. Because we knew that the next step was settling down and having kids, and we just needed to have one last fling, and we wanted to have it with each other.

Our original plan had been to spend a year living and working in China, but without really meaning to we ended up in China *and* Vietnam *and* Cambodia *and* Thailand *and* Malaysia.

A lot of things went right and a lot of other things went wrong. The latter were easier to spot.

This is a book about travel but it's also a book about food. The experience of food, the discovery of it, the sensuality of eating strange things in strange lands and falling in love with the taste of other people's' countries.

Chinese food held a strange allure from my youngest years. We would celebrate family occasions at Mann's Beijing – the beautifully odd, always welcoming, wood-panelled Chinese restaurant in Isleworth, where I grew up. When as a family we had a bit more money, birthdays were marked at the Four Regions in Richmond, where on a quiet December lunchtime we would sometimes see Jerry

Hall feeding her children at the next table. If Italian food tasted of home and family, Chinese food tasted of exoticism and success.

And then there was Anne, my best friend from sixth form onwards. Her dad had come to London from Hong Kong in the 1960s. After several years in London he had returned to Hong Kong, met and married her mother and together they had come to London to make a more prosperous life for themselves and their children.

Watching Anne's parents at work in their Chinese takeaway in Ealing, I observed the very particular ballet of the Chinese kitchen. Anne's baby brother Daniel would be watching television, sitting cross-legged in a dark hidey-hole under the counter by the hatch. His parents worked quickly and efficiently, moving back and forth between two great gas rings; cleaning their vast black woks, seasoning them with oil, their hands flashing over white plastic boxes of bean sprouts, mushrooms and peppers. They worked at a speed that seemed entirely unreal, never bumping into each other, never spilling: hands looping, feet moving in tiny diagonals like a waltz, woks bucking under their touch, ingredients cascading in showers from their fingers.

But it took a spell living in China to really turn me on to the possibilities and varieties of Chinese food. To start to understand the different regions and the thousand different dishes that could emerge from a single wok. And all that was before we travelled the contours of the South China Sea. Down to Vietnam and the Mekong Delta. West to the Cambodian coast and Tonle Sap Lake. On to central Thailand and then down the Malay peninsula to the island of Penang and the city of Kuala Lumpur.

This is also a book about escape. Escaping into the unknown. Escaping big decisions. And the realisation that there comes a time when you have to stop running away.

We start the way our year started: with New Year fireworks, drunken musicians and a table full of dumplings.

Chapter 1

Number One Best Champion City

The man in the tree is firing rockets up into the power lines. Along the street, women jump back as lines of firecrackers are thrown at their feet. Babies and small children crawl under Catherine wheels, untroubled by the screams and cracks and caustic, electric howls. It's like being in a war zone – except *everyone* is happy.

Hundreds of green, pink and white skyrockets are escaping from the dark lattice of streets. It's the Year of the Rat, a great year for China, hosting its first Olympic Games.

Along the *hutongs* – the network of tiny alleyways that connect the houses in the older districts of Beijing – fires are lit and banquets of dumplings, fish and soup are prepared. The sweet, salt smell of chicken stock and rice filters through courtyards that are filled with strings of lights and paper rats, and where three or four generations will gather around tables and countertops to eat. In six months, the *hutongs*, houses and courtyards will be gone –

torn down to build a subway station and chic blocks of flats for young professionals. But no one here knows that yet.

William and Mrs William – veteran owners of the Red Lantern House hostel – are hosting a party for their guests. Mrs William is taking us all in hand, teaching us to make New Year dumplings shaped like crescent moons.

She works with lightning speed kneading the balls of dough, forming them into bagel-sized rings, working and stretching them, cutting them into fat coins and then pressing them thin with a wooden rolling pin: as she turns them in circles on the table with her fine, deft fingers.

She hands her lumbering guests coins of dough with a benign smile and watches us struggle for a while. And then she takes us one by one and shows us what to do; cupping our hands with her own as together we pinch, roll and turn the dough.

The dumplings are variously filled with minced pork, onions, winter greens, cabbage and bean sprouts – flavoured with soy, garlic, ginger, Shaoxing rice wine, sesame oil and salt – then pinched shut and curled into little crescents. Some are boiled in giant pans of fiercely bubbling water; others served as potstickers, half-fried in the wok to form a crispy base before being simmered and steamed.

William plays on his *erhu* (a skinny instrument, tall like a cello, with two strings and a bow), accompanied by his friends on *pipas* (Chinese lutes). Their music reaches us in the kitchen on a choking sea of cigarette smoke that mingles with our hot, white clouds of steam to coat our noses and throats with a cloying, comforting, sticky heat that is peculiarly Chinese.

Chris is curled up on a sofa, drinking Tsingtao beer and swapping stories with Alan and Sonja who are just married. Sonja is from Spain and Alan is from Ireland. Their ridiculous, heady love for each other is obvious. They are at home in the clamour of a hostel dining room but would be equally happy alone, in silence, just grinning at each other. Alan taught Sonja English after they met travelling and Sonja's Spanish-Irish cadences are something strange and wonderful.

Young Western men slouch at the table, eyes glued to their netbooks – blogging, Skyping, lost in their own little monochrome worlds. If our hosts mind, they do not show it.

Barely visible through the cigarette smoke and dumpling steam, Mrs William's female relatives laugh loudly and talk over each other. An extremely old woman carries bowls of boiled dumplings from stove to sink to table and says nothing.

We have been in China for ten days.

From the birth of the Qin dynasty in 221 BC through to the fall of the Qing dynasty in 1911, China was an imperial power for more than two thousand years. The first Qin emperor built his reign on the back of the subjugation of the Han people, and it is the Han Chinese who still make up the largest ethnic group in China today. Under the rule of Qin Shi Huang, political opposition was crushed and absolute obedience demanded from all levels of society. Qin Shi Huang also required the burning of thousands of pages of written material, and between 213 BC and 210 BC, centuries of written history, philosophy and political thought went up in flames. Thus the birth of Imperial China was marked by the destruction of much of her recorded culture and history. This pattern of political upheaval and intellectual vandalism is echoed again and again through China's history.

The Qin dynasty undertook the original building of the Great Wall and the centralisation of government. At this point, China's capital was located near Xi'an, which is best known in the West as the burial place of the terracotta army. The first millennium saw the break up and reunification of China and the rise of Buddhism as a national religion, a belief system that arrived – along with many other aspects of foreign culture – with the opening of the Silk Road. China's capital moved many times, depending often on the origins of the current ruling family. In 1403, half a century into the reign of the Ming dynasty, Beijing – which had been a major trading location for centuries – was instituted as the new northern capital.

It was rebuilt on a grand scale as a vast citadel designed to illustrate the order of the universe. Long walls ringed the city, affording staggering panoramic views across the districts and out to the mountains beyond. The walls formed circles within circles and were mirrored by great moats. To the four points of the compass stood the principal temples: the Temple of Heaven to the south and that of Earth to the north; the Temple of the Sun in the east and the Moon in the west. In the middle of them all was the purple-hued Forbidden City, a palace complex that placed the emperors as secular gods at the very centre of it all.

When Mao Zedong came to power in 1949, he announced the birth of the People's Republic standing on the terrace of the Gate of Heavenly Peace, his back to the Forbidden City, facing south. Symbolically, he was talking to all of China and from 1950 onwards the destruction of old Beijing and the old cultural order began. The walls, which had withstood floods and numerous invading forces, were taken down stone by stone in the dead of night to avoid the protest of ordinary Beijingers. The final pieces of the walls were destroyed during the Cultural Revolution (1966–1976) when political prisoners – many of them Beijing's intellectuals – were forced to tear down these symbols of traditional Chinese culture as a step towards their re-education. Mao baulked at demolishing the Forbidden City and it was finally decided that 78 historic buildings could be allowed to stand for the sake of 'national pride'.

The temples posed a real problem to the new order. Like the Forbidden City and the Summer Palace, the temples were held in high esteem by ordinary Beijingers. But there were hundreds of them, occupying large areas of the city with their vast courtyards and many-storeyed buildings. During the economic reforms of 1958 – popularly known as the 'Great Leap Forward' – moves were afoot to turn Beijing into a centre of production and so a novel solution was proposed. Overnight, engineers and manufacturing experts moved machinery into temple buildings all over Beijing. Little by little, the temples of Beijing became factories, the monks operating in smaller and smaller parts of each temple until they finally gave up and moved out.

The central positioning of so many factories brought new problems to Beijing. Once famed for its blue skies and clean air, the city quickly became heavily polluted as the factories worked round the clock. Beijing's air quality now ranks among the worst in the world and many days a thick fug of pollution hangs just above ground level across the whole city.

The courtyard houses, or *siheyuan*, which ran along the sides of the *hutongs* were redistributed. Traditionally made up of four buildings linked by a single courtyard, the *siheyuan* had given home and shelter to a single extended family before the revolution. Now the owners were evicted and more often than not put on trial for the crime of owning property. All possessions were seized by the state or destroyed, and factory workers were allocated space in the handful of rooms, with as many as ten or twenty families sharing a home that had once housed six or eight people.

When Mao died in 1976, he was succeeded by Deng Xiaoping, under whom the Cultural Revolution was labelled a 'mistake', and some of the half-demolished gate towers were haphazardly reconstructed. Deng's reform led to the end of commune farms and allowed the ownership of private businesses. The old route of the walls became a map for the new ring roads that now circle the city. Building was virtually unregulated and the desperate need for housing meant that prefabricated neighbourhoods were constructed only to fall into ruin within a few years. These dilapidated neighbourhoods became Beijing's new slums, while the end of communal farming and the lack of a clear, long-term financial policy left the area's agricultural economy in chaos.

As Beijing continues to spread outwards, the ring roads grow in number. Planning is piecemeal and slum clearance heavy-handed. Little thought is given to the preservation of old Beijing apart from the great monuments. Building efforts now concentrate on high-rise apartment blocks, gated communities for the wealthy, malls for the new rich to shop in and endless 'British' public schools. The little darlings of the capital can be educated at Eton International School or Dulwich College Beijing, all within an easy drive of home. The financial district shines as bright as that of any other superpower and new skyscrapers appear, shimmering on the skyline, on a weekly basis.

Everything happens in the blink of an eye. All along the city streets, buildings are going up and coming down and everywhere you look unfettered workers climb the sides of half-formed towers and crouch in gaping windows, fitting plastic to steel to brick. China builds and rebuilds herself overnight.

Chris and I stockpile scraps of information against the cold like a pair of Fisher Kings. Some days we are heady with excitement, on others we feel as if we've gone on holiday by mistake.

The scale of everything in China is overwhelming. So much space; so many people; such huge cultural changes; so much loss. She is dazzling. A country of infinite riches: cultural, social, geographical. Yet as scarred as she is by the contortions and contusions of the last 60 years, she is still there, growing, breathing new life, changing. She is all her people, regardless of the prevalent ideology, and a country of so many souls feels like its own world: a universe apart and full unto itself.

Making the most of the New Year festivities, we descend into the subway system at Xizhimen to visit the temple fair at Ditan Park. It's a Saturday morning and the subway is swollen with fair-goers. Bemused by the crush and commuter etiquette, which is assertive though not actively threatening, we let three trains arrive and leave. Chris, hardened by years of trying to get onto the 7.30 a.m. Northern Line at Elephant and Castle, eventually grabs my hand and together we storm the next train. Once inside, we are torn apart by a fast-moving current of bodies and pushed to separate ends of the carriage. We smile at each other in a silly, cartoonish way over the sea of heads. We would wave but our arms are now pinned fast to our sides. In fact, it is only the intense pressure of bodies that keeps me upright as we start with a jolt and rattle into the black tunnels of Line 2.

We disembark giddily at Andingmen station accompanied by about three hundred others and file quietly up the steps. Andingmen is named after the northern gate of the city, which – somewhat ironically – was torn down to allow for the building of the station. Now there is a bridge and a gatehouse. Along the sides of the road white and grey boulders, remnants of city walls and ancient buildings, push through the earth. Sometimes in Beijing it can feel as if the old city is trying to regenerate itself, breaking through the new facades like flinty-grey spring flowers through a frost.

We are carried in a crowd of thousands up Andingmen Outer Street and towards the gates of the park. Great strings of round, red lanterns with dangling, gold tassels swing in the breeze on lines above our heads. From the brightly painted, carved wooden gates – the grand *paifang* – which shimmer with golden characters on a sea of blue and green panels, hang even larger lanterns, each bearing a single character that taken together spell out a welcome to the New Year. Red paper lanterns adorn *everything*, the trees, the stalls, the gates; they hang in great strings up and down the avenues and walkways of the park, and in cascading columns from poles and posts and street lights. At eye level a sea of heads; at sky level a sea of red globes. The effect is overwhelming and thrilling, despite the biting cold.

Before the revolution, temple fairs were a common occurrence, marking the turn of the seasons. For a while after 1949, the party instituted new festivals to celebrate the glorious leaders. When these were quietly dropped, Beijingers were left with few fixed points in the year when they could celebrate as a group. Hence the

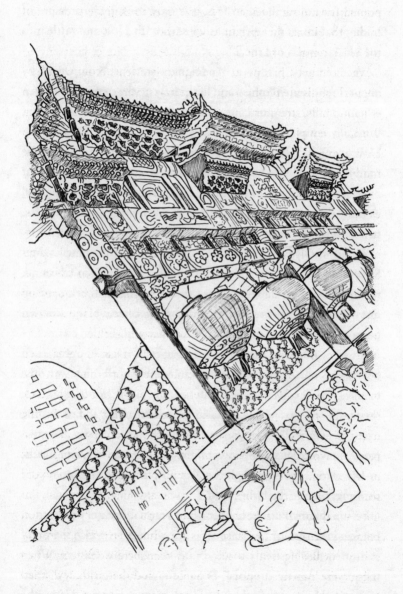

popularity and significance of New Year, and Beijingers' devotion to the few rituals that remain unchanged.

The rich smell of barbecuing lamb hits us: a slice of heat carried on the cold air. Chris perks up noticeably. Meat! Now we are in the park, stalls are popping up on the grassy verges. Many of them sell windmills, streamers, air socks printed with red and gold fish. Within a couple of minutes every child in the crowd seems to have acquired something they can hold aloft. Hundreds of tiny, rainbow-spoked windmills twirl on tall, white sticks.

Rats are everywhere. There are people dressed as giant furry rats, wearing the robes of imperial office. Rats on banners, rats on flags, strings of paper rats, plastic rats with waving paws, stuffed rats in jumpers, Olympic rats (strictly unofficial), rat couples holding hands, rat pillows for children, rat plaques with kitchen advice on them, rat tea towels, rat hats, rat scarves, mechanical rats, dancing rats, wooden 'executive' rats. I spring for a plastic plaque of two imperial-gowned rats in love. Chris stays wisely silent.

Now we are in the middle of the fair. Stalls of games are marked out by lines of 1.5-metre-tall stuffed animals: Snoopys and Garfields; massive, grinning Dumbos: and round, pink pigs. Chris tries his luck on the shooting range. He is easing himself into the spirit of the fair, trying to win me a giant Eeyore. As he shoots, a crowd of young people surrounds us, the boys offering advice and encouragement in Mandarin. There is a convivial atmosphere and the stallholder seems genuinely sorry when we don't win anything. As so often, I'm not entirely sure if we are attracting an unusual amount of attention because we're foreign. Western faces are certainly in evidence around and about Beijing, but I wouldn't say that there were many of us outside the 'American village' of Sanlitun and the business district. Not in the depths of winter at least.

'I have to eat,' and with that Chris strides down another avenue towards the smell of meat. The avenue of trees and lanterns opens out on a courtyard in which there are eight stalls, each one selling barbecued lamb. The posters above the stalls show rolling hills, snowy mountains and attractive, Disney-perfect sheep. Here and there the word *halal* is printed in English, beside it characters proclaim *qingzhen cai* (pure truth food). There are a significant number of Chinese Muslims in Beijing. Most come from the regions that border central Asia and Mongolia. And it is from Mongolian cuisine that the lamb kebab comes. Lamb skewers *(yangrou chuan'r)* are *de rigueur* at festivals and fairs, and you'll find street stalls selling them in cities across China. Small chunks of raw lamb are seasoned with some combination of cumin, garlic, chilli, fennel seed, Shaoxing rice wine, salt and Sichuan pepper (according to the cook's taste and provenance) before being barbecued on skewers and served alone or with fried onions and flatbread. They sell for as little as one yuan (less than ten pence) and Chris assures me they are fabulous. I drink a can of Fanta and eat his flatbread.

When we can no longer feel our hands or feet we head back to the subway. I can't help but look enviously at the stalls full of bright, shining ephemera while Chris mutters: 'It's all crap,' under his breath. One stallholder is demonstrating her plastic birdcages in which mechanical birds covered in brightly coloured feathers come alive at the touch of a button, swinging and spinning and tweeting happily.

Chris takes my hand. 'No,' he says firmly. I buy it anyway.

On Sunday, we take a walk down to Lake Houhai, where we've heard there's good skating.

Lake Houhai, which lies in the northern half of central Beijing, is a long, wavy strip of water bisected by a dainty bridge over which rickshaws pull wealthy foreigners. In winter Houhai freezes solid and the white space is filled with ice chairs and bicycles skidding in circles around small islands mysteriously free of frost and snow. Ask many older Beijingers and they will name skating on Houhai as their favourite memory of childhood.

I make Chris get an ice bicycle so I can see if he falls off. I take the much easier ice chair.

Ice chairs are a revelation. Wooden schoolroom-style chairs are fitted with a pair of long, sharp metal blades and propelled across the ice with a pair of ski poles. They are as much fun as they sound. Unless you're a natural-born coward, in which case you will have to take my word for the fact that they are more fun than they sound.

Chris rides off happily and incautiously on his ice bicycle and promptly falls off. He tries to get up and falls down again. I glide over to him.

'You OK?'

'Yes,' he says through gritted teeth as he falls under the bicycle again. And then, suddenly, he is off, pedalling madly like a small boy round and round the islands in circles. Something about the physical transports Chris. He becomes a child again. Three months into our relationship, we went to Lyme Regis on holiday. On a hot September day, I coaxed him into the warm shallows of Lyme Bay.

'But I haven't been in the sea since I was a child.'

'Well, didn't you like it then?'

'It was Northern Ireland. We used to stay in for 30 seconds and then slide out entirely encased in ice.'

Chris is right. I have attempted to swim off the County Antrim coast. Bracing doesn't even begin to describe it. It's like a form of penance.

'This is southern England,' I tell him. 'We're no good at suffering.'

I literally dragged Chris into the surf, and when the first wave hit him he screamed. With pleasure. Like an eight-year-old girl discovering a room full of Barbies under the stairs.

In and out of the sea he ran, throwing himself into the pounding surf with the other hysterical, sugar-charged children.

I won't lie. It was not his sexiest moment, but it did tell me something very important about Chris. Sometimes he needs to put down *The Economist* and just run into the sea.

It is Sonja and Alan, the lovebirds, who introduce us to the delights of hot-pot dining. They direct us towards a dark restaurant about two minutes away along our narrow *hutong*.

Outside, the dusty windows are covered in paper cut outs of rats in Chinese emperor costumes. Inside, tables covered in plastic gingham cloths are laid out with gas canisters underneath and bubbling iron pots on top. The pots are divided down the centre: one half contains a mild, fishy broth (which grows distinctly trouty in taste and smell as the night wears on), while the other bubbles with a dark red, shiny broth that scorches the roof of your mouth.

At the end of the restaurant a greengrocer's display – with a mirrored back, sloping shelves, lit from above and below – holds dozens of trays containing mushrooms, *pak choi*, tofu, raw fish, meat, offal and hard little cakes of rice noodles. Crates beside it are stacked five deep and laden with bottles of tepid Tsingtao.

The idea of hot-pot dining is that you select from the raw ingredients on display, then dunk it all in the stock of your choice, scoop it out with a sieve when cooked and eat it with a nutty, herby dip and lots of beer to cool your throat. For fifteen yuan (a little over one pound) you can stay as long as you like, eat as much as you like and stew yourself in lager.

The lighting inside is morgue-like, which helps to direct your attention away from all the dirt. It was one of the least salubrious places we've ever visited but something innate is drawn to the warmth and homeliness of its interior. The smell and steam and fiery heat of the food warms us up after freezing-cold days in the snow of Beijing and the restaurant is full to rattling every night with whole families enjoying an evening meal, which takes three hours or more to eat. Every table is another living room, a private space for families to laugh, argue and chatter. I think it's this that beguiles us – this sense of welcome, this non-exclusive club where anyone can eat and drink and chat until closing time.

In China, eating spaces are expansively welcoming. No one will shoo you away. On the contrary, restaurant owners want you to feel at home, to relax and to enjoy time with your companion. This is a culture that, above all else, understands the value of a shared meal.

One evening as we eat, an uncommon hush descends over the assembled diners and we turn in our chairs to find the most enormous rat we've ever seen attempting to pass through the restaurant unnoticed. The vast beast (roughly the size of a rabbit and nearly as plump) is taking a shortcut from a hole in the back wall to the kitchen. Like something out of a Bugs Bunny cartoon, the animal is shuffling quietly along as he eyeballs the floor – because if he can't see us, we definitely can't see him. As one, we watch the giant rodent tiptoe, tiptoe, tiptoe past, and even the cook in his whites stands aside to let the animal pass.

There's a famous piece of graffiti in Paris: *If you speak two languages, you're bilingual. If you speak one, you're English.* I'd give you the quote in French, but...

Not being able to speak a language is one thing. Not being able to read it, quite another. The first few weeks in Beijing we are, literally, illiterate. I walk along the shopping streets in our district and stare at the signs on the shops. Every window is dark glass and the signs tell me... that I cannot read Chinese.

I'm too scared to enter shops. I can't order in restaurants. I have no idea where the toilets are.

Ah yes, toilets. My friend Anne had already warned me about the 'no paper in the bowl' business. Beijing's sewage systems simply can't cope with paper waste, so all toilet paper must go in a little basket beside the toilet. Take a moment and think about it.

Now stop thinking about it. You'll be happier that way.

The 'no paper' rule is only the beginning. In most public toilets there are no toilets. There are cubicles, with a door if you're lucky, and a ceramic floor with a hole. A *small* hole. The toilet makers have helpfully made indentations to show you where to place your feet as you squat. Here's a tip: if you're not built like a Chinese person, don't assume the markings will work for you.

After the first month I invest in rubber shoes. After six months I could represent Team GB in the Olympic peeing-in-a-hole competition. Sadly, as with so much else in China, peeing in a hole is one of those hard-won skills that only impress other foreigners.

At night I lie on my belly on our bed with a Mandarin-English dictionary and a stack of exercise books and carefully copy out Chinese characters or *hanzi*. Within two weeks I have learnt the main subway stops, the sign for an emergency exit and the numbers 1–20. Anything more complex simply baffles me.

I am fine with the very simple:

> *Da* means big. The *hanzi* 大 shows a mountain with a
> line across it – the mountain reaches above the clouds. It
> is big.
> *An*, which carries the idea of good and safe, shows the
> symbol for a cross-legged woman under a simple roof. 安
> A home with a woman in it is good and safe.

But having learned the forty or fifty simplest characters I fail to move out of Dr Seuss territory. The *hanzi* do not tell you how to pronounce the words, and if you do know how to pronounce the words you must also know which one of the four tones you should use to convey your meaning. Spoken and written Chinese are learned almost independently of each other – and neither of them is easy.

We buy food we can point to. We stalk the streets until rush hour and wait for the little hatches to open in the sides of restaurants. From the steamy openings, cooks in overalls sell *jiaozi* (dumplings) and bowls of thick, sticky, white congee – an unholy cross between soup and porridge. *Baozi*, steamed white buns, are light as air. I buy them filled with water spinach and nettle – delicious dipped in sharp, black Chinese vinegar. They are pretty much the only thing I can safely buy.

Did I mention I'm a vegetarian? No? Well, it's a sore point right about now.

Are you a vegetarian? Want some advice? Don't go to China.

No. Wait. Scrub that. Do go to China. Just don't try to be a vegetarian while you're there. Everything is cooked in chicken or pork stock anyway. And d'you know what? It's delicious. I mean, ethics aside and all – it is staggeringly tasty. I digress.

Where were we? Oh, yes. Pointing at food.

Since the rat-infested hot-pot restaurant only opens 4 hours a day we have to find other places to eat.

One night we walk 4 kilometres up a main road because we've heard that there's a proper Chinese restaurant somewhere along there with a menu in English. By the time we arrive it is very late and we are very cold. The restaurant has been taken over by one table on which a group of businessmen are playing something similar to poker. They talk loudly and drunkenly and tell dirty jokes.

You can sense a dirty joke being told wherever you are in the world even if you don't know the language. The voice drops low and a slight growl enters the voice, like a tiger loping on stage and lying down to purr.

The restaurant is filled from shoulder to ceiling with cigar and cigarette smoke. Some of the players have up to three smokes on the go at any one time. The ashtrays on the table look like Jake and Dinos Chapman sculptures – Jenga towers of filter tips. We sit at a small table in the corner and with numb hands we open the English menu that reads as follows:

Cow innard Sechuan sauce fry
Tripe willow herb boil
Kidney hot broth boil
Kidney sauce willow herb boil
Liver eel hot soop
Chicken tripe Sechuan hot sauce boil
Sweetcorn soop

We order two bowls of 'Sweetcorn soop' and Chris chances the 'Cow innard Sechuan sauce fry'. As a rule he will always order the thing that looks closest to beef.

After 10 minutes the field of smoke has given me a raging headache. We both stare at the grubby landscape art. It shows willow pattern images of high hills and tiny garden temples. Puffs of cloud drift over the heads of dainty cattle.

When the soup arrives it is bland, tasteless and full of glutinous lumps. Chris pronounces his dish as 'hot and soft'. A crackle of cursing punctuates the babble. An argument has broken out among the businessmen. Ash flies as everyone gesticulates at once. We stare transfixed into our bowls of 'soop'. More shouting. A pause. Several people start laughing. Then everyone is laughing. The men retake their seats. One of them is sulking.

We eat the complimentary bowls of rice and drink the suspicious-looking, grey-brown jasmine tea. When we can feel our hands again, we walk back out into the cold.

It's after 10.00 p.m. and the streets of Beijing are deserted. We trudge for a while in silence. I'm tired and cold and very hungry. After a kilometre or so I sink onto the step of a dark restaurant and rest my head against a giant fibreglass rat. Chris waits for me, but I don't get up.

Finally, he helps me to my feet, takes off his right glove, and my left, and puts my hand in the pocket of his coat, where he holds it tight. I rest my head on his shoulder and we walk on – awkwardly – like two children misremembering a three-legged race.

One day in the common room at the hostel, Chris catches wind of a noodle and rice stand in a lean-to 5 minutes and a couple of *hutongs* away. He goes to investigate and finds a queue of weary workers waiting to pay three yuan for a hefty pot of savoury heaven. The next evening I go with him and we watch the man perform – two gaping Brits in puffer jackets.

As each person orders, the young man throws a dash of oil into his wok, waits for the heat to rise before adding a handful of fresh noodles or rice, which sizzle and jump about the centre. He swirls a ladleful of thick brown stock over the jumping contents, tosses them to cook the sauce, then pushes them to one side. Reaching into little containers (the cut off bottom halves of plastic Pepsi bottles) for spices, salt and dried chilli, he sprinkles each into the empty half of the wok and lets them cook for less than 10 seconds, as the waiting nose is hit by an explosion of hot, sweet scent. Then, with a toss of the wok the whole is joined together and a pair of chopsticks flick it deftly into a fat, cardboard cup to be garnished with a pinch of sour, sweet pickled vegetables. In just two movements, he has deftly cleaned his wok and is smiling at the next customer.

The whole process takes a couple of minutes and the result is succulent and fresh – full of *umami* and layered with complex flavours. For the uninitiated, *umami* is a Japanese word describing an intense savoury taste found in foods that are rich in L-glutamate and ribonucleotides. In Italian cookery ripe tomatoes and cheese are key ingredients because they give dishes an *umami* flavour. In British cookery, *umami*-rich ingredients include eggs, chicken, cod, meat and fish stock, potatoes and carrots. In Asian cooking, *umami* flavours are added using soy sauce, shiitake mushrooms, fish, shrimp paste, Chinese cabbage, meat stock and the famous additive MSG. For many children *umami* is the first taste they learned to savour because it's found in breast milk.

Street food has been a distinctive part of the culture in China for at least a thousand years. In fact, many aspects of Chinese cuisine were laid down by the time of the Song Dynasty (960–1279) and have only altered slightly in the intervening millennium. Recipes from the tenth and eleventh centuries show Chinese cooks flavouring dishes with ginger, soy sauce, salt, pepper and sesame oil, all flavourings vital to modern Chinese cookery.

In the regional capitals, pancakes, fried meat, fruit and soup were sold along the sides of the main roads just as they are today. Noodle shops were commonplace and important focal points for meeting with friends or colleagues during the day. And 'night food markets' offering hot and cold meals stayed open throughout the hours of darkness, even in the depths of winter.

Food festivals were prevalent throughout China and large cities boasted a huge diversity of restaurants. Restaurants and dishes were already being classified by region, offering southern, northern or Sichuanese cookery. Southern and Sichuanese food was more heavily spiced than dishes originating in the north and travelling officials often found the local food unpalatable, so restaurants catering for homesick and hungry civil servants could be found in capital cities.

There were few parts of life that food did not touch. It was central to the wheels of commerce (trade in foodstuffs driving much economic growth throughout the regions) and shared meals were central to business and political negotiations. Mealtimes were extended by Western standards and provided focal points in the day for workers and families alike. An obsession with food was expected, normal: a sign that you valued your culture and the enjoyments that life had to offer.

In 1082 the poet, painter, civil servant and general polymath Su Shi, finding himself banished to a remote region, wrote 'Poem on Cold Food Festival':

> Rain falls constantly, remaking the Yangtse River in trails across the glass
> Snatched up in a swirl of water, my little hut is a fishing boat shaken by an angry sea
> Cold greens lie in my broke-down kitchen; dripping weeds lie pointless in the hearth
> A letter from home brings a sharp reminder: Cold Food Festival is here again
> All those fine men I've known live in splendour; and I am lost in rain and reeds and dirt
> I long to weep at the way I have been treated; but my tired soul has nothing left to shed.
> Su Shi
> Library of Chinese Classics, *Selected Poems of Su Shi Xu Yuanchong* (2008–12, Hunan Publishing House)

Read the literature of any country and you will quickly realise that the relationship between food and memory is one that crosses all boundaries. There is not a person alive who has not built associations around the taste of certain foods. From our earliest moments we associate the giving of food with the giving of love and comfort. The gift of food is an almost primal act of love.

My mother's family – with its French and Jewish influences – belonged to a tradition of preparing food as an act of love. Though my maternal grandmother Irène was largely uninterested in food, my mother grew up in a house with her extended family and Eliza – her grandmother and my great grandmother – poured her knowledge and experience into the food she made. My paternal grandmother, meanwhile, excelled at cooking in the English tradition; for decades of her life Cicely cooked a two-course lunch every single day, creating a seemingly endless stream of perfect roast dinners, steamed puddings, pies and tarts.

I grew up in a house where both my parents cooked and I learned from a young age, experimenting with new cuisines from the age of twelve or thirteen. My mother was an avid reader of food history and we talked often about the relationship between food and experience, food and politics, food and gender. In my early years we existed on a modest family income and I learned, like billions of others, the secret of how to make food taste good using only cheap ingredients. The popular dishes of the world are dominated not by expensive ingredients – meat, fish, seafood, truffles, saffron – but by the principles of peasant cuisine.

Italian dishes of pasta and tomatoes use the cheapest of ingredients in bulk, augmented with the smallest amounts of luxury products: black pepper and Parmesan cheese. British cuisine is dominated by soups because they make small portions of vegetables and meat go further. Pies use cheap flour, onions and potatoes to bulk out cuts of beef or liver. Rich, thickened sauces became popular because they disguised inexpensive cuts of meat and filled the stomach. In China and Vietnam, bowls of noodles and soup are garnished with tiny slivers of meat, allowing people to fill up for the equivalent of a few pence per bowl. In the cities, where the middle classes eat and socialise, steamed white rice is never eaten until the end of the meal. The most expensive dishes are eaten first, the dishes of meat, fish and vegetables. Only at the end of the meal will those still hungry fill themselves with bowls of broth or bowls of rice: the food of the poor.

Across Asia many people are virtually vegetarian, not through choice or religion, but because meat is too expensive for them to afford. Even those who farm livestock will tend to sell their pigs and chickens rather than eat them. For many of the rural poor, meat is a once-a-year treat: normally reserved for New Year celebrations. The irony for the vegetarian traveller in Asia is that as a relatively wealthy visitor to restaurants in the towns and cities, everything comes cooked in and garnished with meat. With the exception of Buddhist restaurants, chefs in China wouldn't dream of putting vegetarian food on their menus. Vegetarian food is peasant food and no one wants to dream of poverty in a land struggling to escape its grip.

It is Valentine's Day and Chris has disappeared.

I sit and make him a card, carefully copying storks and flowers from a picture on our wall and using my dictionary to fashion a funny message in pictograms, which he will not, of course, be able to read.

I cannot face going out this afternoon. I am fighting my way through my third bad cold of the month.

Darkness falls and Chris returns very flushed.

'Get dressed. I'm going to buy noodles. We have to leave in 30 minutes.'

I stick my head under the shower, rub my head dry and dress. Chris returns with hot, round containers of noodles, pickles and rice and pushes one into my hand.

'We'll have to eat on the way.'

He puts chopsticks in my pocket and we pull on gloves. Outside the snow is 15 centimetres deep and the February night is dry and clear. You can even see one or two stars – a rarity in Beijing.

We walk through the crush of commuters on De Sheng Men Nei Da Jie – a vast street running north to south through our corner of Beijing. Chris hurries us along and we try and fail to eat as we walk. At last he finds a strange, new street and then another and another and we twist and turn until we are almost on the shores of Houhai.

'I think we're still in time,' he says as he bundles me through a door and into the intense warmth of a pitch-black little bar. We stand blinking in the darkness until we make out the line of the bar itself and then an entrance into another part of the room where a projection screen is flickering into life. Chris settles me in a large velvet armchair and goes to order cocktails. The projector is spluttering and stopping and the American in the room above is swearing to himself in English and Mandarin.

When Chris returns I am nearly asleep in the sauna-like heat of the little room.

'Happy Valentine's,' he says and curls his arm into mine.

Sleepless in Seattle is being sharply yanked into focus.

I squint at Chris in the darkness, 'You hate this film.'

'Yes, but you love it.'

The film reel races on before us.

I secretly suspect Chris of replaying Northern Ireland 1–England 0 in his head, but I am extremely happy and very much in love.

We have to find a flat. The hostel is lovely but not cheap enough for the next few months. We must find somewhere to live, register with the police and see if we can scrape up any work.

We have been enjoying the luxury of living in central Beijing, but our future lies in the outskirts, beyond the ring roads, in the ever-blossoming suburbs with their high-rise cities and giant superstores. This is new, urban, middle-class China. Glistening estates and subway commutes and Nike trainers from the sports shop on the corner. There's something of 1950s Americana about it all. A new world of consumerism. Everyone wanting the same chic little home, the same mod cons, the same designer goods.

We decide to save money and live a long way out. Beyond the fourth ring road but before the blossoming fifth. We make an appointment to view a flat in Guo Mei Di Yi Cheng – Number One Best Champion City. It's on the thirty-first floor of a tower block with a spectacular view over Beijing. It has two bedrooms. We joke about how this will come in useful when we argue.

It is a beautiful flat, with fake parquet floors and a vast open plan living room. Two wet rooms, one for him and one for her. Two sweet little bedrooms and a tiny kitchen with a top-of-the-range cold-water washing machine and toaster oven.

The landlady informs me that she will need it back by August for the Olympics. She has been in touch with the British women's hockey team and is hoping to accommodate all their parents here. She says this without humour. My eyes slide around the apartment – all 6 by 8 metres – and I nod politely.

Chris and I gaze down from the giant windows onto the concrete gardens below and marvel at the huge mosaic of Van Gogh's *Starry Night* set into the central amphitheatre. It's very beautiful and very... not Chinese.

Very little about Number One Best Champion City is Chinese, or at least not at first glance. There are ten tower blocks, each one 31 storeys high. Each storey offers four two-bedroom flats, and the flats look out over the other blocks, the tiny flower beds, the mosaic Van Gogh and the shopping street. There is one restaurant, one pizza delivery firm, two beauty salons and Wing's grocery store. Eventually, it will be home to upwards of 10,000 people, most of them young families with their single child and sometimes their parents or aunts in tow. These are white-collar workers, riding the subway to their jobs in retail, business and teaching.

Between the fourth ring road and the fifth, urban Beijing flows into the dusty countryside; wealth living cheek by jowl with poverty. Across the road from our great metal gates, untreated sewage flows thickly beside a ramshackle slum district, constructed from old prefabs and a lot of blue tarpaulin. The district has been tagged for demolition, and within a few months it will be bulldozed. In the meantime it is a source of light, noise and street food in the evenings, as children race along its mud roads paved with sodden cardboard, and working men queue to buy noodles and bags of pineapple. The stench from the river of sewage is so horrendous that we learn to take a deep breath before we step off the bus. After a while we stop looking in at the district gates. The poverty and the knowledge of its imminent destruction are too depressing. Like everyone else around us, we just edit it out.

Wing's grocery store is the common meeting place for everyone on our estate. There's only one supermarket nearby and few residents own a car. Wing's offers copious amounts of fresh veg, shelf upon shelf of cleaning products and freezers full of ice cream. There are large glass tanks with lobsters, crabs, fish and crayfish – whose eyes I try to avoid as I enter.

In the evening, as the packed blue buses pull up outside Number One Best Champion City and deposit commuters, the estate comes alive with street sellers pushing carts. There are popcorn carts and dried meat carts; carts full of Mandarin pulp fiction, romance novels with orange and pink covers, cookbooks translated into English for stunned-eyed long-haul workers fresh off the plane. Every few nights a man appears at the south gate with a little cart of prospective pets: kittens, lovebirds, goldfish and sometimes a puppy or two.

Dogs seem to be favourite in Number One Best Champion City. Mostly toy breeds: tiny terriers and teeny pugs. There are strict rules about the size of dog you can own in Beijing. Each household is allowed just one dog up to 35 centimetres in height. The strict regulation of dog ownership is another hangover of the revolution.

Dogs were extremely popular pets before 1949, but after the People's victory all the dogs in Beijing were rounded up and killed. Numerous theories abound as to the reason. Some said that they disturbed the work of secret policemen, arriving to arrest people in the dead of night. Others claimed that Mao had once been foiled in a youthful attempt to escape prison by a barking dog.

Certainly, pet ownership was seen as bourgeois and eventually all household pets were removed. The destruction of so many beloved pets was met with horror on the part of residents and when rules were finally relaxed, Beijingers re-embraced their love of everything canine.

The Wings are the most notable dog-lovers on the estate. Owners of the almighty grocery store, they also have two ground floor flats next to each other and (uniquely among us estate dwellers) a private garden with picnic tables and umbrellas. They own two large English sheepdogs and a sizeable pig – all of which live in their garden.

The pig is a very lovely creature with kind, tired eyes and an extremely long snout. Preschoolers on their way to kindergarten stop to kiss and talk to the pig over the Wings' garden gate. Some days I walk past a line of more than a dozen toddlers waiting to take a turn.

The Wings don't live as others do. They don't have to. They are winners in the new China. In a community where no one drives, they own a beautiful, shiny black Jeep, and on sunny weekends they pack the children and the dogs (but not the pig) into this and go to the country.

Mrs Wing, supreme matriarch of the Wing dynasty and manager of the grocery store, is extremely kind to me and Chris regarding our horrendous Mandarin. 'Ni hao,' we chorus at her every day and she grins back at us, undoubtedly repressing laughter.

When flustered I fall back on a kind of nervous English politeness rendered in to faulty Mandarin. *Xie xie ni* (the politest form of thank you) and *dui bu qi* (sorry) fall from my lips repeatedly throughout our transactions. I feel helplessly, unstoppably, gallumphingly English – like Eeyore in a dress.

Which is not to suggest that Chris and I have a monopoly on politeness. Our Chinese neighbours are unfailingly courteous. They simply manage to do it in fewer words with less stuttering, blushing and dropping of things.

Even the guards, in their military-style uniforms, present at every gate, are polite in their requests for a date. More than once one of them has broken away from his friends and come up to me as I walk alone to and from Wing's. In very careful English and with slightly downcast eyes I am asked if I would like to go on a date. I explain I have a boyfriend and politely refuse. The guard then thanks me nicely, apologises for bothering me and goes back to his post. The last time I was asked out like this I was 12 and so was he.

I regale Chris with the story over dinner.

'Isn't that wonderful?' I say.

Chris's jaw sets itself at a funny angle and he nods enthusiastically, 'Wonderful,' he says. 'Terrific.'

We hear about a good Mandarin course at a local college and get the details. We can only afford for one of us to attend. Chris speaks four languages – some of them better than others – and has a degree in Russian from Oxford. I dropped out of GCSE French because the third-year oral exam made me cry. The decision kind of makes itself.

While Chris goes to class, I sit in our apartment and try to write.

Writing is my trade. It's what I've done – obsessively – since I was ten years old. Our storeroom back home is stuffed with half-finished novels and plays and books and books of notes. I've written for media companies and websites, magazines and charities, Radio 4 and BBC 7 (now Radio 4 Extra). I've never suffered from writer's block, always been slightly baffled by the concept.

How can you not write? I thought everybody wrote. Not for a living, you understand. Just for the pure joy of it. I'm dyslexic, for God's sake, and I still write for pleasure.

Everyone should write. All the time. Whenever they can. Just for themselves, or for the people they love, or for everyone.

For me, for many writers, published and unpublished, schooled and unschooled, writing is like breathing. It keeps us going. It's our work and our hobby and our therapy and our friend.

But three years ago something happened and all the words went away. And they didn't come back.

I have been in relationships before and I have never written a word. My prolific, if under-published, output has been a side-effect of many years of single life. When I'm single, I can write. When I'm in love, I can't.

So when Chris and I, after almost exactly a decade of not quite getting it together, finally took the plunge it was like turning off a tap. No more poems, no more plays, no more half-started, half-finished novels.

Don't get me wrong now. I'm happy. Really happy. But I can't write.

In a spirit of openness, honesty and blind panic I have decided not to tell Chris any of this.

Chris has heard from an Internet start-up looking for unpaid Western interns. They are working on a language website to teach business visitors Mandarin and they want someone to help with idiom and example. Chris is delighted and relieved. He has somewhere to go during the day, something to do.

I spend my 'blank page' days reading rail timetables and guidebooks, planning weekends visits to Xi'an and Shanghai, Guilin and Yangshuo, Hanoi and Hue.

We start to find a pattern for life in China.

In the morning Chris takes the bus to college and then the subway to work. I stare at the blank page for half a day, give up and go to Wing's to shop, stopping to talk to the pig on the way. Some days I take the bus to the subway and head into town to wander the streets or browse the latest releases in the basement of the Beijing Books Centre. Then it's home before rush hour to cook potstickers and eat together, on the sofa, watching *The West Wing* on DVD.

As evening draws on, Chris sits by the great windows looking over Beijing and does his language homework with a couple of beers. I retire to our bedroom and spend another two hours staring at a blank page, before giving up and cleaning the bathrooms again.

On Saturdays we climb through the wire fences at the back of the estate and walk down the train tracks to Lotus – the Chinese version of Tesco. The tracks are busy with people taking their dogs for a walk or dragging their weekly shop – there is no road yet to take us to the hypermarket. The verges are full of life, rats run beneath the metal rails, grass and weeds break the earth. Beijing soil is thawing all around us.

Huo guo
Hot pot

This recipe looks much more complicated than it is. You are basically making a broth, then cooking meat, fish, vegetables and noodles in it at the table. Other than assembling a dipping sauce and chopping vegetables, the cook has very little to do. I have given the ingredients for two dipping sauces, but you can make whichever one you prefer. The cooling sauce works well with the spicy broth and the spicy sauce with the light broth.

You can use various things to keep your stock simmering at the table. Small camping stoves, electric woks, slow cookers and fondue sets are all possible receptacles for your stock. We like to have two stocks on the go when we eat, so I have given you recipes for a light and a spiced broth. If you only have the equipment to keep one stock simmering at the table, you'll have to choose. Or start your meal with the light stock and then refill with the spiced stock halfway through. You can buy special hot pot equipment in Chinese supermarkets, speciality cook shops or through Hancock Woks (www.londonwok.com).

Serves 6
Preparation and kitchen cooking time: 2 hours

Light broth:
Half a daikon (also known as mooli or Chinese radish),
peeled and sliced into rounds
2 carrots, halved
1 onion, quartered

Half a Chinese cabbage, chopped roughly

6 dried Chinese mushrooms

2 tbsp sesame oil

Salt and pepper to season

Sichuan spiced broth:

3 tbsp groundnut oil

2 cloves garlic, crushed

10 Sichuan peppercorns

2–6 dried and/or fresh chillies, seeds removed if preferred

Half your finished quantity of light broth

1 tsp chilli oil

Cooling dipping sauce:

3 tbsp Chinese sesame paste or smooth peanut butter or

Chinese satay sauce

1 egg yolk

1 tbsp dark soy sauce

2 tbsp light soy sauce

3 cloves garlic, minced (optional)

Half a handful bean sprouts, well washed

Half a bunch fresh coriander, roughly chopped

Spicy dipping sauce: 5 tbsp sesame oil

3 tbsp rice wine vinegar

3 tbsp light soy sauce

1 fresh red chilli, top removed and finely chopped

5-cm piece of ginger, peeled and chopped

4 cloves garlic, peeled and crushed

Half a bunch of fresh coriander, roughly chopped

Raw ingredients for cooking at the table:

Choose items you like from the following, but try to have at least one type of protein, one kind of noodle, one type of mushroom and three kinds of vegetable. A shared *huo guo* will typically offer 10–20 items for guests to enjoy.

Fish: small, filleted chunks of fresh salmon and firm white fish; shelled and cleaned scallops, mussels, prawns and crab.

Meat: thinly sliced beef, lamb, pork, offal, ham or pancetta.

Tofu: chunks of firm tofu or fried tofu pieces.

Noodles: dried ho fun rice noodles (similar in width to tagliatelle) and/or rice vermicelli.

Mushrooms: fresh shiitake and straw mushrooms, and/or *enoki*, broken up.

Chinese vegetables: *bok choi* and Chinese cabbage, roughly chopped; lotus root, peeled and thinly sliced; Chinese radish, peeled and cut into matchsticks; and bean sprouts.

Western vegetables: spinach and lettuce, and carrots and peppers cut into matchsticks.

To make the light broth, bring 2.5 litres of water to the boil in a saucepan. Add the vegetables and simmer, covered, for at least an hour. At the end of the cooking time add sesame oil (especially important if you are serving a vegetarian *huo guo* as it won't have any fat imparted from the meat) and season with salt and pepper. Remove the vegetables from the broth.

To make the Sichuan spiced broth, pour groundnut oil into a medium-sized saucepan and add the garlic, peppercorns and chillies. Gently fry for 1 minute until aromatic. Add half the quantity of light broth and bring to a simmer. Add chilli oil and simmer for 5–15 minutes. (The longer the spiced broth is cooked, the fiercer it will become and you don't want to start the meal with a palate-burning level of heat.)

To make the cooling dipping sauce put sesame paste or your alternative into a bowl. Add a little water to slacken the paste, and then beat in the egg yolk. Season to taste with soy sauce and garlic if desired. Divide the dipping sauce into individual bowls for each diner. Garnish with whole or halved bean sprouts and coriander.

To make the spicy dipping sauce mix all the ingredients together and put in individual bowls.

Lay *huo guo* cooking ingredients onto plates: one each for each kind of meat and fish; one each for green vegetables, other vegetables and mushrooms; one for noodles; and one for tofu.

Set up your stock receptacle of choice on the table and lay plates of ingredients around the gas rings. Set the stock to simmer as you finish your preparations.

Each diner will need two sets of chopsticks (one to handle the raw ingredients, the other for eating), a bowl for cooked food, and bowls of dipping sauces and noodles. Asian supermarkets sell small, wire sieves that are perfect for scooping out the cooked ingredients. If you cannot find these, slotted spoons work at a push.

Open a few bottles of Tsingtao or make a pot of green tea and settle in for a long, leisurely meal.

Add ingredients in whatever order you wish. Noodles take the longest to cook, but meat, fish, vegetables and tofu cook quite quickly. Each diner uses chopsticks to place an ingredient or two into the broth, and when cooked to perfection use the same chopsticks or a wire sieve to fish the food out into his or her bowl. The other chopsticks are used to dip the food into dipping sauces and for eating.

If the level of the broth gets low, top up with reserved stock or hot water from the kettle. Towards the end of the meal you may want to throw bean sprouts and coriander into the broth to make it more of a soup. This can then be drunk at the end of the meal. Any unused broth can be frozen.

Other dipping sauces:

Some people find the sesame or peanut dipping sauce a little sweet and fatty for their tastes. Alternative dipping sauces can be made using soy sauce on its own or mixed in equal quantities with sesame oil. XO sauce, which you can buy in Asian supermarkets, is popular in southern China and in Hong Kong. In Fujian Province and Taiwan, *huo guo* is often served with *sha cha (shacha)* sauce, a kind of barbecue sauce that mixes tangy fish with garlic and chillies. You can find this is in Asian supermarkets, often sold under the Bull's Head brand.

Chapter 2

Parrots are the Things with Feathers

I walk the streets of Beijing, through the snow and the mud and the spatterings of hail. Despite my linguistic limitations I feel at home here because it's a city and I know cities. Like London it is vast, grimy and anonymous, full of surprising neighbourhoods and hidden worlds. As a cash-strapped teenager in London I would sometimes buy a one-day bus pass and get on buses heading for hours into parts of London I didn't know. I would watch my fellow passengers and listen to their conversations. As the bus paused in traffic I would spy on fragments of encounters glimpsed through the window. Having reached a bus terminal in some distant part of the capital I would try to retrace the route we'd taken, often walking for hours along main roads where nothing seemed familiar, until at last I was back again in central London and in a world I knew. And on these walks I'd write. I'd write scenes and chapters, poems and essays in my head. The action of walking seemed to make the words come; it was a kind of meditation.

Here in Beijing I find myself doing the same. The giant ring roads, which encircle the city, are served by plush double-deckers that trace their great trajectory over and over through the day. After Chris has gone to work I pack a little bag and take the bus or subway until I get to one of the ring roads, and then I wait. I have become a connoisseur of bus stop etiquette. The semblance of a queue disintegrates as soon as a bus pulls into view. At evening rush hour male factory workers will literally climb onto the shoulders of the crowd attempting to board the bus. Then on hands and knees they will crawl above our heads, from shoulder to shoulder, until they drop down in front of us and bag the best seats. At first I find this deeply unnerving and occasionally painful. But in time, as with all things, I get used to it and take a kind of strange fascination in looking up and watching their faces as they crawl over the top of us. They are six-year-old boys scaling an orchard wall, their faces full of glee and mischief. I see more in their faces, too. Other faces which lie in layers like masks over that of the six-year-old boy. I see faces lined with exhaustion. I see the mad twinkle of anger and frustration in their eyes. I see the alcohol that lends a manic air to their scrabbling arms and legs.

I ride the buses, sometimes making a full circle of the city that can take two hours or more. And then I get off in some strange and far-flung part and start to walk. I watch the pancake sellers sitting together behind their hatch, clutching steaming cups of black tea in tall Tupperware containers and talking quietly and seriously among themselves. I see the teenage girls in their miniskirts, neon-bright sweatshirts, tartan coats and high fringed boots. They move in packs – little riots of colour and pattern, a tiny phone clutched in the hand of every girl – from fashion emporium to market stall, stroking and cooing over the T-shirts and dresses. They squeal and giggle and gasp, immersed in some intense act of bonding. I walk the hypermarkets and watch the old men in their pyjamas and donkey jackets shopping for frozen squid and packets of tea. Lost in a silent world, they meet no one's eye, make no conversation. I walk the quiet *hutongs*, deserted in frozen winter. Now and then a tiny child wrapped in an unwieldy padded coat will open a screen door and totter out onto the step to see the snow. The children are the only ones who look at me. In this giant city with a million stories playing out I am virtually invisible, despite my height, my colouring and my strangeness.

But the children see me. They stare and point, giggle and clap their hands as if I were a giant mechanical doll. Five- and six-year-olds will shout 'Hello' to me, their only word of English. Mothers will stop me on the street and ask me to speak a few words of English to their son or daughter. One day in an elevator a chicly dressed lady encourages her eight-year-old granddaughter to speak to me. The girl stares at me for nearly a minute and then – her eyes very wide – she says: 'But you are a princess!'

I laugh, both flattered and embarrassed and her grandmother laughs with me.

'I'm really not.'

The girl continues to stare at my white skin and long brown hair. 'You are Belle. From *Beauty and the Beast*. Your hair is so pretty.'

'Thank you,' I tell her, not really knowing how to respond. I don't think I have ever in my life been mistaken for a Disney princess. 'I think you are very beautiful,' I tell her, because she is and I'm not sure what else to say.

The doors of the lift open and her grandmother gets out. The girl hesitates, looking from me to her grandmother, and then she darts towards me and wraps me in a brief, tight, ecstatic hug.

I watch the Beijingers come and go and I wait for the words to come. But mesmerised as I am, nothing forms itself inside my head. Perhaps I am too far outside this world. I don't know how these stories start. I cannot hear their voices because I cannot speak their language.

Beijing can sometimes seem very... muddy. Grey and brown, filled with cars, buses and smog. The sky feels as if it hangs a centimetre above your head and when you do glimpse a view beyond the city, more often than not the desert looks bleak and cold and barren.

In search of a place to escape we come up with four options: Lake Houhai, Chaoyang Park, the Temple of Heaven and the Summer Palace. Of these four, the Summer Palace is perhaps the most beautiful. For us, it becomes a kind of retreat.

The Summer Palace is arguably famed more for its gardens than for its buildings. The grounds stretch over two square kilometres. Walking the edges of the gigantic Kunming Lake, you can spot temples, pagodas, pavilions, statues and *paifang* artfully nestled into the landscape. The principal buildings are gathered together on the sides of Longevity Hill, which rises above the park to the north of the water. The lakes to the south and west are criss-crossed by tiny strips of land – narrow isthmuses – punctuated by ornamental bridges and walkways. It is all incredibly uncluttered and beautiful. Despite being ransacked in 1860 (by the English and the French) and in the Boxer Rebellion of 1900 (yes, that was us again), the buildings have been repaired and restored and the whole complex is carefully looked after and much visited.

The first time we came here, it was like stepping into Narnia. Just three weeks earlier Kunming Lake had been frozen solid, the two-tiered Marble Boat of the royal family trapped perfectly – perhaps immutably – inside a blanket of ice. And while 'always winter and never Christmas' may not have been culturally apt, nonetheless that is what I thought of, as I walked the still paths and frozen terraces. The greens, reds and blues of the pavilion roofs seemed unreal against the natural palate of white snow and brown earth. The smog could not reach us this far north-west and the sky above us was perfectly blue and cloudless. The snow muffled everything and though the park was filled that first day with tourists and Beijingers, we were captivated by the silence. The trees didn't move. The very ripples of the lake were frozen in place. Here and there, ducks perched carefully on the powdery surface as if expecting the properties of water to return at any moment. It was like walking inside a snow globe.

When we visit for a second time one afternoon in March, the grass has just re-emerged from under a blanket of frost and snow. We cross the deep blue and green of Kunming Lake on the cream-coloured stone of the Seventeen Arch Bridge and descend onto a little island, dense with trees. A conical-roofed, red-columned pavilion sits in a clearing and we take a moment to sit and stare and listen to the birds twitter in the tops of the trees. At the water's edge we step down onto the muddy beach and walk the edges of the island where the waterfowl bob and build their nests. It is hard to believe we are still in Beijing. Everything seems so calm, bright and verdant.

The wind is blowing from the north today, bringing cold air down from the mountains and after a couple of hours by the lake (Chris reading, me sketching) we decide to retreat and find something to eat.

Just south of Xinjian Gate is a vegetarian eatery in the Buddhist tradition where monks come from the temples of the Summer Palace to dine and read books and stare out of the windows. There are disappointingly few monks at 5.00 p.m. on a cold Friday, but there's plenty of fake meat and jugs of tea. In Buddhist restaurants almost everything is presented as some form of fake meat to make meat eaters feel more at home. To this end there is vegetarian 'fish' cooked in bamboo leaf and fake 'pork' patties with spice and Beijing 'duck'. It's all very beautifully executed and well spiced but I confess to finding fake meat a bit unappetising, and a bit weird. Honestly, if I wanted to eat meat, I'd eat meat. I like my vegetarian food to be unapologetically vegetarian. And I find myself rolling my eyes at the thought of pandering to the delicate sensibilities of meat eaters. So, there you go. I'm obviously too selfish to be a Buddhist.

After dinner we walk back down the long road to the university district and on to D-22, which we have been meaning to visit for weeks. D-22 is one of Beijing's best clubs and music venues. In the darkness we walk past the entrance several times. It doesn't exactly shout its existence to the world. It's just a doorway in the shadow of a line of shops. Stepping into the warm we find a narrow bar area leading down to tables and then a dance floor and a little stage. Above is a balcony and room for a few extra punters.

We order a couple of bottles of Tsingtao and take in the spit and sawdust glamour: it's very dark and very warm and very basic. It feels like it's been here 60 years. It's also very Western, with its bare brick walls, little framed photos and wooden tables. Nothing feels Chinese about the place. We could be in Brixton or Camden or Shepherd's Bush. Except if we were, some chain would have bought this place out and made it part of a 'music and food concept' or started charging five pounds for a beer.

It's a bit of a free-for-all around the communal tables and within minutes we have been drawn into a drinking game with a group of band members and friends up from Taiwan for the weekend. The game involves some kind of incomprehensible counting and is conducted entirely in Mandarin. Since my Mandarin is horrendous I can get the numbers but not the rules. Every time it's my turn the game grinds to a terrible halt as my attempts to second-guess the sequence fail again and again. Every single person around the table then tries to explain the game to me, which means that I'm getting seven sets of rules fired at me in Mandarin. Above the cacophony of voices I can't work out what the hell Chris is trying to tell me. So, the game continues with eight of us playing a drinking game and one of us playing Mornington Crescent.

As the evening draws on, and we get drunker, the bands start to come on stage. They're a funny mix – electronica, pop, punk, ska and rock. At one point Chris disappears completely and after searching the bar for a while I finally spot a lone blond head, just in front of the stage bobbing in and out of view. In a rush of ska-inspired happiness he is pogoing relentlessly to the sounds of Early Bus.

I decide Chris is having a running-into-the-waves moment, so give up on him and order a Diet Coke in an effort to sober up for the long journey home. Chris fails to reappear at the end of Early Bus's set, but next on are Hedgehog – a bit of a legend on the Beijing music scene. They're a bit punk, a bit indie, a bit rock, and they're really good live. I find myself standing, Diet Coke in hand, in the middle of a crowd of slightly wild, screaming Chinese yoof, mesmerised by the band's performance.

You know that thing with live music where it just makes you smile. I mean really smile. Not just with your everyday 'thank you for my noodle pot' smile but with a smile which erupts from somewhere within you with the fierceness of a hot, bright sun.

The analytic parts of you drop away, past and future disappear and you experience this visceral pleasure being in the present moment.

It doesn't work the same with theatre (and I have sat through a lot of good theatre). I don't get it from opera. Sure, there is a pleasure in the stimulation, in the thought, in the finesse. There is emotion, surprise and revelation that can reverberate for days or weeks or even years. But theatre and opera pleasure you with technique, with intellectual brilliance. Gigs don't reverberate in the same way. They don't unfold themselves at night in your head. You don't suddenly 'get' that bit at the end of the first act. What you remember is the pure unfettered sense of living. Not living in isolation but living at the same point in time as these vibrating others, on the dance floor, on the stage, swirling all around you, the same notes pulsing through each of you at once.

Chris finally makes his way back to me. I try to tell him how much I'm liking Hedgehog, but he's all excited because on the way to the loo he bumped into the lead singer of Early Bus and told him how much he'd loved the set. They'd then proceeded to talk for 20 minutes. In Mandarin. Chris is pretty sure that most of it made sense. Though he can't tell me much about it. He waves a flyer at me, on which the singer has written down the details of their next few dates. He then stumbles off, flushed and happy, to order a last Tsingtao.

It takes us 3 hours and a lot of night buses to get home. Beijing in the dark is rather romantic. With most of the traffic removed and the smog invisible, it's just a big, empty, shiny city through which warmly drunk young people can totter hand in hand.

We run out of buses before the third ring road and decide to walk the rest of the way. We wander the edges of A-roads and motorways, almost silent at three in the morning. Past Chaoyang Park and under the flyovers, through to the great grassy banks of another motorway, past skyscrapers, building sites, office blocks and the foundations of new malls and gated communities. Past an intriguingly Western-looking bar called the Goose and Duck that we'd be tempted to enter if it were still open.

The blocks become more disorganised, soon everything is a building site and we are nearly home. We climb over strips of rubble, over half-demolished walls, over the dead lumps of gateposts. And then the world becomes flat again beneath our feet and the neon signs stretch above our heads advertising Beijing's very own Number One Best Champion City. Back past the sentries who nod us through. Back past the grocery store. Back past the sleeping pig and into the marble hall. We ride the elevator to our own little home made for two. It is four in the morning but we're not ready to go to bed. We lie on the sofas, talking disjointedly, laughing, until the apartment starts to get light and we make coffee and toast and fall asleep.

We're getting addicted to shopping at Panjiayuan – the Dirt Market. Tourists are bussed in their hundreds to the Pearl Market with its shiny carapace and its carefully-aligned rows of stalls selling *thousands* of necklaces, silk scarves and shoes. But we prefer the grime and character of Panjiayuan – a bit mucky, a bit dodgy, a bit like Camden Lock in the 1980s but with fewer Marley T-shirts.

Panjiayuan is set out in a large courtyard in a suburb of Beijing. It isn't on the subway so you have to walk or take a bus. We walk the first time, past the concrete middle schools and long roads of apartment blocks with balconies and tall steps to the doors. It's all a bit reminiscent of the suburbs of a large American city. Past the brightly coloured exercise equipment for elderly (and not so elderly) Beijingers. Past the police station, outside the gates of which relatives queue waiting to see if they can visit those being held. All over Beijing, evidence of the beneficence of the state sits side by side with evidence of its overwhelming control. The unforgiving blankness of the police station, the fear and exhaustion on the faces of the brothers, sisters and mothers waiting silently beside the newly equipped exercise yard and the nicely maintained school. The realities of modern-day China are not always easy to reconcile.

We come to the gates of Panjiayuan. Under a red paper arch, we join the throngs of people milling past the stalls. Nearly half the stalls are simply sheets on the ground, the wares carefully set out on them in lines and towers and mesmeric, curving, tesselated shapes. The remainder of the stalls sit under a metal and canvas roof, open to the elements on all sides. Families of the stallholders huddle around small heaters, perching on plastic chairs and folding wooden stools, watching babies and toddlers who are wrapped in five or six layers of clothing that is tied firmly around their waists like little bundles of bedding. Here and there you see a stallholder slumped forwards onto their arms, asleep. The Dirt Market opens at 5.30 a.m. and stays open most of the day. Tea is constantly on the go, as are noodle pots. Little camp stoves burn behind the counter tops and everyone seems to be eating or drinking to keep out the cold.

We are overwhelmed by choice. It's almost impossible for the eye to settle, as we try to take in the puppets and the painted chests; the teapots and the carved jade and the delicate, wooden scenes of courtly life; the Mao memorabilia, the strings of brightly coloured beads; the vases, the Buddhas and the woven rugs; the bone hairslides, the pre-war coffee tins and the antique shawls; the masks and the paintbrushes and the red-and-black chess sets. There are multiples of everything. Fifty stone lions in a row; 18 gleaming blood-red chests stacked into a single tower; more than a hundred rainbow-coloured string puppets, carefully hung in straight lines, each one with a different face, a different robe, a different hat.

Around the edge of the market are tiny shops specialising in semi-precious stones. The little doorways glow orange and white and blue-green, and peering through the windows is like looking into Neptune's treasure house. Strings of carved coral, jade and freshwater pearl cover – literally cover – the walls and the tiny counters. The effect is at once beautiful and painful to the eyes.

A bird flies past our heads. Spotless tables wait, unlaid, beneath a network of green and brown wooden arbours. Plastic vines, heavy in places with fruit and flower, twist their way up from the floor and form a canopy above the tables set about the edge. The sound of birds is piped into all corners of the room and tiny parrots (Were they really parrots? Did I imagine that?) fly about and cry to each other from the corners of the room. This is Yunteng Shifu – a wonderfully surreal, well-kept secret of a restaurant, hidden in the bowels of a Soviet-era provincial government office, on an otherwise unremarkable elbow of the second ring road.

We have walked some kilometres to be here, circling the lush estates beneath the flyover, where half-dressed chauffeurs clean the family car and where no trace is found of mother, father, daughter, son or illicit offspring number two (wealthy Chinese families sometimes exercising their options differently to the common herd). Where are they all, we wonder? It's a Saturday afternoon and the chic apartments have no private gardens as far as we can see; only communal lawns flood-heavy from the giant sprinklers planted at 10-metre intervals.

On arrival at the government office we are enveloped in a world of coffee-coloured marble. Official buildings in Beijing exist somewhere between the starkness of 1960s and 1970s communism (great empty planes in all directions) and the shiny, monied gloss of 1980s and 1990s new wealth (lush creams, browns and taupe; marble every day and twice on Sundays).

We creep shyly through the corridors towards the sound of plates being stacked and unstacked. A waitress in a spotless apron hurries past.

'*Qingwen. Qingwen. Canting zai nali?*' we call after her. Excuse me. Excuse me. Where is the restaurant?

There is the almost imperceptible flash of suppressed amusement and then the young woman leads us down one coffee-coloured corridor and then another and finally down a little green walkway into a vined and fruited Shangri-la.

Well-trained by now, we request a menu with pictures and pick through the hundreds of choices until we find the famous delicacies we've read up on: *rubing* (goat's cheese) served with a ground pepper dip (the kind you'd eat with boiled quail's eggs), *xuanwei ham* (a kind of Chinese prosciutto), *liangbanbohe* (tart mint salad with strips of tofu), *boluo fan* (pineapple rice) and *guoqiao mixian* (crossing the bridge noodles).

Yunnan lies to the south of Sichuan province and borders Vietnam, Laos, Myanmar and Tibet. With mountains in the north and rainforests in the south, the diversity of the region's people and climate has combined to create a cuisine which, while less unified and refined than that of, say, Sichuan, is exciting and surprising, melding spice and sweetness with sharp and subtle flavours from cheese and cured meat.

Boluo fan and *guoqiao mixian* are two great examples of the strange mix of flavours and styles found in Yunnanese cookery. Boluo fan is sweet and sticky and imparts a feeling of childish decadence to any meal. A whole pineapple is served to the table stuffed with berry-black, steamed short rice. Lifting the spiky lid you uncover a pirate's chest of delight. Candied peel curls in little crystalline caterpillars on top of the glistening, sugary delight. It is food designed to please the four-year-old in you. It delights me. It appals Chris.

Tsingtao is ordered and imbibed while we eat our *rubing*, *liangbanbohe* and *xuanwei ham*. The absence of music, the absence of other diners, the absence of noise hushes us and we do not dare to speak above a whisper.

Guoqiao mixian offers quite another story to the sweet and sharp beginnings. Delicate, romantic, complex, decadent food that nonetheless manages to feel clean and refreshing in your mouth as only Asian broth can, it comes to the table replete with its very own mythology.

In the era of the Qing dynasty (1644–1911) the exams to enter the Chinese civil service were famously the hardest in the world. A scholar named Yang, living in Yunnan's Mengzi County, spent his days studying in a little summerhouse on an island in a lake in the grounds of his family home. Each day his wife would bring him soup and noodles and slivers of meat to eat, but by the time she had walked from the main house and crossed the bridge to the island the noodles and the meat were cold. One day, upon arriving with a bowl of chicken noodle soup she found that the noodles were still hot and deduced that the melted fat from the chicken had helped retain the heat. Experimenting further, she found that by adding oil to her soup she produced a film on top that helped to seal in the heat. Having passed the imperial exam, Yang told everyone he knew about his wife's discovery and *guoqiao mixian* was born.

Guoqiao mixian, as it is eaten today, consists of a large bowl of extremely hot soup with a film of oil floating on the top. It arrives at the table with a host of other dishes from which you choose your ingredients: fat rice noodles; strips of meat and uncooked quail's eggs; chopped cabbage, bean sprouts, spring onions, mushrooms and slivers of chilli. Once you have chosen, your waitress will add these to the soup – first meat, then eggs, then vegetables, and finally noodles – and leave them to cook under the layer of oil. The effect is subtle and savoury and full of interesting textures. It's a dish that comforts rather than shouts in your face.

This is where I write something lyrical about crossing bridges and marriage and commitment. I even wondered whether to call this book 'Crossing the Bridge'. But you could call any book 'Crossing the Bridge'. What else do we write about? Change. Making leaps. That's every story ever told.

To digress for a minute – and this is a digressionary sort of a chapter – I have long been obsessed by the Stephen King novel *Needful Things*. OK, I haven't actually read the Stephen King novel *Needful Things*. (I've sat through the start of the movie several times but it's always on in the middle of the night and as much as I love Max von Sydow, it's not his finest hour.) No, the reason that it obsesses me is that title. That absolutely perfect, universally apt title. *Needful Things*. Every book ever written could be re-named *Needful Things*. 'Crossing the Bridge' and *Needful Things* – tell you everything and nothing at all.

Now, wait. What am I avoiding? Oh yes. I think we have arrived at *mea culpa*.

You see, I made Chris buy a house. A big, expensive house. A big, expensive, run-down house. And just this very morning we got a call from the house agents to say that for a second month running they have received no rent and the tenant won't let them in the door.

So, we are sitting in Yunteng Shifu with the mellifluous broth and the gently poached eggs and we are not talking about this. We are very definitely not talking about this at all.

Eight months previously, I had found myself in the bathrooms of the Prince Charles cinema in London with Jane. Jane of Paul and Jane, as they're known around our way. We have just sat through the shockingly ludicrous *The Departed* and Jane is washing her hands and out of nowhere she says, 'I need one of three things from Paul: marriage, a child or a cat. I don't care which one it is but I need one of them. D'you know what I mean?'

By the way, Paul, if you're reading this – it was another Jane. We know a lot of Paul and Janes and we went to see *The Departed* with all of them. Your Jane definitely never said anything like that and it is entirely coincidental that she now has at least one of the above.

But I do know what Jane means. I really do. Because I have told Chris, I have told him that before I will go off with him on this wild, carefree adventure, we have to buy a house together.

Chris has another plan all worked out. We will sell his flat in Brixton, invest the money and sail off into the Chinese yonder. If we should happen to get pregnant we'll just rent somewhere on our return. In Chris's plan there is no talk about marriage because 'we're not quite there yet'.

Or rather, some of us are there and some of us aren't.

This is turning into a matryoshka set of stories. So, apologies, but to understand the house conversation you have to understand the marriage conversation.

The marriage conversation went something like this:

> INT. LIVING ROOM. NIGHT. CHRIS AND MIRANDA'S
> RENTED FLAT. BACK FROM A NIGHT OUT IN
> LONDON THEY SIT ON THE SOFA AND DISCUSS THE
> CHILDREN THEY PLAN TO HAVE TOGETHER.

Chris: I have this image of the whole family around the table. There's noise and chaos and there are lots of children and we're all eating together and talking and laughing.

Miranda: You know... obviously I don't think we have to be married to have children. I don't think it matters like that. But would you like... maybe... Do you think... We don't have to have a big wedding or anything. Maybe just family and witnesses. But we could... you know... What do you think about getting married?

Chris: [Staring at the cornicing.] Errrr...

Miranda: I mean, not right now. But I just wondered. Is that part of the plan?

Chris: [Staring at his beer, then at the fireplace.] There's no rush, is there?

Miranda: Of course not.

Chris: It's very late.

Miranda: It is. But we were talking about the children and I just wondered...

Chris: [Furrowing brows and still not looking at Miranda.] Is this really a conversation we need to have right now?

Miranda: Well. No. Another time. I just thought I'd put it out there.

Chris: I'm going to find my pyjamas.

CHRIS EXITS SWIFTLY TO THE BEDROOM. FADE OUT.

In some ways I was telling the truth. I don't think you need to be married to have children. Children are a much bigger commitment than marriage. And unless you believe in God or gods, a wedding is just a big, expensive party from which you take away a piece of paper and a slightly different tax arrangement.

But, the knubbly, gristly truth is that before you hand over the rest of your baby-making years to someone, you kind of need to know that they're planning to stick around.

In Jane's formulation: I needed marriage or a house. Some weighty piece of paper needed to be signed before I really and truly believed that he wouldn't blench horribly at the first positive pregnancy test and leave on an open-ended mission to 'find his pyjamas'.

So I gave Chris an ultimatum. We had to buy a house together before we left the country. A house we could come back to. A house we could have a baby in. A house that would yoke us firmly together and make it extremely inconvenient if we changed our minds and decided to 'find our pyjamas' elsewhere.

And so, as we sit beneath the parrots and contemplate the empty bowls before us, we don't speak about the very expensive house. Or the tenant barricaded inside it. Or what I made Chris do to prove he was committed. We just sit there, having our moment of bleaknesss.

Emily Dickinson famously wrote: 'Hope is the thing with feathers.' But right now, Emily, from where I'm sitting, the only thing with feathers also has a beak.

We don't talk. We don't move. We just order another round of Tsingtao.

I'm mentioning Tsingtao a lot, but there's a reason for that. While we are living in China, Tsingtao is the third wheel in our unlicensed marriage.

I spend a lot of awkward/tired/bored/hopeless moments reading the label on the back of the bottle, which is how I come to be familiar with the history of Tsingtao. Don't worry. It's actually pretty good. And pleasingly weird.

The south-east Asian practice of boiling water – rather than brewing it to make it safe to drink as was common in Europe – is generally cited as the reason that many people of south-east-Asian descent do not metabolise alcohol very efficiently. Thus, drinking culture in China today revolves around beverages relatively low in units of alcohol. In this market Tsingtao reigns supreme. It's a light beer, refreshing, very slightly dry and not especially intoxicating. It tastes much like a German Pilsner and with good reason.

In the nineteenth century, the era of Imperial rule in China was faltering. The British had already taken advantage of the 1839–1842 Opium War to take control of Hong Kong and the Japanese were vying for possession of various parts of the eastern seaboard. Germany decided that Shandong, a region on the east coast, south-east of Beijing, offered good agricultural and mining opportunities, so in November 1897 when two German Catholic priests were murdered by a Chinese gang, the Big Sword Society, in south-west Shandong, Germany seized the opportunity to invade. China put up only a token resistance and in March 1898, she signed a treaty granting Germany a 99-year lease over the Kiaochow Bay area.

The German newcomers wasted little time building a complete German town on the banks of the Yellow Sea, replete with opulent thoroughfares, churches, hospitals, the best modern sanitation, a telephone system, and a hunting castle built high on the rocks above the bay for the governor's residence. Within a few years, a complex educational system had been established, with primary and secondary schools, vocational colleges and a university. Within a decade this once-sleepy fishing village had the highest level of student enrolment in the whole of China. Estimates of the time suggest that over a 16-year period Germany was spending up to three million dollars per year on infrastructure and development (equivalent to an annual spend of forty-four and a half million pounds in 2014). Qingdao (Green Island) quickly became a favourite holiday destination for Western expats living in Vietnam and Japan – a little taste of Europe in the heart of Asia. It even boasted its own brewery, which opened in 1903, producing a beer called Germania.

And why was Germany spending so much money on a port thousands of kilometres from Europe? Well, with the building of the Trans-Siberian Railway, they saw a real possibility of linking Berlin with Qingdao and potentially annexing a large part of China.

Both the Japanese and the British, jealous of Qingdao's overnight success and its considerable natural assets, were keen to seize the area for themselves. The outbreak of World War One gave them the opportunity they'd been waiting for. In August 1914, Japan declared war on Germany; Japan and Britain immediately moved to lay siege to Qingdao. The German garrison of 5,000 resisted for three months, no mean feat given that the Japanese force alone numbered more than 60,000. Finally, on 14 November, the German governor surrendered and the Japanese took control of the town.

Facing bankruptcy, the holding company sold the brewery to Dai-Nippon and Germania beer was rechristened Rising Sun. Under Japanese rule, expansion and development continued, with all houses continuing to be built in the German style to maintain the city's unique appeal to tourists. In 1922, the Japanese surrendered and retreated from China and the brewery was bought out by the Tsui family, who rechristened the beer Tsingtao, though this private ownership only lasted until the birth of the communist regime.

Germania/Rising Sun/Tsingtao established itself early on as a quality beer, brewed as it was according to the German Reinsheitgebot of 1516 – the Purity Law that restricted ingredients in beer to water, hops and barley – and using water from the nearby Laoshan springs. The beer is clean in taste: excessively clean to some Western palates. After China took over production, rice was added to the list of ingredients. When rice is turned into alcohol it imparts almost no taste or colour. As such it is looked down on in the West but it suits Asian preferences, where drinkers tend to prefer their beverages light, fragrant and floral.

Qingdao today is a highly popular city of three million, often voted the most liveable in China. Much of the German architecture remains among Chinese- and Korean-style additions. And as for the legacy of Germany's adventures in the Orient – China now produces more beer than any other country in the world.

The phone rings. It is Cody, an Australian student we met in the hostel. 'I've been signed up by an agency and they're short of women, can I give them your number?'

'Sure,' I say.

It is only when I put the phone down that I realise I didn't ask him what kind of agency.

Wei rings me four days later.

'Hi. Is that Miranda?'

'Yes. Sorry. Who's this?'

'This is Wei. Would you like to do a washing powder commercial? It's a one-day shoot. They're looking for a typical English housewife. Cody says you are typical English housewife.'

To say I bristle at this would be an understatement. I am not a typical English housewife. For one, I have a prestigious if insecure writing career. For two, I am delightfully eccentric and not the slightest bit typical. And for three, I cannot be a housewife because Chris will not bloody marry me.

'It's just a poster campaign,' Wei continues. 'For the subway. You just have to hold the box and smile.'

Wei can sense the silence flooding down the phone.

'The money is twelve thousand yuan.'

Oh bugger. That's quite a lot of money, but a strong gut instinct is telling me that this will come back to haunt me.

'I'm sorry, Wei. I can't. I don't suppose there's anything else?'

'Er, OK. We need someone to do a language tape. For schools. A few hours of audio. You interested?'

Earning money for helping to educate the good children of China? My inner schoolgirl shoots up her hand – 'Me, sir! Me, sir! Do we get house points?'

'OK. Cool. I email you address. Sunday OK?'

'Sure.'

We are on a bus heading for Xiangshan (literally: fragrant mountain). Communication is not at its finest. We are waiting to hear back from the house agents who are going to try to enter our house today and find out what's going on. I am attempting to block out thoughts of all our hard work ripped to shreds. Of our possessions taken and sold. Of our furniture destroyed.

Chris is still reading his by now papyrus-like copy of *The Economist* and I am hooked up to my iPod, listening to a series on knitting and trigonometry. I unhook myself briefly and try to tell Chris about this fascinating inter-relationship. He listens for nearly 10 seconds before pointing over my shoulder.

'That's it.'

I turn and watch as the bus climbs through the suburban, tree-lined streets and the mountain grows higher and higher and blacker and blacker above us.

As we get closer, the black mass starts to reveal itself. There are rivers of rock and tree, walls and walkways, each of them cascading down the side of the mountain in hazy, fragmentary lines.

We are poured from the bus with the Saturday-afternoon family outings and the teenage lovers, and set out. From the first few walkways, we spy a jutting platform with a building on it and confidently predict that we will reach the top within 30 minutes. The sky grumbles and flocks of dark pigeons move in flurries from one tree-filled promontory to the next.

We walk in single file, trudging damply through a fine spray of water that seems to arrive from the ground rather than the sky. We pause at a bench to rearrange the things we're carrying and a collar of squirrels shoots from the tangle of branches above our heads, bouncing like pinballs down the zigzag paths we've just climbed.

The Chinese families have evaporated, as if into the mist. Are they above us or below us? The paths are lost behind rocky outcrops and lines of trees. The Chinese equivalent of a park ranger shoots past us in sodden uniform as the first lightning bolt flashes above us, disappearing into the haze below.

I look thoughtfully at the night-black sky as another lightning bolt crackles and sparkles less than a kilometre away.

'Is this the best place to be in a storm?'

Chris doesn't answer. He is re-tying his shoelaces. Chris's shoelaces are only tied for about five per cent of any day. It drives me mad. I follow him around trying not to sound like his mother: 'But don't you think you should do them up?'

Mysteriously, the only time he chooses to tie them is when I want him to look me in the eye and answer my bloody question. It occurs to me now that perhaps this is why he never does his shoelaces up. I consider asking him this but he seems pretty annoyed already and it's not the kind of conversation that's going to end well.

I settle for, 'Did you check the bus times home?'

Chris stares at the platform above us and, accessing his startling ability to wrongly estimate any journey time, says: 'It's only another ten minutes.' Chris starts walking away.

I stand there for a while, getting wetter and wetter, struck by the very tangible lack of wisdom 'we' are displaying. But Chris is gone, somewhere above me, and I must follow or abandon him altogether.

A mere 40 minutes later we approach the platform. After a desultory 20 minutes of trudging separately, I have caught up with Chris and we have climbed in an almost companionable fashion with the promise of the summit binding us temporarily together. Steep steps take us from the path to the edge of the platform. A painted building waits for us promising the possibility of tea and chocolate. We twist and turn and Chris starts to bubble with cheer as the lightning sails past us in the night-black afternoon. As we mount the platform, we look as one at the empty painted building – a glorified bus shelter with broken wooden seats – and then, behind us, at the absolutely gigantic mountain that has materialised above us.

We are not at the top. We are not even near the top. This platform is barely on speaking terms with the upper reaches. But there above us, disappearing into the clouds, is another peak and another painted shelter promising tea and chocolate and beef strips and packets of cake.

The rain is falling in sheets and it's too late to think about staying dry. We keep climbing.

The next hour is spent in silent trudge. We are alone: all the Chinese day-trippers apparently knowing a magic, step-free way off the mountain. I want to talk to Chris. I want to talk to him about how awful everything is back home, but he is radiating his own private wall and I can't. Somehow, on this wet, miserable mountain I am struck by how lonely I've become.

In a very different story the storm would pass and as we made the top the sun would have broken through the clouds and a rainbow would snake its way through a last fine mist of rain to point the way back home.

What in fact happens is that the lightning and thunder finally pass to reveal a day thick with dark grey cloud and an oppressive, humid, constant mist of rain. It transpires that there is not a magic path off the mountain, known only to the Chinese. Instead we reach the summit to find a tea and chocolate shop heaving with all the people from our bus who just walked much faster than we did.

We buy cups of tea and, ignoring the rain that falls gently, we stand on top of the great stones and stare down the mountainside. On a clear day there is probably a fantastic view from here. Today there are rocks and clouds.

Chris poses for a photo under a lone tree, clouds floating beneath him like sullen magic carpets.

The following day I am in the studio with Cody and the Chinese producers from the language course company.

'John's bag is blue and his new shoes are red.'

'My cousin will visit us this summer and we shall go the beach.'

We take a break halfway through for cups of tea and pastries and I decide to impress the producers with Chris and my feat of mountain climbing.

'Coffee, please. Still a bit knackered today. Climbed the fragrant mountain yesterday.'

They turn slowly and look at the talking puppet.

'You went to Xiangshan?' The sound editor does not seem overly impressed.

'Yes. We got all the way up. To the top. All the way. In a thunderstorm...' I am losing impetus under the weight of their collective boredom.

'You went to Xiangshan and climbed up the hill?'

'The mountain.' I correct gently. I am the English expert here, after all.

'It's a hill,' the sound editor says, frostily. 'Old people and children climb it for exercise.' She and the producer exchange a look.

Cody giggles into his script and I shrink and shrink and shrink until I am so very, very small that I am able to exit the recording booth under the door.

Our visas require us to exit and re-enter the country after three months, in early April. Tibet is currently a 'sensitive destination' and Mongolia has started to make things difficult for anyone who isn't a Chinese or US citizen. One of our friends went to North Korea for the weekend to renew his, but he says the high point was coming back and being able to say 'I went to North Korea for the weekend.'

Vietnam is 2,995 kilometres, two days and one train ride away. And we need to escape. We need a holiday from this holiday. We book our berths.

Suhongdou
Crispy red beans with mint

This side dish adds piquancy and texture to any meal. It's deceptively simple and very moreish. The recipe below is pretty authentic, but you can add spices or black pepper to the mix if you want to raise the level of heat. Suhongdou can be served as a main course with rice or noodles.

Serves 2–4 as a side dish
Preparation and cooking time: 15 minutes

40 g fresh mint
400 g precooked beans (red beans can be bought from
some Asian grocery stores,
alternatively kidney beans can be used)
40 g plain flour
4 tbsp groundnut oil
1–2 tsp salt

Roughly chop your mint. Drain the beans. While still wet, toss the beans in the flour until coated. (You may find it easier to do this in small batches.) Transfer the beans to another bowl and discard the remaining flour – you don't want any additional flour making it into the wok.

Heat the groundnut oil in a wok and add the floured beans. Fry for 4 minutes, tossing occasionally. Scoop out the beans with a slotted spoon, then fry the mint in the remaining oil for 30 seconds. Put the beans back into the wok with the mint. Season with the salt. Toss together and serve.

Boluo fan
Pineapple rice

White glutinous rice is fine for this recipe, though Yunnan restaurants tend to serve it with black rice, which tastes slightly nutty and gives the dish a dramatic appearance. It's really a kind of sweet but you can serve it alongside other dishes for a large family meal.

Serves 4–6
Preparation and cooking time: 4 hours (minimum)

200 g glutinous rice (black or white)
75 g rock sugar or palm sugar or white sugar
100 g pine nuts
1 ripe pineapple (it should have a slight give when squeezed)
50 g dried longans or sultanas

Rinse the rice and soak it for a minimum of 2 hours or even overnight. The rice needs to be relatively soft and crumbly. When you are ready to cook the rice, drain it.

If using rock sugar, bash it into small pieces. Toast the pine nuts in a dry pan until they are just turning golden.

To prepare the pineapple first wash the outside then cut off most of the top leaves.

You now need to cut your pineapple in half. Look at your steamer and judge what shape will best fit. Restaurants serve a whole pineapple with just the top removed, but few home steamers are big enough for this. You will need to cut it in half lengthwise or widthwise. Now cut most of the flesh out of the pineapple. Do this over a bowl so you can save the juice.

Retain the pineapple shells and cut the flesh into small cubes. To the flesh and juice add the rice, sugar, pine nuts and longans or sultanas. If using rock sugar, let the mixture stand for 30 minutes to allow the sugar to dissolve slightly.

If using a steamer that sits in a pan, put a pan of water on to boil.

Spoon the mixture into the pineapple halves. Put the pineapple halves into the steamer or steamer basket, propping them upright if necessary. Now steam them for 30–60 minutes. Black rice will need longer than white. Taste a few grains to judge when they're cooked through. Don't worry if you leave them to cook for longer, the dish won't suffer, but remember to check water levels and top up when necessary.

Take the pineapple rice in its pineapple shells to the table and let everyone serve themselves.

Chapter 3

Only One of Us is Paddling

Two weeks before our visa is due to expire we roll up at Beijing (West) railway station to board the sleeper train from Beijing to Hanoi. We have booked two first-class (soft class) berths in a shared compartment and are reliably informed that we are in for a premier travel experience. Images of the Orient Express and other classy trains of the 1930s and 1940s – gleaned entirely from Poirot adaptations and old films – flash in my mind. There is a dining car where we'll eat and I imagine sitting there in white fur like Cybil Shepherd in *The Lady Vanishes* – Chris making an excellent if noticeably goy Elliot Gould.

The train from Beijing to Hanoi takes 40 hours over the course of three days. You leave on the evening of day one, travel through the whole of day two, cross the border in the early hours of day three, arriving in Hanoi in time for an imagined breakfast of thick Vietnamese coffee sweetened with condensed milk and pieces of crusty baguette smeared with butter.

DAY ONE

We board the train and make our way to our cabin, which is charming: white linen on the beds, a tablecloth and a vase of flowers on the little breakfast table and thick, creamy jacquard curtains at the window. The upper berths are folded up against the walls and the lower bunks kept down for seating. We stow our stuff under the lower berths and practise lowering the beds. We figure out that whoever goes on top will have to stand on the lower berth and then use a one-rung ladder to vault into bed. I don't really fancy being trampled in the night so I decide to go on top. The train is filling up with Chinese families and businessmen but our cabin remains just ours.

We sit on the lower berths and watch people pass by through the open door. It's all terribly exciting in its novelty.

A little before 5.00 p.m. the train draws out and we rush through the Beijing suburbs, the industrial parks, factory-land and then we are into the country which goes on and on and on. Endless flat green/brown fields with occasional fences, hedges, paths, and houses in the distance.

We roll up to the dining car at 8.00 p.m. to find it a little less chic than expected. The businessmen in the dining car sit at Formica tables sharing huge numbers of dishes. There are no free tables. There is no menu. We wait and we wait. There seems to be just one waitress and she staggers from tiny kitchen to table intermittently, looking grim. When we finally get a table I order vegetable soup and Chris orders boiled beef and rice.

The food is not good. The soup is like water with no discernible vegetables, the boiled rice is one solid lump in its little polystyrene cup. My dreams of being a vegetarian in furs have gone up in smoke.

On the way back to our cabin we look in at the other soft-class travellers and note the multi-generational families gathered around the lower berths all eating giant pots of noodles in soup. We pass people ferrying to and from the boiling water tap at the end of the carriage, filling flasks of tea and yet more noodle pots.

We need noodle pots. We definitely need noodle pots. But we are stuck on a train for another 35 hours with only a packet of custard creams.

I haven't eaten much and I can't sleep. The train rocks us on into the night and after midnight the sounds of voices fall silent. Lying on my upper berth I peer disconsolately at *Lanark: A Life in Four Books* by the dim glow of my reading light. I'm too tired. The words are swimming in front of me. I try to read the same page four times. Chris is snoring loudly in the berth across from me. The bed below me is still empty. I drop down onto it and then out into the corridor. Even by the pale light of the moon I can see how the scenery has started to change. The flat expanse of northern China is no more. We are in a land of undulating hills and vast farms. The corridors are empty now. I love travelling by train. I relish the fact that no one can reach me here. I am in a liminal world. I feel anonymous. Hidden from real life.

Many things have given me this drive to hide myself away. Dyslexia is one of them. I realised by the time that I was seven or eight that something was wrong with me because although I could read well – if slowly – I could not make my hand form the letters that my brain told it to. My rs came out as vs, my bs as ps, my ws stood up and became ms. By the end of junior school I was both top of the year in many subjects (our tests were mostly oral) and unable to do joined-up handwriting.

As I got older I heard about dyslexia but only through jokes and insults. Dyslexic was another name for stupid. And I didn't want to be stupid. My cleverness and my articulacy were my strengths. They were my ticket to university and my reason to feel good about myself, and so I hid my terrible writing from my parents. I squirrelled my exercise books away. I put up with comments from teachers that I was lazy because my written work was always such a mess. I couldn't concentrate to read in class so I stayed at home whenever I could and taught myself from books found on my parents' bookshelves. I developed dozens of strategies to cope with my unruly mind.

Despite my struggles to write by hand, books and ideas were my passion. I would sit up for hours at night writing stories, poems and novels, unbothered by my illegible writing because I wrote only for myself. In sixth form and working towards a place at Oxford, my English teacher Hugh kept me back after class one day and asked me if I knew I was dyslexic. It was a surprise to hear someone say the word out loud.

'Yes,' I told him.

'Do you want to do something about it? Do you want to take a test? Make it official?' he asked.

'Not really,' I said and walked out of the classroom. I was trapped within my own mindset about the condition. Dyslexic meant stupid and if the world knew I was stupid then they would take my options away from me. I was playing a trick on everyone. Pretending to be clever and getting away with it.

At Oxford I found myself overwhelmed in lectures. I couldn't write notes because the lecturers talked so fast. I had to copy out my essays two or three times to weed out the mistakes. And so my essays were shorter than everybody else's. My writing style was brief and journalistic because that meant I had fewer letters to form. Unsurprisingly I did badly in my exams. But this only confirmed to me the belief I already held: that I was secretly stupid.

The autumn that I was 22 I finished my Masters in Playwriting and went to stay with my parents for a little holiday. I felt an immense surge of relief. No more exams. No more essays. I'd got away with it. I had two degrees and no one could take them away from me. On Saturday, *The Guardian* arrived with a pull-out section dedicated to understanding dyslexia. I took it to my bedroom that evening hidden inside the pages of a magazine. I was ashamed even to hold something with that word – dyslexia – on the front cover.

I remember quite vividly sitting on my bed and starting to shake as I read it. I learned that dyslexia varied hugely from person to person and in how its symptoms presented. I learned that my bad memory for figures and confusion over foreign languages was probably one aspect of the condition. I learned that my lack of coordination – my inability to catch a ball despite years of sports lessons, my tendency to walk into furniture and to fall down stairs – could well be features of dyspraxia that often overlaps with dyslexia. Huge parts of my life and personality suddenly became explicable.

I turned to the section on notable figures with dyslexia and found it full of people I admired passionately. There was Eddie Izzard, Roald Dahl, Charles Rennie Mackintosh, Auguste Rodin, Pablo Picasso, Steven Spielberg, Agatha Christie, Hans Christian Anderson, William Butler Yeats and Benjamin Zephaniah. I felt as if my world had been tipped upside down and all the pieces were fluttering down around my ears.

When I think of her now, I feel sorry for that younger version of myself. Not because of the dyslexia. I'm lucky. My dyslexia is fairly mild and as an adult it has helped more than hindered.

It helps me to think creatively, to be a more inventive writer, a more natural artist. But I had 12 GCSEs, three A-levels, a BA from Oxford and an MA from Birmingham and still I could not believe the evidence of my own experience. Without that little pamphlet I would have gone on – perhaps forever – as someone desperately trying to hide her own stupidity.

My eyes have started to droop. I climb back onto my bed and fall asleep face down on top of *Lanark*'s open pages.

DAY TWO

We are woken at 6.00 a.m. by the conductor with a pot of coffee, which he leaves on the table.

We have been joined by a young female student, who is up and eating a noodle pot, sitting on a fold-down seat in the corridor. We ask her if you can buy noodle pots on the train.

'No. But we stop one, two hours in Nanning. You buy them from shop in station.'

'When do we get to Nanning?'

'Nine, perhaps.'

'In three hours?'

'No. No,' she laughs, 'Nine tonight.'

'Ah.'

Outside, the green and brown fields flash by. For. Hours.

Actually, it's extremely restful. Nothing happens. No one gets on and no one gets off. We have given up on the dining car. We are forced to daydream, read our books and nap on our rocking bunks.

As we near Guilin, the earth ripples in the distance. Great brown hills, huge curved mountains punctuate the horizon. In time, the great hills get nearer and nearer, greener and greener. The landscape

has erupted into a kind of life, full of lush grasses and trees, which seem to burst every which way into the sky like firecrackers.

I pull Chris from his bunk where he is hunched over *The Golden Bowl* with furrowed brow. 'Come and look.'

We stand in the corridor and stare at this new China flashing by.

'It's the plates,' I say, 'the willow pattern plates. With the curvy hills and the ox and the streams and the weeping willows. I always thought it was a cartoon. I never thought it would actually look like that.'

Just before 9.00 p.m. we arrive into the vast station at Nanning. Chris and I are the first ones off the train. We walk through white marble corridors along the edge of which women and children sit on benches watching fat orange goldfish swim in circles in a deep pool. We are ushered into a waiting room with overstuffed armchairs and plush curtains. The doors are locked. Chris asks the family sitting beside us what happens next. They shrug. Eventually a guard appears and tells us we have 45 minutes to go and get some food. The doors are unlocked and we are led out like eight-year-olds on a school trip. In the huge, bustling plaza outside, the guards mysteriously vanish and we are left alone. We wander dazed around the square in the muggy evening looking for a shop selling noodle pots. The square is full of kiosks, but they're all closed. Huge streets lead away from the square but they're full of office buildings and shops, long since shut up for the evening. The sky is streaked red and purple and the air is damp and clinging. We are in southern China now. And in southern China there is water: water, humidity and heat.

On the third side of the square we spot some of our fellow travellers sitting at little white metal tables in a large restaurant open to the night air. In front of them are deep bowls of noodles and soup. We clutch each other's arms and hurry over with indecent haste.

A couple of people from the train nod hello as we hover on the edge of the action trying to work out how you get food. There are no waiters but everyone is being fed. A group of workers arrive in blue boiler suits (just off shift) and make straight for the open kitchen in a corner of the dining room. They give their order to a woman with a vast ledger, pay their two or three yuan and chat as a chef in whites beats and pulls a hunk of dough.

The chef grabs the long rectangle of porcelain-white dough and flings the centre into the air, keeping tight hold of each end. The two halves wind around each other as they fold together, making a sort of barley sugar twist. He folds the barley sugar twist and stretches it out again into a long strand of dough. Then, keeping tight hold of both ends, he starts to fling the strand of dough away from his body – almost like somebody shaking out a towel – so that the line of dough between his hands stretches thinner and thinner. He folds the thin strip and starts to stretch it again, in just the same way: flinging the line of dough up into the air so that it makes an arch above him in the air. He repeats the process over and over again. Folding it and stretching, folding it and stretching. And now we begin to see what he is doing. There are multiple strands now moving between his fingers and slowly forming themselves into noodles: fat at first, then longer and thinner. Now he holds 30 and then he folds them over and there are 60. Suddenly he stops, lays the noodles down, cuts off the joined ends and curls them into a line of white bowls.

The woman with the ledger ladles hot broth from a vat beneath the counter over the waiting noodles. Then they get a sprinkle of seasoning. Some roasted, green, chopped nuts. A little chopped, roasted pork for those who paid three yuan. The men take their bowls and sidle over to a table in the corner.

We approach the counter with some hesitation. We don't want to do the wrong thing. The woman nods at us: business-like. She must be used to wide-eyed foreigners. We point at the bowls. She holds up two fingers. We nod. She points at the meat. Chris holds up his hand. We hand over five yuan and realise with disappointment that in the time it has taken us to make our order the chef has performed the noodle dance again and our bowls are nearly ready.

We head to the back of the restaurant where we can watch the chef work as we eat. The soup is mellow and salty and piquant, with layers of subtle flavour. The noodles, which cook in the hot broth as you carry it to your table, are slippery and meltingly fine.

Soothed by the hearty meal we return to the waiting room from where we are escorted back onto the train and off into the night.

DAY THREE

All the lights come on at once. We are awake. It's 2.30 a.m. Everyone is packing their bags and pulling on their clothes. Businessmen rush past us in Y-fronts and jackets, their trousers hung over their arms. Conductors walk the suddenly bustling corridors. We have arrived in Dong Dang, frontier station between China and Vietnam.

It's warm for the middle of the night. We push our belongings into our rucksacks and drag ourselves out of bed. We have to get everything off the Chinese train so that we can board a Vietnamese one in 2 hours. We step out onto gravel and scramble over a couple of sets of train tracks and onto a long, dark platform.

ONLY ONE OF US IS PADDLING

An imposing building glows in front of us, partly shrouded in creeping plants. Art Deco arches of glass and wood sit high above the entrance to the waiting room. It's our first view of French colonial architecture. The ticket hall looks like something out of Casablanca. There's a winding staircase, large, dusty chandeliers and a balcony overlooking the main hall.

We carry our train tickets, visas and passports from counter to counter, window to window. We wait on long lines of chairs to have our temperature taken. People with HIV and other infectious diseases are forbidden from entering the country and the procedure for establishing health involves filling out a form and having your temperature taken.

There is a table of American candy for sale. It is as unfamiliar as Chinese sweets. Boxes and packets of things we've never heard of. Mysterious tubs of pink marshmallows, red liquorice and sugar-paper astronauts. A pair of American backpackers swoop down and buy handfuls of candy bars.

Finally, at 3.50 a.m. they call us to the platform. A large and battered train is waiting for us. The berths are a little more rustic than the Chinese equivalent. There is a lot of blue plastic.

As the sun rises we pass rice fields and yellow/brown towns and dusty, stone-coloured stations. Now the scene becomes industrial. Windswept streets with great windowless factories, dusty outreaches of the city. Then suddenly roof ornaments and coloured eaves can be seen on either side of the raised tracks. Potted trees sit on ornate iron balconies and washing hangs between the top floors of the buildings. We could be in nineteenth-century Amsterdam, Paris or Madrid, except that tropical vines cover the green, yellow and orange houses. It's like arriving in a sweet shop after the desert colours of Beijing.

The train disgorges us at 8.30 a.m. and we wander dazed through Hanoi's wet heat and yellow light to the road, where a mixed-vehicle speedway is in full swing. Cars, vans, cyclos (rickshaws pulled by bicycles or motorbikes) and mopeds career past us.

We look for a crossing. There is no crossing. A woman of 80, carrying a carpet, steps out into the melee causing me to have a minor seizure. The cars and mopeds slow fractionally as she walks across unharmed amid a swirl of traffic.

We consult our map. Can we get to the hostel without crossing the road?

We walk for more than 10 minutes, but we're starting to go in the wrong direction. We have no choice but to cross the road. So we stand and we wait for a break in the flow of traffic.

We wait.

And we wait.

Finally a cyclo driver pauses fractionally and Chris steps out, grabbing me by the hand. He walks with determination into the path of a moped, which curves around him and keeps going. I am, without quite realising it, emitting a low-throated squeal of terror. I want to close my eyes, but that seems unwise. I squint instead, trying not to look at the van speeding into our path. Chris pauses fractionally. A moped gently grazes my thigh as it rushes past. Then another and another. I stand tight against Chris as mopeds stream past our bottoms and cars whoosh past our toes. Chris squeezes my hand very, very hard and steps into the flow of cars... which cut behind us as we hurry... through another stream of cyclos... through a line of bicycles and... pavement!

We've done it. Six streams of traffic. No broken bones. We stand there and hold hands for a minute.

'Let's never, ever do that again,' I say.

We arrive. The hostel is charming. We deposit our stuff and go for a walk. We traverse the sides of Hoen Kiem Lake, noting the bookstores, the ice cream parlours, the bars and cafes. Legend has it that a turtle from this very lake once stole the sword of the emperor Le Loi To. Le Loi accepted the loss of his sword on the basis that it had been given to him by the Golden Turtle God to help him defeat his Chinese overlords. A carved-stone Turtle Tower was erected on an island in the lake in honour of this event and rare turtles can be spotted in its depths to this day.

Heading back to the hostel, we pass one of many tiny travel agencies and read the excursions board. We have already been seduced by pictures of Ha Long Bay in our guidebook. Like a million tourists before us, we are utterly beguiled by the great stretches of blue-green sea and thousands of mountainous prehistoric islands. Year-round, dozens of orange- and red-sailed junks sail from island to island taking tourists out to swim, kayak and spot the monkeys and eagles that live on and around the peaks. We book an excursion and retreat to our hostel to find something for lunch.

On every other street corner dozens of tiny plastic stools in primary colours are set out around the opening to *pho* restaurants. There are no vegetarian options here but Chris is desperate to try some, so I send him off while I go and look in the boutiques near the lake.

Pho is one of the great traditional dishes of Vietnam. A broth made from the bones and meat of either chicken *(pho ga)* or beef *(pho bo)* is served with rice flour noodles and thin slices of the relevant meat. It arrives in a little bowl covered with lime juice, Thai basil, coriander, beans sprouts and fragments of fresh chilli and spring onion. It is a staple street food in Hanoi and one of the city's main contributions to world cuisine.

In Vietnam, as in many South-East Asian countries, you never sit on the ground. While the head is considered sacred and spiritual – and the head of a child may only be touched by family members – the feet and the ground they walk on are considered lowly and base. Hence the tiny plastic chairs (about the right sitting height for a short three-year-old) set outside every *pho* restaurant. In many Vietnamese homes shoes are never worn but since restaurants cannot enforce such a custom their floors are washed several times a day and nothing that might touch the lips may also touch the ground. When one evening Chris places his glass of beer onto the road to move his chair out of the way of a delivery van, the owner of the restaurant screams with anger and alarm and rushes to pick up the glass and press it back into Chris's hand.

And why did Chris have to move his chair out of the way of a van? Because the little roads we walk along and eat on have no pavements. As you sit eating your bowl of *pho* you are effectively in the stream of traffic. Apparently there isn't much in Hanoi that cannot be accomplished standing in a stream of traffic.

We dress for dinner (well, I put on a dress and Chris wears his least-torn shirt) and take ourselves to Ladybird, a cheap but unexpectedly glorious Vietnamese restaurant in the old quarter. We ask to sit upstairs and the waiter leads us to a table on the balcony overlooking the street.

Dusk has fallen but the shops in the street below glow with light and activity. The ironwork balcony is covered with twisting vines, set with two cafe tables and lit from overhead with paper lanterns. We are brought an English menu and I order aubergine cooked in hot and sweet sauce. Chris orders beef strips in a fiery sauce. The scene from the balcony is magical and unreal, like stepping inside a theatre set. The macaroon-coloured townhouses; the wrought iron balconies; the lemon and orange trees planted in bright blue ceramic pots; the electric lines and the washing lines; the shadow tableau of women in the lighted windows opposite, feeding their young children and washing their hair; the stream of bicycles with Hanoi traders – some in woven conical hats – returning home, carrying goods from their stalls: mats and feather dusters and watermelons tied in bundles and rolls to the back of their bikes.

The aubergines when they arrive are cut into thick strips, bloated from the frying pan and juicy with oil, covered in sticky, sweet, hot chilli sauce and sprinkled with finely chopped fresh herbs. The piercing heat combined with the sweetness is addictive. Chris's beef is so wildly hot that he gives up halfway through and smiles apologetically at the waiter.

We don't want to leave. And we return twice more.

If I could eat anywhere tonight... if I could eat anywhere on any night, I would eat at Ladybird. Partly for the delicious and deliciously simple food but even more for the sheer romance, the theatre of that balcony, the charm of friendly service and the warm breeze of an evening in Hanoi.

On the way home Chris pauses to buy some bottles of water from a late-night food shop and I stand and stare into the window of a pharmacy. My period is a week late. My period is never late. I have not mentioned this to Chris.

If it doesn't arrive tomorrow I will tell him. I will have to tell him.

By way of diversion from, well, everything, we shall take a moment to contemplate the history of Vietnamese cuisine. Unlike its near neighbours – Myanmar (Burma), Thailand and Malaysia – Vietnam never enjoyed a close enough relationship with India to take on board its curry culture. In most other parts of South-East Asia, you'll find the Indian influence riding high with local curry pastes essential to many staple dishes and thick sauces accompanying meat and vegetables. In Vietnam, however, it is Chinese cuisine that has shaped the national palate. Indeed, China controlled Vietnam from 111 BC until Vietnam finally won back her independence in the battle of Bach Dang River in 938. During this 1,000-year occupation, China introduced Confucianism, Buddhism, feudalism, writing, silk production and a taste in everyday food that embraced clear soups, lightly cooked noodles, steamed buns and fried rice.

There is a great emphasis on fresh, uncooked herbs and vegetables added to cooked dishes in their final stages. Non-Chinese ingredients such as *galangal* (a sort of cousin to ginger), fish sauce, shrimp paste, lemongrass and tamarind have been added to the repertoire thanks to several thousand years of maritime trade. And latterly, French colonial rule introduced baguettes, patisserie, butter, yoghurt, coffee, sausage-making and the habit of cooking with onions, potatoes and carrots.

Vietnamese cuisine celebrates delicacy of flavour. Cooks aim to deliver food that still retains some rawness, bite and texture. Vietnamese spring rolls, for example, diverge dramatically from the Cantonese counterparts that we are all so familiar with. Wrapped in rice paper pastry so fine it's translucent, they're stuffed with uncooked slivers of carrot, bean sprouts and onion and flavoured with fresh, green herbs and tiny amounts of deseeded chilli. They arrive at the table rolled in pre-soaked rice paper without even a nod to a wok or frying pan.

After a while, I start to think of Vietnamese cuisine as fairy food, imbued with a lightness that is almost ethereal.

Next day, we head for the Temple of Literature, just off Van Mieu. On the way, we stop at the pharmacy to buy suncream. Chris goes in and chats to the young lady behind the counter in French. I stare through the window at the shelves of boxes and bottles behind the counter.

The Temple of Literature is one of the world's oldest universities, operating as a centre of learning between 1076 and 1779, when the rulers of Vietnam made the move to establish a new capital at Hue. The university buildings are hosted within an imposingly beautiful Confucian temple, which stretches over many buildings and courtyards. The four sacred animals of Vietnam – the dragon, the unicorn, the turtle and the phoenix – are much in evidence. To a Western sensibility, one can't help feeling that the turtle rather drags down the mystical mean value of the group.

We tour the gatehouse and the gardens, marvelling at the sense of openness and calm, the subtle engraving, the delicate topiary, the Well of Heavenly Clarity (a reflecting pool, rather murky with weed), the elegant beauty of the low, red-roofed buildings.

In one temple, giant lacquered figures of Confucius and his followers sit, reaching out their hands to us, looking us in the eye. The whole room is oppressive with the glare of shiny red lacquer – like being trapped inside a Chinese paper lantern that has just been lit.

In another temple, 3-metre-high metal storks stand on the back of turtles, guarding the entrance to a courtyard where people come to honour their ancestors. Throughout the day – as we have seen before in the lama temples of Beijing – people will come with sticks of incense to pray to their ancestors, to grieve, to observe tradition, to ask questions. It is at once very intimate and very public, tourists and fellow worshippers observing the bowing down, the clasping of hands, the lighting of the incense sticks. Some faces are immobile; others are contorted with grief or worry.

In the next courtyard, stone turtles carry on their backs huge, stone stelae: tablets carved with the names and birthplaces of men who took exams here from the fifteenth century onwards, affirming the importance of exams and praising the officials who oversaw them. One cannot help thinking that no one will ever erect a stone turtle in honour of Edexcel. But I could be wrong.

We cross the road and head to KOTO for lunch. KOTO is a very chic corner of hipster Hanoi. KOTO – know one, teach one – is an Australian/Vietnamese charity that takes kids off the streets and trains them in culinary and hospitality skills. It is decorated in a Westerner's version of the East, all tasteful wall hangings and sumptuous pillows.

It is, however, a delightful place to hang out and ignore the fact you might be pregnant. The service is terrific, the food delicate and well balanced, the drinks sublime. The honey and lemongrass cooler becomes an especial favourite.

I am definitely not thinking about the fact that I might be pregnant. No, not even one little bit. Well, maybe one little bit. I

go to the bathroom (The bathrooms! So chic! So *Elle Interiors*!). Nope. Still nothing.

We check our emails. Still no news from the agents. I stare out of the window and contemplate our current position. I want to lose myself in work but I can't. I have exhausted all my plans. Plan A was to work as a paid intern-come-consultant for a Chinese magazine or website who wanted to expand their English language presence. Two months before we came here this was perfectly possible and I was talking to an agency that arranged such placements. But one week before we arrived the Chinese government suddenly changed their requirements for work visas and I was unable to get a visa to work paid or unpaid. Plan B was to get on with my normal freelance work for BBC Radio 4, but they decided they would rather not employ me when I wasn't resident in the UK. Plan C was to work freelance for one of the charity websites I'd worked on in the past five years, but nothing had come up in the past three months. Plan D was to get work through Cody's agency – though this plan made me deeply uneasy, as I have no visa to work and no desire to habitually break the law. There is no Plan E.

After lunch we go our separate ways. Chris to some far-flung and worthy museum and me back to the hostel.

I turn on the telly. *The Pursuit of Happyness* is just starting. *The Pursuit of Happyness* is an 'inspirational' true story about a single father (Chris Gardner played by Will Smith) conquering the corporate world to make a better life for his son (who is also called Chris and is played by Will Smith's real-life son Jaden). It is highly sentimental and politically questionable. It's exactly the kind of film that I would normally avoid like the plague.

I sit and watch it. When Will Smith hugs his son to him – his son played by his son – I cry and cry. When he gets the good job and the great apartment my heart threatens to burst with happiness. Sorry: happyness. When it is over, I lie exhausted, consumed by emotion. Then it starts all over again. Oh very wondrous wonderfulness! This film channel obviously plays the same film over and over all day. Halfway through the second showing Chris (my Chris) arrives back.

'What are you watching?'

'*The Pursuit of Happyness.*'

There's a pause. 'Really?'

'It's wonderful.'

'Are you OK?'

'Yes.'

'You're crying.'

'It's very moving.'

'Is it?'

I don't look at him. My eyes are glued to the screen, devouring every minute, tears streaming down my face.

'Did you want something?' I ask him, testily.

'I was thinking about going out for a little bowl of *pho* and a beer.'

'Have you got your book?'

'Yes.'

'Good. Take your time.'

Chris backs out of the room.

When he finally returns at 11.00 p.m. I am watching *The Pursuit of Happyness* for a fourth time. And still crying.

'Honey, seriously, what's wrong?'

I don't look at him. I am so dehydrated, I can barely speak. I lick my lips. 'I think I might be pregnant.'

There's a long pause. 'Right.'

'I'm nine days late.'

Chris's voice goes up a full octave. 'Right.'

I start to sob uncontrollably. Chris hugs me. 'It's alright,' he says. 'It's going to be alright.'

We fall asleep on top of the blankets. I'm still crying as I drift off. But at least I've turned off *The Pursuit of Bloody Happyness*.

The next morning we go out to buy a pregnancy test kit. We head for the only pharmacy we have seen since we got here, the one where Chris bought the suncream, a very chic affair with French beauty creams in the window.

We hold hands tightly as we step through the traffic. Finally, we are standing outside the pharmacy.

'Do they speak English?' I ask Chris.

'No,' he says, 'but the young woman speaks French.'

'OK,' I say, 'You're going to have to do the talking.' My French is minimal at best and my brain is in utter chaos.

'OK,' says Chris. He squeezes my hand and we head tentatively towards the door.

'Wait,' Chris cries.

We stop.

'What is it?' I ask him, beyond anxious, 'Do you want me to ask?'

'I can't remember the French for pregnant.'

'What?'

'What's the French for pregnant?' Chris stares at me with wild eyes. He's been comfortable speaking French for the past 20 years. But now...

'Embarazada?' I venture.

'That's Spanish.'

'Errrr... Preg... I... Em... Preg...' We both start to gesture wildly with our hands – big bellies, big bellies.

'Well, what's test in French?' I ask him.

Chris stares at me, his eyes like two full moons. 'I don't remember.'

'It's OK,' I say, 'Deep breaths. *Je voudrais...*'

'*Je voudrais...*'

We gesture at each other silently.

'*Je voudrais* what?' I snap at him.

'I don't remember,' Chris wails.

'Do you have a dictionary?' I ask him.

Chris digs around in his backpack. 'English-Mandarin.'

'Do you think they speak Mandarin?'

'It's worth a try.'

'OK. Come on.'

We head inside, Chris brandishing his Mandarin dictionary.

'Bonjour,' says the young woman, recognising Chris from yesterday.

'Bonjour,' says Chris, his voice faltering. He points at me, '*Huai yun. Huai yun?*' Pregnant. Pregnant?

The young lady blinks at us. Chris shows her the character for pregnant in the English-Mandarin dictionary. She shakes her head.

My eyes scan the shelves. I cannot see a pregnancy test.

I try looking quizzical, '*Estoy embarazada. Si?*' I am pregnant. Yes?

There is a deathly silence. My eye is caught by a line of Durex packets. Could I perhaps ask for one of those? Then mime one breaking...

'*Un moment,*' says Chris. He leads me out of the shop and we stand in the street staring at each other as mopeds and cyclos stream around us.

'How can you not remember the French for pregnant?' I ask him.

'When would I ever need to know the French for pregnant?'

'If you were a woman—'

'Well, I'm not. Let's try another pharmacy.'

'We don't need another pharmacy. We need you to remember the French for pregnant.'

We start to gesture at each other again – big bellies, big bellies. *'Je voudrais,'* we chant, *'Je voudrais un...'*

'We'll mime,' Chris says, in desperation.

'We'll mime?'

'Big belly. Pregnant belly. I'll point to you. I'll mime a pregnant belly on you and then I'll look confused.'

'You'll look confused?'

Chris shrugs gallically.

We re-enter the shop. The girl smiles at us. She has been pretending not to watch us through the window.

'Bonjour,' she says.

'Bonjour,' says Chris.

He points at me. Big point. Big point. Then he mimes a huge pregnant belly. I hold it, gamely. Stroke it. Chris looks at me and then at the girl. He shrugs again. Shakes his head. Strokes his chin. Throws his hands in the air. *Zoot alors*, he seems to be saying. *Boof!* I am French. I have maybe got this girl knocked up. What am I to do?

Despite myself, I am mesmerised by Chris's performance.

The young woman watches our dumb show with slowly widening eyes. Then she quietly produces a small white bag from beneath the counter. I scurry over to her. It's a pregnancy test. *'Oui!'* I squeal, holding it up, *'Oui!'*

She smiles sympathetically. We buy three.

We walk back to the hotel, giggling and dodging traffic. Our merriment lasts until we are in the room, standing by the door to the bathroom.

I stop. I feel cold all over. Chris's hand drops from my arm.

'I need you to go out,' I say.

'Really?' he sounds desperate, stretched.

'I need to be alone. Sorry. Can you give me half an hour?'

'OK,' he says, 'OK.'

He takes his books and leaves.

I go into the bathroom, pee into the little cup, dip the stick and put it down on the sink to develop. The instructions say to wait 3–6 minutes.

I go back to sit on the bed. I feel terrible that I sent Chris away. But I'm still not sure that we're in this together. Not completely. If I am pregnant, then first and foremost it will be my problem.

That's the thing – the house, marriage. That's what it's all about. Not wanting to feel that you're in this on your own. Wanting to know. Wanting to know that someone will be there for you, no matter what.

I feel so alone. I don't want to find out I'm pregnant, not like this. Full of uncertainty. In a foreign country.

I stare at the clock on the nightstand. It's been 20 minutes. I have to look. I have to look before he comes back. I walk over and grab the stick, not looking at the little windows. I go back to sit on the bed again.

Chris doesn't understand why I feel like this. As far as he's concerned we're in this together. Why am I so full of doubt? Well, you see, it's like this...

Before this relationship, Chris and I had another relationship, six years ago.

One Saturday in September we went out for drinks, and late into the evening Chris got up to go to the bar and I fell in love with him. One moment, we were talking and he was Chris, my friend who I'd always fancied a bit but not enough to really do anything about it. And the next moment, he was the only person I wanted in the whole world.

I honestly cannot tell you what made me fall in love with him. There was nothing exceptional about that evening or that conversation except that I fell completely in love with this man and that was that. I loved him from that day to this.

I tried to suppress my feelings, but I couldn't stop thinking about him. I couldn't function at work. I couldn't sleep. All I could think was that... perhaps... perhaps we could be together.

I made it through six weeks of head-curdling obsession before I asked him out. He was walking me back home through the dark, on a warm evening in October and I asked him whether maybe he thought we should 'go out'. He stood and looked at me and then he kissed me. In my crazily obsessed heart, that was that. It was him. He was the one I wanted. And now we were together.

We started seeing each other. We went out, I cooked him dinner, we sat up late into the night and talked. It was immediately familiar and intimate and warm. I was transported with happiness. Sorry: happyness.

Chris: not so much.

It was all too much. Too much. Too fast. There was no casual dating. We already knew each other. We'd already sat up night after night, talking. We went from friends to partners with nothing in between. And he wasn't ready. Wasn't certain. Didn't know if this was what he wanted. Didn't know if it was me he wanted.

He turned up for Sunday lunch, held my hand over the dinner table and told me he didn't think it was working.

This was news to me. We seemed incredibly happy. (Well, I was incredibly happy.)

He wanted us to cool things off. He said maybe we could see each other next week or the week after. Then he sat there and ate Sunday dinner while I tried not to be sick.

I emailed him to make an arrangement to meet. I heard nothing back.

I tried again. He arranged to meet me the following Saturday. Saturday morning I got an email, cancelling. He had to work. This carried on for ten weeks. He'd make arrangements and then break them. He was always working. Always busy. I knew what was happening but I couldn't quite believe it. We had seemed so happy together. It didn't make any sense to me.

I didn't see him again for a year.

It doesn't look like much written down, I know. But it broke my heart. Literally. I could feel the broken pieces lodged in my chest. And I never stopped loving him. I never stopped wanting to be with him.

Time passed. We resumed our friendship. We had some honest talks about what had gone wrong. We got past it. We liked each other too much to let it fester on.

I started to see someone else. And then one evening, while over at Chris's house, he told me that he thought maybe I was the one after all and maybe he'd made a big mistake and maybe I could stop seeing my current boyfriend and we could get back together.

I pretended to think about it but really there was nothing to think about. A week later we were back together and that was that.

Except... Except... I couldn't quite get past the first break-up. The unexpectedness of it. I found it hard to trust him. I just couldn't get rid of this feeling that at any moment he might change his mind. And that would be that. Again. Except now... perhaps... with the messiness of children involved.

I sit on the bed and stare at the back of the stick.

Deep breath.

I turn the stick over.

Two vertical lines.

I am so dazed that I can't remember what's positive. I scrabble for the piece of paper.

Two lines. Two lines: negative. Positive has a cross in window number two.

I peer at the second window. Is there a very slight shadow of a horizontal line? There is! What does that mean?

There is a tap at the door and a little voice.

'Can I come in?' Chris asks.

'Yes,' I tell him, distracted.

His head appears around the door. 'Well?'

'There's a line,' I say, staring manically at the second window.

'Is it positive?' he asks very slowly.

'I don't know.'

We stare together at the stick.

'It's two lines,' Chris says. 'What's that?'

'Negative.' I can feel him exhale. 'But look. Look closer. There's a shadow of another line.'

'I don't think there is.'

'Really look at it,' I tell him.

Chris stares and stares and then he looks at me. 'Did you pee on this?' He drops the stick. 'There is a teeny tiny shadow of a second line. That's all. D'you want to do another one?'

I do another one. We sit on the bed together and wait. It's nice to have him back.

After 6 minutes I go and check. There are two very clear vertical lines. No horizontal.

We go out to dinner to celebrate.

Cyclo is a bit of a Hanoi institution. A French/Vietnamese restaurant filled with refurbished cyclos for seats. It's what I shall politely describe as a 'fun environment'. I order Vietnamese spring rolls, Chris the steak frites. We sink gratefully into our food and share a bottle of wine.

As Chris mops up the last of the steak juices with a sliver of baguette he throws one hand in the air and cries: *'Enceinte! Enceinte!'* Pregnant! Pregnant! The entire restaurant turns to look at us, then at me. Thanks, love.

The next morning we board the bus for Ha Long Bay. The bay is a marvel of natural history, thousands of islands bursting from the sea, many of them virtually untouched by human hand or foot. The little islands are limestone monoliths, covered in dense jungle and ill-suited to human habitation.

We take the bus travelling east from Hanoi. The towns and cities on the way to Ha Long Bay are ramshackle, the modern buildings stark and stained, the older, wooden houses missing windows, porches and sections of walls. As in Hanoi, the roads are thick with cyclists and motorcyclists, most travellers carrying goods at least as big as themselves. Here and there we pass a toppled cyclist, or witness someone pulling their precious goods out of a ditch and rewrapping them in blue and white plastic. The impression one gets is of an entire country engaged in business.

To come from a land of corporations, chains and multinationals, it is fascinating to travel through countries where people are so obviously engaged in hundreds of thousands of small businesses. I feel like we're being given access to a part of our own history. Witnessing a less industrialised state, a less centralised economy where the working parts of capitalism are little bigger than the individual in most cases.

As ever, reality is a bit more complicated.

Vietnam is still officially a single party state and that party is Communist. Since 1986, her economy has been run as a socialist-centred market economy. In effect this means that all major institutions and large-scale industries are controlled by the state, but that small businesses are allowed to operate in private hands. Vietnam's government claims that this is one phase in a transition to a full socialist economy and as such is compatible with Marxist economic thinking.

A less idealistic explanation might run like this: for thousands of years Vietnam's economy was based on farming; she was self-sufficient and traded little with any country outside her borders. Under French rule in the late nineteenth century, Vietnam was 'encouraged' to stimulate wealth by trading her natural resources, for instance, by selling coal and rice to neighbouring countries.

Then in the mid-twentieth century, she was hit by two national earthquakes. The first involved the division of the country into a communist north and a capitalist south. The second, leading on from the first, was the staggering list of casualties from the subsequent war. One and a half million people were killed. One million more fled the country. Almost all of Vietnam's scholars, economists, scientists, inventors and industrialists left or were killed. After re-unification, the country was briefly kept afloat by trading agreements with the Soviet Union. But by the 1980s it had become apparent that the state had to give the working classes the ability to trade their way out of poverty, and that Vietnam needed to relax her rules to allow herself a wider field for export. And so the socialist-centred market economy was born. A model that China would later follow (albeit using a more complicated and controversial model).

Vietnam is now one of the fastest developing nations on earth. To visit Vietnam is to be impressed by a seemingly open, modern and dynamic country. Tourism and trade thrive, and as a consequence of this, many of its population speak at least one European language. More than China, Vietnam is very good at helping you to forget that she is a single-party state. That the well-attended elections only allow you to vote for Communist candidates. That when dissenters are elected (from within the party) they are barred from the most influential committees. That censorship is widely practised, both in the printed press and in the restriction of websites relating to political comment and human rights. That the arrest and imprisonment of those who question the government is both commonplace and underreported. But Vietnam is... cuddly in a way that China is not. Vietnam is very good at image.

All of this might give the impression that we did not warm to Vietnam. Quite the opposite. Vietnam is beautiful and friendly and very beguiling. You could explore Vietnam for months and only touch the surface. In some ways though she's an even harder country than China to get to grips with.

When the houses and shops give way to the flat plane of sea at the edge of Ha Long city, the scale of Vietnam's tourist success is only too apparent. Fat red junks stretch as far as the eye can see. They jostle and queue to eject island visitors onto the quay and welcome more aboard. It's like that moment when the man with the megaphone calls all the pedalos in, except the pedalos in this case are 70 metres long and 20 metres high. There are forty or fifty large junks all trying to dock at once. I've never seen a port in such chaos. But, as with the giant, swirling roads of Hanoi, there must be some basic, underlying order because no one falls in, no one falls off, all the boats make it in and make it out again. We scamper obediently down to the quay and wait until told to embark. When a man with a clipboard finally waves us on, we rush to claim a cabin and then listen to the terrible scraping of wood and metal as our junk tries to pull out while completely surrounded by other boats.

Our junk is one of the smaller ones. It sleeps eight (plus the crew) and we are joined by a couple from London and four students from Hong Kong enjoying their spring holiday.

We set sail for a nearby island where we're allocated two-person kayaks and lifejackets. Always a bit of a control freak, I take the front and Chris takes the back. We paddle around a headland and then into the dark of a cave. We follow the voice of the guide as we rock single file towards the chink of light at the end, emerging into a vast lagoon whose high rocky sides are covered with trees, bushes and vines. Birds of prey cry and circle the peaks. The lagoon kinks and bends and we follow its contours.

Someone is shouting ahead of us. We crane to listen.

'Monkey?' says Chris. Where's the monkey?

We look around us. There is a shaking, rattling tree above us on the left. The people ahead of us are squealing with delight. We sit there slightly grumpily, and later we shall pretend that we saw the monkey so as not to be left out of dinner conversation.

By now my arms are really starting to ache. They've been hurting since the cave. We've only been going for 30 minutes or so.

'How are your arms?' I ask Chris.

'They're fine,' he says, breezily, 'Are yours hurting?'

'They really are. I'm obviously not cut out for this.'

'Oh,' says Chris, 'Do you want me to start paddling?'

I turn around to look at him. 'You mean you're not paddling?'

Chris gazes innocently back at me. 'You were doing so well on your own. I thought you were enjoying it.' He pauses. 'Were you not enjoying it?'

'Start paddling,' I tell him.

On the way back to our junk we buy bottles of Coke and dried jackfruit from the floating grocers on the bay. Jackfruit is common in India and South-East Asia. Dried it tastes like a cross between a banana, a pineapple and a mango: starchy and sweet but with a peppery bite. The fishing families of Ha Long live in pastel-coloured shacks, large porches sheltering the fishermen from the sun as they gut and clean their catch. These shacks and porches float in tethered lines on huge rafts of wood and empty plastic drums, allowing the fishermen to tie their little boats up outside their front doors. Whole villages bob in neat grids on the water. The women of the community buy American snacks – Coke, Red Vines, marshmallows – from the mainland and sell them from the side of wooden dinghies to passing tourists, many of them kayaking or in the middle of a swim.

At dinner, we sit opposite the couple from London who tell us all about their various trips to Vietnam and how they mainly come to buy pirate DVDs and ship them home. They reel off the vast number of American series they've bought this time round:

'And then we found *House*, seasons one to five and *Lost*, though that's only up to three and *Bones* and, what was it? Oh yes, *CSI: Miami*; and the other one... And *Smallville*. We love *Smallville*. And *The OC*. And some old episodes of *The X-Files*. Did we remember *The X-Files*, John?'

We're served great plates of savoury rice and prawns. As we tuck in, the older of the two men starts to complain about all the MSG used here.

'It's like at home, in those Chinese restaurants. Heart attack in a box. It's just a complete con trick. To fill you full of rubbish and then you're hungry an hour later.'

The four students from Hong Kong are listening to this and the temperature drops noticeably. Our dining companion continues, oblivious to the bad feeling he is causing in the dining room, next reeling off his list of 'great Asian con tricks'. The word cunning is used. I try repeatedly to change the subject but he's on his fifth bottle of beer and talks without drawing breath. As he talks I realise that he is entirely oblivious to the students from Hong Kong. I don't think he has talked to them once. He probably assumes they don't speak English.

It won't be the only time that we're treated to a racist diatribe in Asia, though in my experience it is the exception rather than the norm. There is an odd attitude, prevalent among some travellers, that the whole of Asia is one giant scam machine where everyone is out to trick you and take your money. Only rarely do people make mention of the tiny amount of money that most people charge for their time and services. Of the poverty in which the majority of the population live. Of the great amount of graft involved in trying to feed yourself and your family. They will snort about being made to pay more than one pound for a meal. They will roar with outrage if someone asks them for thirty pence for a bowl of *pho* when you can buy it for twenty-five pence down the block. 'Does she think I was born yesterday! I'm not paying thirty pence for that.'

We return to Hanoi the next day, stock up on noodle pots and pack our belongings. We have mixed feelings about going back. Hanoi has been a space outside reality: no work worry, no talk of tenants and no blank page.

More and more I realise that I am looking for a space outside my own life. As each new space fills with noise I am forced to find another one in which to dwell. Beijing was one space, Hanoi another, the train a stretch of space between the two. They feel like stepping stones, which disappear under the pressure of my foot.

In my head, I am already planning the next flight into glorious anonymity.

Nem cuon
Vietnamese spring rolls

Nem cuon in the north and *goi cuon* in the south, spring or summer rolls are a classic Vietnamese dish. We ate these often in Hanoi – in fact they were the only vegetarian food available in many restaurants. The lovely dipping sauce comes courtesy of a class I took back in the UK from Van Tran and Anh Vu, authors of *The Vietnamese Market Cookbook*. If you skip forward to Chapter 7 you will also find a recipe for *nuoc cham*, another dipping sauce often served with these rolls. Though I invite you to pick your own fillings I highly recommend including noodles, for substance and texture, and some kind of pickled vegetable for the kick and the bite.

Makes 8 rolls
Preparation time: 35 minutes

8 rice paper wrappers (available from most Asian supermarkets)

A selection of at least six of the following fillings:
Large soft lettuce leaves, hard stalks removed and chopped
50 g rice vermicelli, cooked and drained
1 carrot, grated
Do chua (recipe in Chapter 8) or another finely sliced pickled vegetable
10-cm piece of cucumber, unpeeled and cut in matchsticks

Half a handful of mint, stalks picked out and leaves chopped

Handful of coriander, larger stalks picked out and rest chopped

Half a handful of Thai basil

Handful of bean sprouts, well washed

2 spring onions, very finely sliced

80 g cooked chicken, shredded

80 g cooked medium-sized prawns, halved

50 g firm tofu, cut into small strips and dry fried

2 tbsp peanuts, crushed with a little salt

Half a handful of chives, cut into 8-cm lengths

Half a handful of perilla leaves, stalks removed (available from some Asian grocery stores)

Lemon and ginger dipping sauce:

1 tbsp sugar

3 tbsp water

1 tbsp lemon juice

5-cm piece of ginger, peeled and sliced

A few drops of fish sauce (or light soy sauce for a vegetarian alternative)

Make the dipping sauce by mixing together quantities of the lemon, sugar and water until you're happy with the contrast. Then sprinkle in the slices of ginger. Last of all, season with fish or soy sauce, until the saltiness has just started to heighten the taste of the other ingredients.

Wash and chop all the filling ingredients first and lay them out so you can assemble the rolls speedily. Boil a kettle and fill a medium-sized bowl with hot water. Now, one at a time, submerge the rice paper wrappers in the water for a few seconds. When they feel pliable, use tongs or fingers to remove the wrappers from the water then lay them on a clean surface. Assemble your selection of fillings on one half of a wrapper. Roll the wrapper over and when the roll is half done, tuck the ends in at top and bottom (so the fillings don't fall out when eating), then finish rolling the wrapper. Repeat for the remaining wrappers. You have to work at a reasonable speed, but don't stress: the process of making the rolls is a lot of fun.

Serve with the dipping sauce.

Chapter 4

The Happy Melon Farmer

The farmers of Lintong County, Shaanxi Province knew only too well that spring usually brought with it drought. So one morning in the spring of 1974 Yang Wenhai, Yang Yanxin, Wang Puzhi, Yang Peiyan, Yang Zhifa, Yang Xinman and Yang Quanyi set out to dig a new well in a persimmon grove.

The digging of a new well is no easy feat and they worked hard, hacking open the earth, cutting and shaping the sides for nearly a week. But then on the fifth day they hit a layer of red earth, red baked earth, unlike anything they were expecting. Taking it in turns, they buried their picks into the hard-baked layers until they found what seemed to be the curved edge of a jar. This was good news. A solid, well-made jar could be used for storing eggs so they carefully pulled the earth from its edges. It was enormous: far larger than anything they were expecting. They brushed the earth away to find the neck of the jar, to make sure they didn't crack it. One end of the jar seemed to divide into two legs and at the other they discovered a head. Perplexed, they continued to dig, until they had unearthed an entire pottery man.

They went back to their village – Yang – and reported on their find. What did people think it was? What were they meant to do with it? The village elders were suspicious. Some were even scared. It didn't seem appropriate to disinter a man of any kind. Incense was lit and prayers sent to heaven asking for forgiveness. Some suggested that they had found a statue to the God of the Earth, buried by an ancient religious sect. Some elders even remembered stories from their youth of other pottery men being discovered. The digging of wells or graves in the fields around Yang had produced a host of giant red men over the centuries, and each discovery had brought with it fear and suspicion. Sometimes the pottery men had been flogged to drive out evil spirits. Sometimes they were burned or broken into pieces and reburied. Incense was lit. Prayers were offered up. And the men were returned to the earth.

But this normal pattern of events was about to be interrupted by a force stronger than ancestry or superstition: the arrival of a government inspector. Lao Fadre was in charge of water resources for the region and the very next day he arrived to inspect progress on the new well. He was less than impressed to find most of the villagers standing around the great hole in the persimmon grove – and no one actually doing any digging. The farmers led him into the hole: 'Look!' they said, 'we found a man. And a bow. And arrows. And pots. And tiles.'

Lao Fadre stared at the great haul before him – the tiles reminded him of those he'd seen unearthed near the Qin Shi Huang Mausoleum – and then he went home and wrote a report to someone higher up the chain of officialdom. And so the word spread from Yang to Xi'an and from Xi'an to Beijing. And as a team of archaeologists prepared to make the trip down south, the farmers carefully transported the great red man to the County Cultural Relics Administrative Department, where they were given thirty yuan to share (equivalent to forty-five pounds in 2014) in recognition of the work time they had lost.

What the seven farmers had discovered, of course, was the terracotta army of the Emperor Qin Shi Huang: a beautifully executed yet fundamentally monstrous vanity project of the third century BC. The first emperor of a unified China, Qin Shi Huang ruled for just 11 years until his death at the age of 49. He was the one who burned many of China's cultural treasures including tens of thousands of books on philosophy, politics and history. In addition to this he put thousands of scholars to death and sent hundreds of virgin boys and girls out to sea to search for the elixir of immortality (which was supposedly held on a divine island somewhere). When he wasn't busy conquering other states, sending teenagers on fruitless missions and destroying his country's intellectual legacy, he was overseeing the construction of his final resting place, a network of rooms, passages and chambers that occupied an area nearly 3.5 kilometres square. The Qin Dynasty had unified China with the help of an army that numbered over a million, and now the Emperor planned to place an army of 8,000 terracotta soldiers 1.5 kilometres to the east of his mausoleum, to protect him from evil spirits. Not coincidentally, all of Qin's conquered states lay to the east of his final resting place.

There are many things I could say about Qin Shi Huang, but none of them would be good. He dragged thousands of slaves across the country to help build the mausoleum. He arranged that after his death dozens of concubines and the architects of the mausoleum itself should be walled up alive alongside his corpse.

I don't believe in monsters. But Qin Shi Huang spent most of his life doing a damn good impression of one.

These strange and macabre facts drift through my head as I shuffle in line along the edges of a sort of aircraft hangar on a misty Saturday in Xi'an. In trenches to my right stand hundreds of dusty, red-brown troops. In their great numbers, they have a power to inspire awe, but only briefly. Yes, the army before me represents might: its rows of dull copper-coloured men standing straight and true. The very size of this moulded infantry is almost beyond comprehension, the eye cannot reach to its furthest extent, and the scale of Qin's enterprise is hard to wrap one's head around. To speak truthfully though, I am underwhelmed by the whole experience. Where is the beauty? Where is the art?

It isn't until we walk through the second hangar, where teams of restorers are carefully working on the chipped bodies of soldiers lifted from the trenches, that I understand what it is about this find which has captivated people for the past 50 years. The beauty of the warriors can only be appreciated up close. It lies in their individualism, in the astonishing experience of standing one to one, nose to nose, looking into their eyes and seeing the humour, alertness and life that the artist put there. Each warrior is – taken by himself – a thing of tremendous beauty, thought and craft. A striking sensuality lies in the curve of those mouths and the slope of the brows.

It's hard to know what to think of art commissioned by tyrants. But then if one dismissed all the art and architecture commissioned by despots, you really wouldn't have much art left. And if one were to take it further and actually start hiding or destroying these works, you would have yourselves a cultural revolution. The men who crafted these figures weren't monstrous (well, some of them probably were: ill treatment of human beings not being the preserve of any single class). But an artist is not the regime he works under. Thought and hope and creativity have a habit of finding light, burrowing their way up through the rubble like moss between the paving stones or wild flowers growing in a wall.

From Xi'an we make our way east to Banpo, home of another archaeological site, this time a Neolithic settlement, consisting of 40 houses, 200 tombs, six kilns, two animal pens and around 10,000 artefacts and implements: making it one of the most notable sites of its kind in the world. Radiocarbon dating estimates that it was actively used as a settlement anywhere between 5,600 and 6,700 years ago.

The settlement at Banpo was situated near a large river and surrounded by a deep trench. The village was carefully organised, with an area given over to pottery production, another to their place of worship and an extensive burial ground outside the perimeter of the trench.

Walking the site, you can see the remains of the semi-subterranean houses that were cut in large squares into the mud. Poles were erected in the earth and these were used to support a high conical roof, surrounded by walls made of earth and mud. Once the cut mud floor inside the house had dried out, it was ready to live in and was accessed by an entrance hall with a slope leading up from the living quarters to the exterior.

Among the graves that have been excavated are those of women who have been buried alongside a plethora of jewellery, pots and clay figures: suggesting to some that this site was once a place of matriarchal lineage.

The artefacts recovered from the site are exceptionally beautiful, with an abundance of painted pottery. Terracotta jars and bowls are covered with geometric designs of waves and triangles. Elsewhere there are bowls painted with deer, fish and human faces. Fish – as the principal food source for a riverside community – are particularly prominent. There are designs involving fish nets, human faces surrounded by a halo of fishes and geometric patterns made from fish tails rotated in an almost Escher-like fashion.

We spend hours walking through the site, the museum and the gardens. On the bus back to Xi'an my mind starts to whir: plots for plays or novels set in Banpo unfolding and developing. I have a passion for other worlds: sci fi and fantasy and dystopian strangeness. Bronze and Iron age societies feel like another world, so much on the edge of our understanding and imagination that they sometimes feel like another planet. Liberated from the culture that we know – the major religions, the established empires – they are free to be anything, at least within the scope of our imagination. I think about an older woman, a mother, a leader in this place and her desire to control the passage of power after her death. I think through her options. Will she pass one of her own lovers on to her daughters? Will she choose someone to follow her outside of her own children, someone she might better control? What if she has no children? What then? Will she make use of a younger lover who she can manoeuvre into a place of power and influence? Her character forms in my head and then a daughter and another one and then a male lover, one who is entrusted to keep power alive after the death of the old woman. And they start to talk to one another and their voices get clearer in my head.

Day two in Xi'an and we're off to explore the Muslim quarter, with its art communities and markets, mosques and museums.

Islam arrived in Xi'an during a Golden Age. The Tang Dynasty (618–907) was ruling, using Xi'an (then called Chang'an) as their capital. The nation was enjoying a period of massive growth with numerous trading routes operating through Asia and the Middle East. Thanks to the merchants and the political ambassadors, Chang'an was a city open to foreign influence and investment. Scriptural texts, translators and missionaries arrived on the Silk Road, bringing religious thought and philosophy from the Mediterranean, North Africa, India and the countries of the middle and near East.

The Great Mosque at Xi'an is a quarter of a kilometre long. Its buildings are spread over four courtyards, each one planted with shrubs and trees and decorated by carved stone fences, steps, platforms and gateways. A tall, multilayered pagoda in the third courtyard takes the place of a minaret, a few words in Arabic the only sign of Islamic influence. There are no domes in evidence and the prayer hall in the furthest courtyard resembles, at least from the outside, a state room from Beijing's Forbidden Palace. Scholarly opinion tends towards the view that Islam established itself slowly, quietly and unobtrusively in the city over more than a thousand years. And it helps to explain the strikingly un-Islamic style of the mosque itself. The colours here are mellifluous, complementary rather than contrasting. Grey, green and brown predominate, with only a little touch of red, blue and yellow, here and there, on a painted ceiling tile, or the top of a stela.

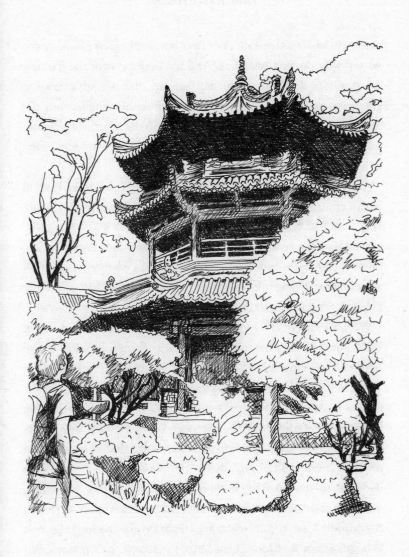

As you pass through the raised stone gateways between the gardens you occasionally catch what appears to be an optical illusion. A tiny – *Alice-in-Wonderland*-sized – gateway, framed in a larger gateway, framed in an even larger gateway, framed in the gateway that you stand in. The effect is unsettling: like looking the wrong way down a telescope. And for that moment the gardens disappear and all that you can see are doors and gateways, gateways and doors. The effect is profoundly intellectual, the architect inviting you to take a journey into the heart of a religion, or into the heart of a god; the multiple gateways and doors hinting at a journey of many stages, or boundaries.

Arriving in the fourth courtyard, the eye is suddenly blasted with colour from above. Against a northern Chinese grey-white sky, a roof of pure turquoise shines like a great jewel above the carved wooden columns of the colossal prayer hall. As we watch, prayers end and a little flood of worshippers emerges, men of all ages in neat black suits, padding away from the hall and back through the gardens to their workplaces in the city.

We walk out of the mosque and into the streets to find lunch. We're already familiar with lamb kebabs *(yangrou chuan'r)* and flatbread from myriad stalls on Beijing streets and temple fairs but Xi'an has a wealth of good Islamic restaurants.

Islamic cuisine is set apart from traditional Chinese cooking by its exclusion of pork (hugely popular in Chinese dishes); its inclusion of the less popular mutton and lamb; and its observation of *halal* practices in regards to the slaughter of animals. In addition to this you'll find there is a heavy reliance on wheat, which is perhaps unsurprising, since wheat cultivation started in the Middle East and it was travellers from this region who first brought Islam to China. Unusually for China, rice is not often served, noodles tend to be the wheat variety and flatbreads are a common accompaniment.

This reliance on mutton and wheat means that Islamic cuisine is hearty rather than delicate, occasionally even a little heavy on the stomach. If it lacks anything in refinement it certainly makes up for it in flavour, offering sweet, salty sauces; sour, pickled vegetables; and rich, slow-cooked meat.

We go for lunch at one of the restaurants near the main mosque. There are tables set out on the pavement, covered with black and white gingham cloths and shaded by trees. We order a pot of green tea and chat while we wait for our food. I have ordered the only vegetarian thing on the menu: *niang pi*. Large flat noodles of wheat dough are steamed and then tossed with mustard, soy sauce, chilli oil, vinegar and slivers of shredded cucumber. Served cold, the dish is hot and sharp and thoroughly refreshing, though I confess to missing the lightness of rice flour noodles. After nearly five months without much wheat, the Western staple has started to feel unpleasantly heavy in the mouth and in the stomach. Chris orders a bowl of lamian: hand-stretched noodles in beef soup that is spicy with chilli and fragrant with cumin.

We pick over the latest news about the house. Our tenant has allowed the agent in to negotiate with her. Though she then refused to discuss the rent. She seems to have rearranged the beds in the house and there are a number of men staying there who are unrelated to her. The agent has come to the conclusion that she is running a boarding house for construction workers, from which presumably she is taking an income. We have offered, via the agent, to reduce the rent or work out a payment plan but since she won't actually discuss money the agent can't get an answer out of her. And what about our stuff? All of our worldly possessions are boxed up in a storeroom in the basement. It is locked and padlocked, but it wouldn't take much to break the door down and take what you wanted. She knows what's in there because we told her. Because we trusted her. This was obviously a mistake.

I can feel pieces of myself being chipped away by this. We moved to Wales because London became unbearable after we fell victim to a string of crimes. In the seven years I lived in Camberwell I was twice mugged outside my flat, always for little bits of money by people obviously desperate for the next hit. About a year after Chris and I got back together I started a new and well-paid job at *Mother & Baby* magazine, in an effort to save some money in the run up to buying a house and going on our last big adventure. In the second week of working there I was on my way to work when I was assaulted by a man in the throes of a schizophrenic episode, again outside my flat. He was an outpatient at the Maudsley Hospital – which I lived beside – and he was on his way into the hospital to tell the staff he needed to be admitted. This was the final straw in terms of living where I lived. I went and talked to the police and that afternoon I moved into Chris's flat, 15 minutes away from mine.

Chris's flat was in a large block just by Loughborough Junction on Coldharbour Lane in Brixton. It probably wasn't the optimal safe haven but it was Chris's flat and Chris made me feel safe. I was extremely shaken after the assault and stayed indoors for three days. On the Sunday of that week, Chris suggested that I come out with him and walk two minutes down the road to the local Japanese takeaway to get some sushi and edamame beans. We made our order and as the young ladies disappeared to get it all together a couple walked in and stood behind us. Almost immediately they started to hurl racist abuse at the young women and then to rip the shop apart. We couldn't get back out the door so the young women pulled me into the kitchen while Chris tried to calm the situation. A year before, he had left his work in corporate copywriting to train as a drugs worker in East London, and he was experienced in dealing with people who were both angry and high. As I squatted behind the central cooker in the kitchen, the angry couple proceeded to throw parts of the fixtures and fittings through the door towards me and the terrified young women. Chris finally managed to get hold of a policeman and together they defused the situation.

Back in Chris's flat – over our box of edamame beans – we decided to leave London. We'd had enough. We had no chance of affording a home in one of the posher areas and I couldn't face bringing my kids up around this much angst. We would move away, somewhere near a city so there were jobs for Chris. I would go freelance so that we weren't tied to my work and we would find a cheap but relatively safe town with a park and a beach where we could take the kids at the weekend. Cardiff was a good city for Chris to work in so we bought a house in a small town nearby. Having spent some months feeling low and shaken by the attack, I felt liberated by the move to Wales. I did up our wreck of a house, learning to tile and make curtains and strip paint and hammer drill concrete floors. It was all quite physical and therapeutic. Taking a year out in China was meant to be a way of stepping out of the shadow of these difficult events. I didn't want to go into motherhood feeling scared of my own shadow. I wanted to regain my confidence; regain my travelling spirit.

But now everything is unravelling. And I begin to worry that I might unravel with it.

Chris has a yen to look at lots of stelae – carved stones commemorating people and events – and, not to put too fine a point on it, I don't. So I go souvenir shopping in the Muslim Quarter, where along covered aisles, market stalls offer jade animals, wooden boxes, scarves and jewellery. Lost in yet another market my mind wanders over the strange moment of my life I find myself in.

I have begun to get the sense that I am somehow disconnected from my own life. I seem to have lost some pieces of who I used to be. Once upon a time I was a fearless traveller, going where I wanted – quite alone – unbothered by my gender or my youth. Here in China, I find myself cautious, often shy. Is this age, I wonder? Is it everything I went through before I left London? Or is it travelling with a partner, with a man? Was I only brave when I had to be? And if that's the case am I destined to remain a more timid creature than I once was? I don't want to be timid. I don't want to be afraid. More to the point – I do not want to be a fearful mother. The point of coming here was to shake off all that, to challenge myself.

Since Chris and I have been together a lot has happened, and I cannot seem to pick apart how much the change in my character is down to these events and how much is a reaction to being with someone. I am by nature somewhat solitary; perhaps I am not meant to have relationships. I don't like being dependent. I see dependency as a weakness. Left completely alone I simply refuse to unravel. Whatever life may throw at me I just persevere. In a relationship I am required to open myself up emotionally, which gives me the sense of becoming more vulnerable. Rationally, I know that emotional support is a good thing and I don't judge others when they need it, so why do I judge myself?

I love Chris. If I only focus on that everything seems so simple and clear. And yet I am fighting decades of instinct that tell me to stay on my own, to run away, to remain invulnerable.

In less than a month it will be our third anniversary of getting back together. I browse the tables for something small and funny and personal. A grumpy jade monkey sits on his haunches, staring out from the lines of little elephants and horses. I feel the need to laugh at our anger and frustration, so I buy Chris the furious little monkey and squirrel it away.

I walk on, past tables laden with painted fans, wooden instruments, pens and brushes, paper lanterns, string puppets and painted plates. From some distance my eye is caught by a striking image – a white page filled with hundreds of red leaves. The leaves belong to graceful, arching trees rendered very simply with a few black lines. Below the trees, viewed from above, as if we're hovering in the sky, are a group of farmers pulling fruit from the trees with long sticks. As I get nearer I can see it's a woodcut printed in shining crimson and black – extraordinarily graphic but still approachably human, gentle and joyful. I get closer and closer and I can't stop looking at it.

It is hanging to one side of a shop, a three-walled space along an alleyway in the market. The walls of the shop and the tables in the shop are filled with prints. In one, a little troop of lambs is being driven up a mountain, forming a curving trail through the picture. Delicate, fragile creatures, they are starkly white against a mountain executed in brown and black lines. In another, a school sits atop a tree-covered mountain. Above it a black sky swirls with snowflakes. Looking closer we can see a little procession of children climbing the mountain dressed in coloured suits, one of them bringing his dog along with him. Above the school a small red flag blows in the winter wind.

I stand and stare for a long time, completely lost in these extraordinary pictures that seem to speak both of fairy-tale romance and a kind of glorious, uplifting mundanity. They have names like *Picking Persimmons*, *Herding Back* and *The Happy Melon Farmer*. A woman leans over the counter and asks in English: 'Can I help you?'

I point to the pictures: 'They're so beautiful.'

She smiles. 'Thank you. My father did them. Would you like to meet him? His name is Ding Jitang. He is a leading artist from the peasant art movement.' She gestures to an open flap in the plastic curtain at the back of the shop. Behind it I can see a long bench set out with a couple of presses. A man in late middle-age wearing a stained apron is bending over one of them applying a layer of colour to a print. He looks up from his work, smiles, wipes his hands on his apron and comes out into the shop. We shake hands and he welcomes me. My Mandarin isn't good enough to express what I want to say about the prints so his daughter translates. Ding listens and accepts my compliments with a modest decline of the head.

In the mid-1950s, as a self-trained artist, Ding Jitang moved from the southern part of Shaanxi Province to Huxian County to study and, later, teach art. In the following years, as China began her Great Leap Forward, Huxian County would be chosen to take a cultural lead, and Ding was employed to help orchestrate the Mass Art Movement. In an effort to model the ideals of Mao's romantic notion of every peasant being both a labourer and an artist, groups of artists from relatively humble backgrounds in Huxian County were provided with the supplies, tutoring and time to develop as artists. They were taken in groups to observe the farmers at work on the land and encouraged to sketch *in situ*. Chinese folk art, with its brightly painted carved animals, paper cut-outs and woodcuts of New Year festivities, was popular in the region and this was their model for development. Meanwhile, artist-tutors taught the more formal skills, such as use of perspective and composition. Artists from the movement were encouraged to take their skills into the villages and paint murals exemplifying the joy of hard work and the pleasure found in engagement with the earth. The paintings were supposed to demonstrate the principle of *haoren haoshi* – good people doing good things – and the strongest images would be used again and again in waves of propaganda campaigns over the second half of the twentieth century.

The Great Leap Forward was a time of social and economic turmoil as Mao sought to enforce sweeping reforms: the end of private farming, enforced collectivism, the movement of millions of workers from farms into the burgeoning steel industry and the application of a range of risky agricultural experiments. The use of propaganda was widespread – as was the use of coercion and violence. In 1958, with millions of workers missing from the fields much of the harvest was left to rot. So desperate was Mao to save face that he continued to export millions of tons of grain to Africa and Cuba, leaving his own citizens to starve. It is a strange and uncomfortable truth that at the same moment that China was living through her most terrible famine, the artists of Huxian were enjoying an explosion of creativity and paintings began to flood out of the peasants' art centres into galleries around the country.

There are no official records for how many people died as a result of starvation, state violence and suicide during this period:

but 30 million would be a middling estimate. In the wake of so many deaths, Mao's authority was tainted and he took a step back from front-line politics for a number of years. When he returned to prominence it was with a new scheme for nationwide change: the Cultural Revolution. The Cultural Revolution set groups of peasant artists against each other. Painters were encouraged to denounce others in the movement who showed bourgeois tendencies. Throughout the late 1960s, many artists from the movement went into semi-retirement, fearful to produce or say anything lest they be branded rightist: a kind of inverse McCarthyism.

After the death of the military leader Lin Biao in 1971, the Cultural Revolution lost some of its momentum and the peasant movement found themselves once again in favour. In 1973, a large and important exhibition of peasant artwork – which had been put on hold throughout the years of the Cultural Revolution – was mounted in Beijing and visited by 10,000 people. Ding Jitang, who due to his prominence and authority was regarded as an intellectual, was not allowed to attend. At the suggestion of Mao's wife the Huxian exhibition was sent on a tour of China and the fame and prestige of the movement began to grow.

Throughout the years, the peasants' art movement would be picked up by one faction or another within the Communist Party to be trumpeted or used as propaganda only for that faction to fall out of favour and the champions of the art movement to have to defend themselves against repeated charges of disloyalty and ethical corruption. Yet the movement was stronger than the party that created and manipulated it. It has changed and adapted over the decades, and a third generation of artists are now training within its schools.

Ding Jitang is proud of what they have created over the years – of the beauty and integrity of much of the art that has flowed out of Huxian. He worries about the future. The huge global trade in Chinese art is seducing young artists into becoming lazy: into finding the most commercial images and then repeating them *ad infinitum* rather than taking the time to develop, learn and experiment. His own work is exemplary: naive in style but with a breathtaking understanding of composition and colour and an unerring ability to find the expression of joy in the experiences of everyday life.

Back in Beijing we visit 798, a factory-chic complex of modern galleries in the city's art district. 798 is full of Westerners. Chinese modern art is currently very fashionable in the Western capitals and the Beijing art scene is busy capitalising on this with great success. We have been warned that the art we see might be a little underwhelming. It is.

There are a lot of large oil canvases, the subject matter of which tend to be cars, cartoon-like figures of people and animals, trees, sky. If any of these pictures are saying anything, I can't work out what. Aesthetically and intellectually, they're pretty unengaging. Now, that might be down to my lack of cultural sensitivity or it might be because Chinese artists are allowed to 'say' very little.

There is an underground art movement, but any reference I can find to it tells me where you used to be able to find artists working, not where they're working now. Anything faintly political or critical can end your career before it's begun. As with many other contentious aspects of Chinese culture and society the best place for all but the best-connected to study Chinese art is anywhere other than China.

Many Chinese artists have moved to work in other countries and spoken out against state censorship, and they paint a vivid picture of the difficulty of safely expressing any truly engaged idea. I search in vain for anything by Wang Peng – sometimes he shows here – but today I am not in luck.

Wang Peng, one of my favourite modern Chinese artists, was born in Jinan in 1964, two years before the start of the Cultural Revolution. He exists within the first wave of a Chinese avant-garde, demonstrating an extraordinary level of intellectual sophistication in work that is both deceptively simple and philosophically playful. His work and public reactions to his work offer a kind of alternative narrative history of Chinese society in the years since the Cultural Revolution.

Wang's early training in art focused on line drawing, with students pressed to represent nature as accurately as possible. In 1980, at the age of 16, he got the opportunity to study art in Beijing. He found art school in the capital no less restrictive, and the fields he was allowed to work on were narrowly drawn and strictly policed.

In 1982, China moved to a system of 'market socialism' and rewrote her constitution, opening up to trade with Western economies. In the autumn and winter of 1983, wary of Western influences creeping into Chinese culture, a conservative faction within the Communist Party instituted an Anti-Spiritual Pollution Campaign, targeting – among other things – excessive individualism and the use of nudity in the modern media.

In June of 1984, aged 19, as Wang prepared to take his entrance exams for the Central Academy he conceived the idea for a nude performance piece. So sealed was China from Western influences that he had never seen or read about performance art. Within days he had recruited a good friend, Li Tianyuan, to photograph what would become Performance. Hidden away from fellow students and teachers, Wang stripped naked and his body was covered in ink; ink normally used for the students' daily calligraphy practice. He then used his limbs and his hair to create prints as Li Tianyuan photographed the process. Some of the prints from that day are extraordinary: splattered canvases holding the shadows of splayed limbs and prints of Wang's face, his mouth open, his face bursting with surprise and delight. Wang developed the film himself and, too scared to make prints, packed all evidence of the work away into boxes, where it stayed hidden for many years.

He went on to study at the prestigious Central Academy, later becoming a tutor there. In 1989, a student-led movement pressing for democratic rights and freedom of speech was crushed: most famously in Tiananmen Square. In the aftermath of this uprising, the limits of what you could do as an artist were rigorously enforced. Installations and performance art were banned. In 1993, having been awarded his own show in a contemporary gallery in Beijing, Wang Peng paid bricklayers to wall up the entrance to the gallery the night before his opening. The audience who arrived the next day found only a freshly dried wall and a poster stuck to a board proclaiming '93 Wang Peng's Installation Exhibition.

In the 1990s, Wang moved to teach in the US and his work, *Passing Through*, was started in New York in 1997 and completed in Beijing in 2006. In these parallel performance pieces, Wang Peng carried a ball of fine string in his pocket, feeding it through a tiny hole in his jacket. He then tied one end to railings outside his apartment and went for a walk, creating a taut trail of string that looped its way around city blocks, through underpasses and across roads. The accompanying videos document the way in which passers-by react to the newly-created barriers. On the whole, we can see that the witnesses react with surprise and curiosity but no one tries to divert Wang or cut the string, instead most people try to work around it, with strangers helping each other to get untangled. As with so many of his pieces, *Passing Through* studies two things simultaneously: what happens when people encounter art and what happens when people encounter barriers.

On his return to China at the start of the twenty-first century, Wang staged his follow-up to the 1993 installation: *Gate*. A large group of artists, curators and critics were invited to see Wang's show at a modern art gallery in Beijing. When they arrived they found the doors closed. There was a monitor outside and a camera trained on the doors. They waited. And they waited. In time, Wang opened the doors and the audience flooded in. The space inside was nearly dark and as the audience started to realise that the room was empty, Wang closed, chained and padlocked the doors shut.

Time passed. Nothing happened inside the gallery. Anger started to grow. The crowd became restless. People needed to pee. They decided to force the door. One or two of them made an experimental push. But they needed more force. The crowd behind the door grew in number: the pressure on the chained doors increasing with every new body pressing against it. With vast effort from the crowd inside and some latecomers outside, they eventually broke the chain.

Wang's video captures everything: from the waiting; to the chaining of the doors; to the break out; and the aftermath: the good, the great and the influential, out in the street again, joking and laughing and peeing. It says quite a lot about the Chinese art world that *Gate* was widely dismissed as nothing more than a silly joke.

✳

To people who grew up believing that communism was the big bad wolf, the left's attachment to the movement is incomprehensible. And to those who grew up on the left – as I did – the vilification and conflation of communism, Marxism and socialism can be perplexing in the extreme.

Put very, very simply, communism aimed to eradicate class boundaries and promote social and economic equality for every citizen. Karl Marx identified the intrinsic weakness within the capitalist system, which is that it tends towards cycles of boom and bust. He also demonstrated that capitalism required a large percentage of the population to labour for very low wages so that a smaller percentage could benefit disproportionately further up the chain. He suggested that capitalism be replaced by an economic system that did not make use of the market, but instead placed the allocation and dispersal of wealth in the hands of a centralised government committed to lifting the labouring population out of poverty.

To achieve these aims the major powers who adopted communism did two things. Firstly, they instituted a one-party system, to stabilise the transition from one order to the next and to wrest the reins of power from the bourgeoisie – the business-owning classes. Secondly, they removed the right of people to own and profit from private business. All large businesses were moved into the control of central government. Smaller businesses, such as farms, were collectivised and had to hand over whatever proportion of their produce the government deemed appropriate. In return, central government made a commitment to feed, house, clothe and provide medical care for its citizens according to their need. This last promise was crucial to winning over the support of the people. It was a promise that talked to a country's poor, those living on the edge of society with no economic safety net. And in countries like Russia, Vietnam, China, Cuba and Korea many millions were living in just those conditions.

Leaving aside the mismanagement of the change from one system to the other, two very crucial things went wrong. Firstly, the one-party system transitioned quickly into dictatorship. The leadership was virtually unaccountable and could only be removed by a coup. The slightest murmur of dissent was leapt upon as a bid to undermine the revolution. The end of democracy effectively silenced not just the bourgeoisie but everyone at every level of society. Free speech was trampled underfoot. Journalists, political commentators and writers – those who have traditionally questioned the social order – were intimidated, jailed, murdered or sent into exile.

The second problem was the complete removal of the market. Since very earliest time markets have existed not just as an economic tool, but a means to communication. If you are going to produce goods you need to know what people in disparate parts of the nation want to buy and how much of it you can sell. The market provides a way for one part of society to communicate their want and need to other parts of that society. If you replace the market with highly-centralised government you are trusting a very small group of people to do a job previously in the hands of millions. Plenty of nations have managed to regulate their markets, but none has been successful in completely removing them.

After decades of economic hardship, China and Vietnam finally reinstated the market but they retained the one-party system. For the Chinese and Vietnamese people it's a pretty raw deal. They've regained the notoriously unstable capitalist market system with its drive towards a two-tier society yet are denied democracy and remain voiceless in the face of their countries' turbulent political progress.

One of the great ironies for the left in the West – who so love to engage with political theory, to discuss and debate – was that successive communist governments silenced the great conversation within their own countries. Without democracy and under threat of censorship there can be no true political debate. By removing the market they removed the discourse that is fundamental to the functioning of any large economy. The great march of knowledge and debate and creativity, the one that happens between millions of people over hundreds of years through the means of art, science, trade and social interaction was stifled and suppressed. The writers, artists and political campaigners who strived to break out from this silence are heroes and heroines of their age. They kept the conversation alive. They are keeping it alive: in pockets, fragments. They are the cultural and social memory of their country. They are its future. Some of them, like Ding Jitang, are working inside the system. Others, like the artist Ai Weiwei are working in exile. Still others, like Wang Peng, are trying to straddle both worlds. And that's the point about the conversation. It isn't linear. It doesn't have a single course or moral. Its diversity is its strength. A single voice may be easier to listen to but a billion voices tell a greater truth.

Liang pi
Fried noodles with lamb

This dish is a good example of Chinese Islamic cuisine and originated in Xi'an. As with many Chinese noodle dishes it can be served cold or hot. This dish is unusual in that I don't offer a vegetarian version. The lamb is a vital ingredient. It gives the stock depth of flavour and adds texture to what would otherwise be very soft, slippery fare.

Serves 2
Preparation and cooking time: 45 minutes

300 g lamb, chopped into bite-size pieces
100 g bean sprouts
Spring onions to garnish
250 g wide, dried rice or wheat flour noodles
Pinch of salt
Groundnut oil

Marinade:
1 tsp Shaoxing rice wine
1 tsp light soy sauce
½ tsp cornflour

Sauce:
2-cm piece of ginger, finely chopped
2 small cloves garlic, finely chopped

1½ tbsp light soy sauce

1 tbsp Chinkiang black rice vinegar (available from most Asian grocers)

1 tsp sugar

Generous pinch of salt

180 ml stock (lamb/mutton or vegetable)

Seasoning:

1 tbsp cumin

1–3 tsp dried chilli flakes or chopped dried chillies (adjust according to preference)

To make the marinade, mix the rice wine, soy sauce and cornflour in a shallow dish. Add the lamb, toss and leave to marinate for 30 minutes while you prepare the rest of the dish.

Wash the bean sprouts thoroughly. Chop the spring onions. Leave both to one side.

In a bowl mix together the ingredients for the sauce.

Bring a large pan of water to the boil, and then add a pinch of salt and the noodles. Cook according to instructions (normally 3–8 minutes). Use tongs to remove the noodles but keep the water bubbling. Add the bean sprouts to the pan of water and cook for 1 minute. Drain the bean sprouts and refresh in cold water. Arrange the noodles and bean sprouts in two bowls.

Heat several tablespoons of groundnut oil in a wok. When hot, add the marinated lamb in its liquid and cook for 1 minute, sprinkling with the cumin and chilli as you move the lamb around the wok. Tip the sauce mixture over the lamb and turn off the heat.

Pour the lamb over the noodles and bean sprouts and garnish with the chopped spring onions.

Zhi ma da bing
Sesame bread with spring onions

A traditional Chinese Islamic bread, *zhi ma da bing* is cooked in a lidded pan on the stove. It's commonly found on the table at big family meals and celebrations, as it looks rather wonderful. It's also nice as something to eat with a glass of wine while you're waiting for your supper to cook.

Serves 4–6
Preparation and cooking time: 2–3 hours

1 packet instant yeast
1 cup hot water
1 tbsp sugar
½ tsp salt
450 g strong white flour
Groundnut or other mild tasting oil
1 small bunch spring onions, finely chopped
Sesame seeds

In a jug, dissolve the yeast in the water. In a large mixing bowl combine yeast water, sugar and salt. Add about a third of the flour and mix thoroughly. Add the remaining flour and start to knead it in. When soft and pliable, cover and leave in a warm place to rise. When the dough has doubled in size, knock it back, cover it and leave it in a warm place to rise again.

Prepare a large, floured surface to work on. Knock the dough back and then divide it into two portions, roughly one-third to two-thirds. Roll out the larger portion into a rough rectangle until it is less than 5 millimetres thick. Brush with oil, avoiding the edges. Sprinkle the oiled part with the spring onions. Roll the rectangle into a long sausage shape, as if you were making a roulade. Starting at one end, coil the sausage tightly into a round loaf – it will look like a snail's shell. Put the loaf to one side.

Now roll out the smaller portion into a circle 30–40 centimetres across. You are going to use this circle of dough to completely enclose the loaf. Place the loaf in the centre of the circle and then wrap the edges up and over the top of the loaf, pinching them together at the top to seal. Smooth the dough where you've pinched it together. Make sure the loaf is quite wide and flat or it won't cook in the middle. Brush with water and sprinkle over sesame seeds.

To cook the loaf you need a large frying pan or large, shallow saucepan with a tight-fitting lid. For the bread to rise and cook successfully it must be allowed to steam as it fries. Heat 2–3 tablespoons of oil in the frying pan over a medium heat. When the oil is hot, add your loaf and put the lid on. Turn the heat down to medium and allow it to bubble and steam without being tempted to take off the lid. When the loaf has cooked for roughly 10 minutes on one side, turn the loaf over, replace the lid and cook on the other side for 8–10 minutes. The loaf should go golden brown on the outside but not dark brown.

Allow the bread to cool and then cut into six or eight wedges and take it to the table.

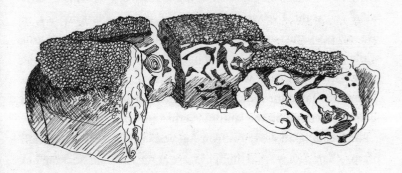

Chapter 5

Hot Spike Bitter Willow

The following Monday, Chris disappears at 6.30 a.m. to language class as normal. I get up, eat breakfast and set myself up to work at the dining table. I'm still writing up notes on Banpo, researching early matriarchal society, digging around for interesting details.

It's a warm day in the second week of May, which means it's sweltering in our apartment, the air conditioning making little difference. I strip off my jeans and T-shirt, throw them down beside me and keep working. I've always felt one of the great perks of writing is that you get to sit at home for work wearing exactly what you want. I've written in a ball gown, in silk kimonos, in five layers of knits and produced hundreds of thousands of words while wearing pyjamas. In China, in the spring and summer the most sensible (private) work attire is as little as possible.

I make a salad for lunch: leafy greens, bean sprouts and tofu. I watch something on the laptop. I return to work.

I am reading an essay on Iron Age societies in Asia when I fall off my chair. Sideways. Thump. I stare at my own feet sticking out in front of me. That's odd, I think. I go to get up and immediately fall down again. This is what goes through my head next:

> I'm drunk.
> When did I last have a drink?
> Last night. One bottle of Tsingtao.
> Oh my God, the bean sprouts. I didn't rinse them properly.
> I've given myself food poisoning and now I'm going to be massively sick on this floor.
> Why are the buildings waving at me?
> What's that crashing sound?

Above my head, a glass chandelier is jumping up and throwing itself at the ceiling.

With great effort, I get myself onto all fours and crawl towards the windows, collapsing onto my front at least once along the way. Not only are our neighbouring tower blocks waving at me, but the ground itself is swaying, the horizon is swaying.

> But ground can't sway. It can't do that.
> Oh! We're swaying! The tower block is swaying.
> It's an earthquake.
> I'm going to die.

I think about this for a moment. I feel slightly panicked and a bit sad. Then I think:

> What do you do in an earthquake? What do they do on television? They hide in doorways and under furniture. But I'm on the thirty-first floor. A sturdy door frame is not going to help me if the tower falls down.

I'll get the lift. No. You're not meant to use lifts. There must be a fire escape. I've never looked.

I need to get out of the apartment. I'm not wearing clothes. I can't run out of a building in knickers. I'll put some clothes on. What if I die because I stopped to put clothes on? I should just go. But I'm practically naked! No. I can't. I can't do it.

I crawl over to my clothes, lie down flat on the floor and pull them on, not bothering with fastenings. I pull myself upright on the dining table, but now I can't let go. I feel sick. I try to balance on two legs. It's not working so I shuffle my feet further and further apart. When my legs are more than a metre apart and I am effectively squatting I can just about balance without the table. I shuffle forwards, as fast as I can go, looking like a cross between John Wayne and a Cossack dancer.

I need the keys from the bowl to unlock the apartment door.

Do I lock the door? It's an earthquake. Who's going to come in? But that woman's in our house back home. What if she or her lodgers have stolen all our stuff? What if all we have left is in this apartment?

I lock the door behind me and totter across the landing. No one else is around. There is an emergency exit to the right of the lift. It's a concrete staircase, pristine with a sturdy handrail. I lean on the handrail and start to stumble and hop down the stairs, managing two at a time when my balance is good. My sandals are flapping and banging on my feet. I pull them off.

I can feel myself panicking under the surface, heart bouncing and drumming. I decide to count floors to give me a sense of focus.

We are 31 floors up. I can now tell that there are two flights of stairs per floor. So I must run down 62 flights to get to the lobby. I start to count them off.

Every two floors or four flights there is a small window looking out to the south. The first few times I pass these windows all I see is tower, sky, tower. About a third of the way down, I catch a proper sight of the ground. A surge of human beings – a river – is flowing out of a tower block to the south. Four more flights down and there is the river again, further on now, flooding the concrete. This, more than anything, terrifies me. Up to now, I was alone in this experience. I still half-doubted that it was an earthquake at all. But the mass of terror I can see through the windows just serves to reaffirm my panic. I run faster.

As the ground becomes the only view from the windows two things happen. The first is that my balance suddenly returns and I can run normally. The second is that I am now running so fast that I overshoot the ground floor and keep running – down into the basement. I plunge into darkness, grab the handrail and haul myself back up the stairs into the peachy fake marble of the entrance hall and then out into the light, queasy and confused. Nothing is shaking now. Seventy or eighty people – young women with babies and old men – are sitting on the pastel-coloured steps of the amphitheatre, bordering Van Gogh's *Starry Night*. Most people are wearing pyjamas.

I expect to see something on people's faces. Terror perhaps? Or curiosity. Instead everyone looks blank. Stunned. No one is talking. People continue to run from the blocks, but the running has slowed. As the minutes go by, a few more people amble out – sleepy nightshift workers, elderly men and women. I look up at the tower blocks. What if it starts again? Where do we run then?

How is Chris? I have to speak to Chris. But I have no phone with me. And he is on the other side of Beijing.

I look around me, pleadingly, thinking that perhaps someone will take pity on me and tell me what the hell is going on. It's their country, isn't it? They must know what's happening. I'm just an idiot who rolled up here looking for an adventure. What's the Mandarin for: 'Was that an earthquake?'

I sit on the pastel steps and watch the mood change. The pacing mothers are sitting now and the old, shirtless men in pyjama bottoms are chatting away. Now and again they wave at the sky in a general way. There is a solemnity here: no one knows what's happened or if it will happen again.

Time passes. Nothing happens. My panic settles into a kind of misery. Where's Chris? Is he OK? Is he dead? Were there other earthquakes? Were we on the edge of one?

After 30 or 40 minutes a man in a grey army uniform appears. He shouts to get our attention then he proceeds to tell us something in Mandarin. He leaves.

No one moves. I look across at a young woman, point down at the steps and look quizzical. 'Do we stay here?' She shrugs, nods.

I stare into space. It's eerily quiet. I feel tired and confused and sad. Was this how it always was? For those thousands and millions of years, no Internet, no phones, science in its very infancy. The earth picked you up and shook you and then it stopped. No wonder people thought the earth, the gods or their ancestors were angry with them. This makes no sense at all. How are we meant to know if the earth will shake again? Did the whole of China shake? Or just Beijing? Did we get the worst of it, or the best?

I want Chris.

A Beijing smog descends. The afternoon gets colder. The shops are closed, the Wings sitting by their garden gate. Now a group of five men in uniform are striding towards us. They talk at us for a couple of minutes and everyone rises and starts to filter back towards their tower block.

Back in the apartment I check our phone. No messages. The Internet is still working and *The Guardian* is running a breaking news report from AP – Associated Press – about a massive earthquake in Sichuan Province. I email Chris (who has no mobile phone) and while I wait for a reply I phone my parents on our landline.

It's 3.30 p.m. in Beijing, 8.30 a.m. in London. My father is awake but bleary.

'Hello?'

'Hi Dad. It's me. You might hear on the radio that there's been an earthquake in China. I'm calling to say I'm OK.'

I listen to the sounds of my Dad making coffee in a kitchen in Isleworth. He doesn't say anything for a minute. Then:

'There's been an earthquake?'

'In Sichuan. A huge one. Something happened here too. The tower blocks were swaying. It was all very scary. But I'm fine.'

'An earthquake?'

'Yes.'

'My God.'

'I know. But I'm fine.'

I ring off and send Chris another email. I watch the news reports roll out across the BBC and *The Guardian*. The earthquake in Sichuan has been vast. Two smaller earthquakes followed it, tiny in comparison, one of them the quake I felt, which was centred on the Beijing district of Tongzhou to the north-east of us.

With the television on, the laptop scrolling pictures and AP flashes, I am back in known territory. The world's media is consuming this earthquake so I don't have to. Everything is mediated, everything is familiar.

I want to ring Chris but I don't know how to find the number. I struggle to search Baidu (the Chinese Google) with my limited Mandarin. I ring the Chinese version of directory enquiries and give the lady the name of Chris's company. She doesn't understand my accent. I try another operator. She doesn't understand either. I give up and send another email.

As I wait for Chris to tell me he's OK, I flash back to the July heat of a Thursday in 2005. I'd just started working at Mencap National Office and I was in love with the morning commute, a bus from Camberwell to Liverpool Street – crossing the River Thames in the glittering morning light – then a winding walk through the City of London to the offices by the Barbican. Chris and I had been back together one month. Two days previously London has won the 2012 Olympics. It's a beautiful summer.

As I settled in to work at 9.15 a.m. we started to hear reports of a bombing on the tube. Then another one. Then a bomb on a bus. One of the tube trains bombed was running on the Piccadilly Line, on a stretch that Chris used for his commute. The timings were wrong; the bombed train was running 20 minutes later than the one he normally caught, but all the same... Mobile phones weren't working, the phone networks were suspended. I emailed him. And waited. And emailed him. And waited.

Morning became afternoon. By 3.00 p.m. I had received no fewer than three emails from my ex-boyfriend (the one who I broke up with to get back together with Chris). Am I OK? Do I want him to walk across London and take me for a drink? Do I have somewhere to stay tonight, because I'm very welcome to come to his? Hmmm.

Nothing from Chris. Not a sausage. It's like he'd been fitted with a non-communication device.

> In the event of emergency:
> do not pick up the phone,
> do not check your messages,
> do not use your computer.

Back in Beijing it is evening, 8.50 p.m. It is 6 hours and 20 minutes since the earthquake. Chris walks back through the door swinging a blue bag of Tsingtao. He drops his keys in the bowl.

Chris: Did you hear about the earthquake?
Miranda: WHERE THE HELL HAVE YOU BEEN?
Chris: At work.
Miranda: There was an EARTHQUAKE! I sent you EIGHT EMAILS!
Chris: I wasn't checking email today.
Miranda: There was an EARTHQUAKE!

It carries on like that for a while.

So, the big picture probably isn't my strong point at moments like this.

Chris is fine. I am fine.

In Sichuan, nearly 70,000 people are dead or dying – though we have no idea yet that the number will be so high or that so many of the dead will be children, crushed in their schools and kindergartens.

Ten days after the quake, the artist Ai Weiwei posts a response to the disaster on his blog. He enjoins his fellow countrymen to turn themselves from thoughts of the dead and focus instead on the living, on themselves.

> 'The true misfortune of the dead lies in the unconsciousness and apathy of the living, in the ignorance of the value of life by those who simply float through it, in our numbness towards the right to survival and expression, in our distortions of justice, equality, and freedom.
> 'This is a society without citizens.'
> Ai Weiwei
> Ai Weiwei, From *Ai Weiwei's Blog: Writings, Interviews and Digital Rants 2006–2009*. Translated by Lee Ambrozy. (Published by The MIT Press).

A week after the quake there is a minute of remembrance for the victims. In the UK this would mean silence, but not here. Chris is on his way from our flat to the subway when, unbeknown to him, the minute starts and suddenly every car on the road has started to blare its horn. The sound crashes down on him and he looks around wondering what on earth has happened. On and on it goes, horns beeping over and over again for a long angry, anguished minute: half the length of the earthquake itself.

The mood in China is slightly shell-shocked. Everything is grey and subdued. Beijing is a very long way from Wenchuan (the county where the epicentre was) so there's really not much you can do. Except give money and blood, both of which we do. We check if they need volunteers, but right now they're using people from neighbouring provinces – fluent Mandarin speakers and specialists like engineers and medics – and besides we can't volunteer for an organisation because we don't have a visa to do so. We had planned to travel to Sichuan in July to visit the Wolong Nature Reserve but Wolong has been badly affected. Who knows when the reserve will reopen.

We visit the Sichuan Provincial Government Office for lunch. Stuck up north, so far from the devastation, it feels like a very tiny mark of solidarity to go and eat in the embassy of the province.

We mistime our arrival quite significantly and find the restaurant shut, though a kindly waiter lets us in and tells us we can wait at an empty table until service starts. He brings us a couple of beers and then leaves us in the great empty dining room of one of Beijing's best Sichuan eateries.

The restaurant at the Sichuan Provincial Government Office is (unsurprisingly) the counterpart of Yunteng Shifu, though its interior is rather grander, befitting a region that has a staggering amount of agricultural production and a world-famous cuisine.

As we wait in the shadowy dining room, 20 or 30 staff troop out, dressed in a smart uniform of black and white. The manager calls order and they form themselves into a circle. He calls out questions and they answer, stumbling over the answers, sometimes giggling. He takes a kind of register and then quite unexpectedly they break into song. They seem completely unaware of our presence and we watch fascinated. The final chorus is met with a round of applause, more giggling and then the lights come on and a surprised young lady shows us to a spotless table in an inner room.

We order our favourites: water nettle salad, sizzling beef, fish-fragrant aubergine, steamed rice. The restaurant quickly fills up, mostly with native Beijingers, and the walls hum with chatter and laughter. While we wait for our food we people watch, look at the Chinese landscapes on the wall, pick over snatches of conversation in Mandarin and peel the labels off our bottles of Tsingtao.

The archetypes are all there: your classic Chinese diners who you encounter in smart restaurants from north to south and east to west. There is the business lunch table. Two to four businessmen in suits – jackets off if they know each other – joking, laughing, more intent on talk and drink than on the food. They will order platters of sizzling beef and pick at them as they discuss the finer points of business and mergers. When the conversation ebbs they will fill themselves up on bowls of steamed rice and order another round of beers.

There too are the thirty-something professionals taking their parents out to lunch. They can be single or in couples. More often than not the parent will be alone: widowed or divorced. These are the least raucous tables and the ones most likely to order a lot of sensible vegetable side dishes.

Then there is the birthday lunch. In a country of 1.3 billion, more than 3.5 million people will celebrate their birthday on any given day. So, it's perhaps not surprising that it is virtually impossible to go anywhere without encountering a birthday party.

Certainly no where as nice as a good Sichuan restaurant. These birthday meals, though, are the preserve of twenty-somethings and college students. Ten to twenty people, men and women, in restrained party outfits (more likely to be smart blouses than tiny, sparkly tops – think 1950s Britain) will gather round an enormous table on which the restaurant has placed a lazy Susan. The table will quickly fill up with giant bowls of fried rice, huge tureens of soup or slow-cooked meat, great platters of fish and stir-fried vegetables. The younger ones will get giddy and giggly on Coke while the more mature partygoers will get quickly sozzled on wine or beer. There will be a lot of discreet flirting across the table and the hands of the girls will continually sneak beneath the tablecloth so they can text their friends (possibly the same friends sitting across from them at lunch).

When it comes, the water nettle salad – or hot spike bitter willow as it is called in our English menu – is wildly sharp and moreish with morsels of fresh chilli, salt and lots of vinegar. Chris kindly allows me to eat all the salad; he is waiting for the sizzling beef, which arrives crackling like a firework in a deep, black iron skillet on legs. It sits, 25 centimetres proud of the table, looking like a witch's cauldron and emits angry crackles. Inside, long strips of beef, onions, enoki and wood ears have been fried and doused in a deep-red combination of chilli oil, dried chillies, Sichuan pepper and stock. Chris digs in: I help him with the wood ears. The first taste warms the mouth and fills it with *umami* flavours of meat and stock. By the time your chopsticks have gone back in for a second piece the Sichuan pepper is starting to tingle on the centre of your tongue. You take another bite and the chilli heat gets stronger, the Sichuan pepper a little more numbing. By the time it's been sitting there for 15 minutes you can no longer taste very much at all, so numb is your mouth and throat.

What would the other diners see if they looked across at us? They would see a tall white man with sandy hair and glasses chatting away as he picks through his bowls of food and gesticulates with his bottle of beer. And they would see his girlfriend (who everyone would assume was his wife), trying to look presentable in her cleanest T-shirt and grey cardigan, long brown hair falling everywhere as usual, laughing and talking and dissecting everything on the table before her boyfriend has a chance to finish it.

Because this is what we do, Chris and I: we go to restaurants and I tell him about the food. When we first got together it would not have occurred to me that this was something that anyone outside my family would want to talk about. Of course *we* talked about food. My mother and I can easily fill four hours discussing one meal. And not just the meal we're currently eating. We will discuss what we just ate. The last interesting food we read about. What we plan to cook for dinner. Where we plan to go for our next meal out. We will discuss recipes and compare notes on how we cook things. The discussion and preparation of food fills a vast proportion of our lives.

To my great surprise, Chris loved this. He wanted to know about the food he was eating. He wanted to know its history and how it was prepared. It blew his mind that I would decide that next week I would learn to cook curry from the Seychelles and the week after that sauces and flatbreads from Mexico. His was not a foodie family in the same way that mine was. They did not spend 40 per cent of any given day thinking about and preparing food. He was a bit startled that anybody did.

Back in London, when we were earning fairly well, Chris would find strange and interesting restaurants to take me to. I would read the menu and tell him what the most interesting or promising dishes seemed to be. Then I would carefully dissect his dinner and mine. Tasting everything. Eating around his meat to tell him how his sauce had been cooked. Why the tart pickle alongside the pork complemented the vegetables it came with, and which herbs and vinegars had been used for pickling the fish. A lifetime of cookery and classes and reading and discussion meant that I could dissect most dishes with a fair degree of accuracy. We could go somewhere for dinner and then I could attempt to recreate things the next night. He took me out to eat and I educated him in food. It was one of the cornerstones of our relationship.

Chris seems to like the fact that I obsessively make things. Or at any rate he looks upon it with a benign and accepting eye. I get nervous and fidgety if I'm not making something. I cook. I write. I draw. I paint. I sew. I knit. I tiled our house. Relaid our floors. I can't stop making things. Building things. I am currently cooking and knitting and drawing every day to make up for the fact that I cannot write. I find the act of making to be deeply soothing. I love the concentration and skill it requires. I love that it takes me out of myself, out of the world. I cannot quite pin down in words why the act of creation is so satisfying, but it talks to something deep within the human psyche.

It is a tragedy of our age that fewer and fewer jobs require us to create. There may be an economic benefit in moving away from a world where people farm, sew clothes and build ships; where people are signpainters, carpenters, wheelwrights and leatherworkers. But there is also a great loss. It's easier to feel personal pride in a job where you go to work and make things, than a job where you go to work and sell things, or sit on the end of a phone and talk to people who have bought things – things that then don't work.

I believe there are two truly satisfying things you can do with your life. You can care for and nurture people, and you can make things. For centuries, women staying at home have ploughed their energies into these two activities unpaid. They have raised children, cared for their families and lost themselves in their hobbies.

I can feel Herr Marx eyeing me beadily from across the stretch of a 130 years. 'Ah,' he is saying, 'but these are bourgeois concerns. The peasant in the rain-soaked field isn't thinking – oh good, here's another day I don't spend at a desk in a call centre.' In China, jobs in the new industries are dragging families slowly out of poverty. Increased wealth is raising life expectancy and lowering infant mortality. But you can't help wondering if people will look at their brave new world of developed living in 30 or 40 years and wonder when the soul was sucked out of the world of work.

My parents – Jenny and Oliver – come to visit us in Beijing. I am close to my parents, but when they arrive I realise that I can't bring myself to tell them the extent of our problems: with work, with the house, with the pregnancy scare.

I am an only child and grew up knowing my parents well, but at times I was more like a third adult in the house than a child. My mother and father were parents of the 1970s permissive mould. I grew up with few rules, few boundaries, no punishments. They talked to me about politics, religion, sex and relationships, theatre and family strife. As they were both actors, I grew up in rehearsal rooms and on sets, listening to hours of actors talking and arguing and bantering. I knew the ins and outs of who was sleeping with whom, whose marriage was over and who had just come out. I enjoyed the freedom of this world, the intellectual curiosity and wit, but I also longed for more stability. Often one parent or the other would be away on tour for months or even years. We moved a lot when I was still small. I changed schools, made new friends. I envied the stable home life of other children I met, just as they envied me my somewhat glamorous parents.

As I grew older I learned to parent myself and was far stricter than either of my parents would have been. I remember watching *Absolutely Fabulous* for the first time and wondering how Jennifer Saunders had come to write a documentary about my life. I was Saffy, socially and sexually conservative, overly earnest about my own education, occasionally horrified by the excesses of the world my parents worked in. I focused on doing well at school and getting into university. By the age of ten, I had mapped out the next 20 years of my life. When asked if I knew what I wanted to be I would say: 'I'm going to read English at Oxford and be a writer.' In reply, there would be one of those friendly but embarrassed nods that mean: I don't quite know what to say to children like you. But my plans made me feel safe and ordinary. When many of my contemporaries at school started smoking and sleeping with people at 14, I touched neither cigarettes nor boys. I didn't even go on a date until I was 19.

I loved my parents but I wished that they could be more normal: more parent-y. As a child I considered them to be the least parent-y parents I'd ever met, though I now wonder how parent-y any parents really are. I think all children have an idealised sense of how fathers and mothers should be. It is gleaned from years of reading books and watching films and rare is the parent in reality who can live up to these imagined idols.

My mother and father were lovely interesting people, full of ideas and passion for their work and beliefs, but I sometimes struggled to understand what place in the family I was supposed to have. I alternately confided in them and kept them at arm's-length. My mother in particular was extremely keen that everyone should be honest about everything so I never directly lied to my parents, but I did learn to lie by omission. Complete emotional honesty can be overwhelming, a bit like living inside a therapy session that never ends. In my teens I took a step back and decided to keep hard things, for the most part, to myself. I was able to see my parents, and enjoy their company while maintaining an emotional distance. Like many coping strategies this served me well for some years but would come to be problematic later on. I found it hard to confide difficult truths to my boyfriends. In times of crisis, I would just stay silent and keep everything inside. If things got worse, I would simply run away and start again.

My parents allowed me to travel from a relatively early age. My grandmother Cicely had left me money in trust to pay for a university education and I used the interest from this to go on trips every summer from the age of 16 until I was 22. I had grown up reading travel books from the 1930s and 1940s, by writers like Laurens van der Post, and had a highly romantic idea of the relationship between travelling and being a writer. At 16, my friend Dulcie and I travelled across Canada by train from Toronto to Vancouver and back again, and then down to New York State and New York City. We were, it must be admitted, not the most worldly of travellers. On our first day in Canada we found ourselves hiding from a shoot-out on an industrial estate on the edge of Toronto, and our stay in a hostel in the red-light district of Vancouver was educational. The trip created strange and indelible memories, like the day our train broke down in the middle of an aboriginal reservation and we ended up exploring a vast stretch of land which looked like the surface of Mars, while its rightful inhabitants stood in a line on the rocks beyond, watching us carefully.

With my friend Alysia, I travelled to Poland the summer we were both 17, exploring Krakow and Warsaw and the countryside around. We both had Polish heritage, but since her family was Catholic and mine Jewish only one of us had relatives we could visit. I walked the streets of the ghetto where some of my family lived for a while before being transferred to the camps, but I could not bring myself to visit the camps themselves. I had had a picture in my mind of buying a bunch of white flowers to lay on their graves. Strange as it might sound, it had not occurred to me that there would be no graves to lay flowers on, no plaques, no tombstones, no names written up on a wall somewhere. I bought a bunch of flowers and laid them instead beside the eternal flame, the very existence of which made me angry. For I was not a believer. For me there was no eternal flame, those lives snuffed out were ended for all eternity, there was no hope to find within the picture, all was bleak.

The summer I was 18 and on the verge of leaving for university, myself and three friends: Alysia again, Sophie and Tamara, made a plan to spend July and August living in a barn in the middle of the French countryside, drinking wine and vodka, reading books and lying in the sun. None of us owned a car and when we arrived we discovered that we were many kilometres from any town or supermarket. We lived on what we could buy nearby – which was mainly bread and butter – and trekked around the countryside fairly happily, frequently getting lost, occasionally spending several hours finding our way home in the warm, pitch black of a summer night in the Loire. One night we woke to find that the whole barn was shaking. Though it was 2.00 a.m. the light through the shutters was as bright as a midday sun but hard and white. And there was a deafening noise crashing and churning and thundering into us from the world outside. We shouted to each other but our voices could not be heard above the roar. Thinking that a plane had crashed metres from us, we joined hands and, pinned together like a little line of paper dolls, ran away from the blinding light and into the darkness on the far side of the hill. At the edge of a field we stood and watched the giant white lights sweep the countryside. There, beside our barn, a combine harvester the size of two houses put together was cutting and processing a field of wheat with all the sound and fury of an alien invasion.

The summer I was 20 I travelled alone for the first time. I devised a meandering trip of many weeks around north-east USA. I travelled through the Midwest on Greyhound coaches and trains, spending a couple of very happy weeks in Chicago, a city that I fell in love with. Then I took the bus across to Boston, and down the east coast, visiting Ithaca, New York and Washington DC. I walked the city streets for hours, people watching and writing in my head, seeking out strange and interesting art. The following summer, having thoroughly messed up my finals, I felt myself coming apart at the seams and timidly took a package holiday to Rhodes, before being restored to my travelling self at the age of

22 when I spent most of the summer in San Francisco, trying to turn a set of Isaac Bashevis Singer short stories into a script, and making friends.

All through my diverse adventures, my parents seemed quite happy to encourage me in my desire to escape and explore. Many years after my first trip to Canada and the US, I asked my mother if she'd really been comfortable with me going away at 16. 'Well,' she said, 'in hindsight you were probably too young, but you were always such a determined child there didn't seem much point in saying no.' I am pleased to see my parents when they come, taking comfort in their conversation and familiarity, but I keep the fragility of my current state to myself.

I wonder now what kind of parent will I be. I have a horrible feeling that like so many others I will overcompensate for my own upbringing by erring much too far in some direction or other. Perhaps I will become so authoritarian that my children will spin completely out of control, or else my own crises will make me hopelessly neurotic and I will wrap them up in cotton wool. Years ago – when Chris and I were still just friends – he had a running joke that I would end up living in Hampshire, married to a stockbroker called Harold, a stay-at-home mother to little Tarquin and darling Jaquenetta and a stalwart fundraiser for my local Conservative Association. This amused me and annoyed me by turns. I felt as if he was daring me to stay true to myself yet somehow doubting my ability to do so. I wonder what my friend Chris – as opposed to my lover Chris – would think of my choices in life?

My parents are staying in the Bamboo Garden Hotel, which is tucked down one of the *hutongs* near Lake Houhai, and was once home to an imperial eunuch. We decide, on balance, that we won't take them to eat anywhere where we've spotted an enormous rat in the dining room. So for my mother's birthday we go to a rather chic Yunnan restaurant, where you can eat in a conservatory perched on the roof, surrounded by pot plants, ethnic hangings and friendly cats. We order *boluo fan* and crispy beans and lots of *rubing* with salt and pepper and gaze out over the rooftops to Lake Houhai, where the water lies still and calm and the skaters have long ago been replaced by giant pedalos in the shape of swans.

My father wants to visit the Great Wall and the hotel arranges a car to take the three of us out there (Chris will be in work). This is my second visit to the Great Wall. The wall was originally made up of disparate sections built by warring states to preserve and defend boundaries in the seventh century BC. After the unification of China in 221 BC, large sections of wall were joined together by the first emperor Qin Shi Huang – that noted humanitarian and book lover whose handiwork we so admired in Xi'an. At this point the wall was entirely constructed from stamped earth, mud, gravel and wooden boards. Under the Ming Dynasty in the fourteenth century the wall was reconstructed using brick and stone – and 25,000 watchtowers were added to it – as a means of keeping out Manchurian and Mongolian tribes to the north.

On our first visit to the Great Wall, Chris and I went to the Badaling section by bus. Gazing out at the strange panorama I noticed how the wall seemed to hang like bunting between the mountain peaks, sagging gently down, then rising up to be pinned by watchtowers at each and every summit. It was the second week of January and the stones were slick with frost and powdery snow. Behind the forested peaks, an echo line of hills stretched into the distance, growing ever more blue and indistinct. The sun shone brightly and the sky was a clear, unclouded shade of deepest cornflower.

I remember staring in wonder at the female halves of Chinese couples, many of whom wore 10-centimetre-high heels to make the climb. The wind blew fiercely that day and as we reached the

peak of the first hill along our route my mind started to swirl with a strange and unfamiliar feeling of vertigo. I left Chris to make the rest of the walk alone and climbed down to sit on a rock and wait. I sat there and stared out at the retreating hills. At the unfamiliar contour of those peaks, rippled like the backs of dragons. Everything was different here, the light, the colours, the biting, burrowing cold. But it was a kind of heaven: to have made it here, to China.

The car myself and my parents are travelling in is taking us far outside Beijing, into the countryside where public transport doesn't reach and the wall is quiet. As we leave the suburbs the perpetual blanket of smog disappears, leaving no trace over the countryside. We drive past palatial mansions, closed off behind iron gates and 10-metre-high white walls. We pass fields of cows and orchards. The poorer neighbourhoods and squalid hamlets have given way to affluent villages with prettily painted houses. I suspect we are in the Chinese equivalent of the home counties. The kind of place one might retire to or keep a weekend house if one were doing well in the administration.

We have been heading towards the line of mountains for nearly an hour but like a mirage, they never seem to get any closer. Then, suddenly, they are growing in size and we see the wall, honey beige in the May sunshine, draped across the peaks above us. We take a cable car up the mountainside, which drops us off on a modern stone platform with a picnic area. On the way up, I am grasped by that same rocking, swirling sense of vertigo (something I have never felt before this visit to China) and when we get to the platform I let my parents go on without me. My dad walks the wall in the late spring sunshine and pronounces himself content that he has visited one of the places he always dreamed of. The historian in him is satisfied with this visit into the past. My mother walks the wall quite briefly, decides it's very high and comes back to sit with me. To distract both of us from the sheer drop to our right I point out *hanzi* on the memorial beside us and give her a crash course in reading dates in Chinese.

I feel conflicted when they head back to the UK. I wish I could have been more open about our current troubles, but I always find it hard to decide how much of anything to share. Perhaps if we were one of those families where people have stiff upper lips it might be different. If I could tell them that everything feels like it's going to hell in a handcart, and if they would respond by patting my hand or giving me a bracing punch on the shoulder that might be easier. As things are, everything has to be thoroughly talked about and picked over. All angles must be scrutinised and considered. Nothing ever goes unsaid. It's both very honest and completely bloody exhausting.

I cannot sleep. I get up night after night and sit in the silent living room staring at the walls trying to figure out what is going on inside my head. I feel anxious about so many things. I feel a sense of dread. I try to separate out everything I'm feeling. To make sense of it.

I feel guilty. Guilty that I insisted we buy a house, a house that is now causing us no end of problems. I feel guilty that I'm not earning any money. I've tried and failed to get work from my normal employers and though some might emerge in the coming year, I'm used to contributing financially and I can't cope with the fact that that has changed.

I feel impotent sitting in China, while everything unfolds back in the UK without us. I feel resentful. Resentful that Chris's way of dealing with things is to disappear into work and into himself and into books and into beer. Monday to Friday I barely see him and I feel so lonely. Will this be what it's like when we have children? Will I sit alone at home, stare at the walls and never have another adult to speak to?

And I have started to write again. Will that continue? My experience is that I don't write well when in relationships. Now that I have an idea for a new project, would I not be better off running back to singledom and trying to make the writing work?

We thought we were ready for a baby but now everything's up in the air again. We're barely seeing each other. In Hanoi, we were so relieved that I wasn't pregnant; now the plan is to start a family at the end of this year. How will I get from here to there?

Things are not going that well and my default response in times of trouble is to leave. If I leave I can travel back to Wales and help to untangle the house mess. If necessary I will attempt to evict our tenant myself. I'm itching to be off. To dive into another adventure. To do something which will be successful.

At the point of exhaustion, with these thoughts whirring around my brain, I decide to leave Chris. This is not a cry for help. I am deadly serious. I am going to go.

It takes me a couple of days to plan how I am going to leave. I look up cheap hostels. I look up flights. I have a little over two hundred pounds available in my bank account, and that is the bottom of my overdraft. I have no credit cards. No savings accounts. I have enough for a hostel but not enough for a flight. So I can leave the flat, but not the country.

I pack my rucksack and an extra bag. I decide to leave Chris the computer because he needs it for work and Skype. I'm not going to ask him for any money because I've taken enough already.

The night I plan to leave he disappears for hours after work. I sit on the sofa with my rucksack waiting for him to come back. I don't want to be talked out of it, but I don't want to leave him without explaining what's happening. When he does come through the door it's 11.00 p.m.

He sits down and stares at me as I explain that I am leaving and that it is best for both of us to make a new start. Then he asks me not to go. Then I cry a bit. Then suddenly, it's midnight.

'But where are you going to go at midnight?' Chris asks.

This is a good question. I can't waste my money on a hotel, and hostel receptions tend to close at 10.00 p.m. or 11.00 p.m. And I have to find a cab. In the outer suburbs. After midnight. And while my Mandarin is adequate to direct cabs back to our estate, can I manage directions to a new part of town?

'I'll just have to wait,' I say.

Chris's eyes are like saucers. He just looks... stunned, really.

'Are you coming to bed?' he asks.

'No. I'm leaving.' I sit on the sofa with my rucksack balanced against me. I am ready to pop with frustration. How dare he come home late and make me miss my window for leaving him! That is so... Chris.

'You can go to bed,' I tell him. So he does. Which annoys me further.

I sit there. All night. On the sofa. With the packed rucksack. As my brain starts to melt with tiredness.

I can't let myself go to sleep. If I go to sleep I will lose impetus and that will be fatal. I have reasoned things out. I know what I have to do. I'm leaving.

I stare at the living room wall for 6 hours. Then the sun comes up. My body, which has been coursing with tension and adrenaline, starts to sag. In the bad old days of my teens and twenties, when I suffered from chronic insomnia, I often found that dawn was the trigger for sleep. As the room starts to glow grey and yellow with heavy morning sunsmog, I can feel emotion prickling on the surface of my skin like needles. My guts have collapsed, heavy with a sense of doom.

But who is doomed? Not me. Not Chris. Not anyone I love. Just this enterprise. This ridiculous enterprise of leaving. Because I love him. And in the 8 hours I have been forced to sit on the bloody yellow sofa, the weight of that remembrance has undone everything. How can I leave the only person I have ever loved this much? I haven't fallen out of love with him. I'm angry with him for disappearing into himself but I'm the one who's threatening to run away completely.

Chris gets up and comes and stands in the doorway of the bedroom, not sure whether to come into the room.

'You're still here,' he says.

'Mmm.'

'Are you going?'

'Don't know.'

'Can I go to work?'

'Yes.'

'Will you be here when I get back?'

'Don't know.'

'Can I hug you?'

'Not yet.'

'OK.'

And he goes to work. I make myself a cup of tea (I feel too sick to eat) and sit on the sofa. Out beyond the tower blocks there are cabs on Qingnian Lu. The hostel receptions will be open now. Bowls of congee and banana pancakes will be steaming on tables. I could open the computer. Choose a hostel. If it was the right thing to do last night isn't it still the right thing to do this morning? Surely leaving is the noble thing and staying the cowardly thing.

But I am so tired. I can't even face trying to lift my rucksack without sleep, let alone set off on a new Chinese adventure all on my own. I lie down on the sofa and fall asleep.

When I wake it is 4.00 p.m. and I feel even less inclined to leave. I try to separate out my various reasons: measuring my love for Chris against my lack of money for a plane ticket against my need for a shower. Even if I am still leaving I might as well wait until Chris arrives home because I forgot to discuss anything practical last night. I make myself some coffee and sit on the sofa listening to the silence in the apartment.

As it happens, my decision to leave has the magic effect of making Chris come home from work on time. I hear his keys rattling in the door and then it opens and his big, surprised eyes seem to enter first on stalks.

'You're still here.'

'Mmm.'

'Are you leaving?'

'I don't know.'

He shuts the door and sits down on the far end of the sofa.

'D'you want a hug?'

'Little bit.'

Chris hugs me and I hug him back. Then I start to cry. And I carry on crying for a while, pressing my forehead into a bone in his shoulder. Eventually, Chris draws away and gestures to his chest. One half of his shirt is completely soaked.

'I can't stop,' I tell him.

'Can I go and change?'

'I guess.'

'Will you leave while I'm in the bedroom?'

'Probably not.'

He changes his shirt and comes back to sit with me on the sofa. For a long time we sit and hold hands and don't speak. Then Chris says: 'I was so happy when I came in and you were still here.'

I nod. I stay.

I stay for love. And I stay for loyalty. I stay knowing that I may run away sometime in the future if things get harder still. I stay because I am not financially in a position to do otherwise. I stay because I have run away so many times and I fear that if I never stop running I will always and forever be alone. I stay because when I hold Chris he feels like home.

Yuxiang qiezi
Fish-fragrant aubergine

Sichuan cuisine is full of different preparations, ways of cooking things and sauces to cook them in. Fish-fragrant is a description given to this particular sharp and sour sauce classically served over aubergine. There are no fish products used in it. It is very spicy, so cautious first-time cooks might want to halve or even quarter the amount of chilli bean sauce they put in. Served over boiled rice with a handful of chopped spring onions and maybe some nuts on top, I think it makes the perfect winter lunch. If you enjoy the taste of this dish, I recommend you seek out Fuchsia Dunlop's *Sichuan Cookery* – the ultimate Sichuan cookbook in the English language.

Serves 2
Preparation and cooking time: 30 minutes

5 Sichuan peppercorns
2 small aubergines
2 tbsp groundnut oil
3 garlic cloves, chopped
2-cm piece of ginger, finely chopped

Sauce:
1 tbsp Shaoxing rice wine
2 tbsp Chinkiang black rice vinegar (available from most Asian grocers)

2 tsp sugar

1 tbsp light soy sauce

1 tbsp dark soy sauce

2 tbsp chilli bean paste (this can be found in Asian grocery stores and some supermarkets, under the Lee Kum Kee brand)

3 tbsp chicken or vegetable stock

1 tsp cornflour

Garnish:

3 spring onions, sliced

Toast Sichuan peppercorns in a dry frying pan for a minute and then crush. Set aside.

Make the sauce by mixing the rice wine, vinegar, sugar, soy sauces, chilli bean paste, stock and cornflour together in a small bowl.

Cut aubergine into bite-sized cubes.

Heat the groundnut oil in a wok over a medium to high heat. Add the aubergine and stir-fry for 3 minutes or until the outsides have browned. Add the garlic, ginger and reserved ground peppercorns and stir-fry for another 30 seconds. Pour the sauce over the aubergine mixture and cook on a medium heat for 4 minutes, until the sauce has started to thicken.

Remove from heat and serve with spring onions sprinkled over.

Alternative version with pork:

I've given you the classic recipe, but meat eaters might want to add pork. You'll need 100 grams of minced pork. After you've heated the oil in the wok, add the pork and cook until it's just starting to brown. Now add the aubergines and continue with the recipe as given above.

Ma la kong xin cai
Water spinach fried with spices

Green Chinese vegetables tend to differ from Western produce. If possible, go to your local Asian grocer and pick up some water spinach or ask for an alternative if not in stock. Water spinach is a much firmer vegetable than the spinach we're used to. If water spinach is not available, this dish works equally well with lots of other green vegetables: shredded cabbage, kale, broccoli, green beans and cucumber. Remember to blanch all but the softest vegetables first. Like the recipe above, this dish is extremely spicy and needs to be served with lots of plain rice and possibly a milder meat or tofu dish for balance.

Serves 2
Preparation and cooking time: 15 minutes

1 bunch of Chinese water spinach
2–3 tbsp groundnut oil
10 Sichuan peppercorns
3 dried red chillies
1 garlic clove, crushed
1 tbsp sesame oil

Blanch the water spinach in boiling water for 2 minutes. Drain and refresh in cold water and set aside.

Heat the groundnut oil in a wok until hot. Add the peppercorns and chillies and fry for 30 seconds. Remove the peppercorns and chillies from the wok and keep to one side. Add the garlic and fry for 30 seconds.

Add the blanched water spinach to the garlic in the wok. Cook for 1 minute. Take off the heat, and then toss through sesame oil and reserved fried peppercorns and chillies. Serve.

Chapter 6

Though We Have Not Been Called

Back in April we booked advance train tickets to visit Suzhou for a long weekend, and now the moment is here. We are both wrung out emotionally but I welcome the chance to spend more time with Chris, because the weekends we go exploring are the only times we really see each other.

Sometimes called the Venice of the Orient, Suzhou is a city of romantic boat rides, late-night dining, classical Chinese gardens and silk shops. If it weren't all so damn old I would imagine that it had been designed by the tourist board. And perhaps it was. For the affluent Chinese, Suzhou has been a tourist destination since at least the ninth century.

We are staying in a little hostel on the edge of one of Suzhou's many canals. The canals form their own grid below the level of the streets, allowing an alternative way to navigate the city. Tall, stone houses with black-tiled roofs, white walls and ornate wooden balconies overlook them. Many of the houses have little patios that look onto the canals and the roofs of these are hung with long strings of large red paper lanterns. The hostel is arranged around a central courtyard – open to the elements – and long wooden balconies ring the courtyard at every level. In the evenings, it's particularly nice to take a chair and sit on one of the balconies reading by the light of a lantern under a clear night sky.

Unfortunately, canals plus heat equal mosquitoes and we wake from our first night to discover we have been thoroughly bitten.

Our guidebook directs us to a chemist in the suburbs, where a succession of pointing and grimacing rewards us with a strangely beautiful art deco-style bottle of emerald green liquid. The liquid is to be applied regularly and will discourage mosquitoes and soothe the itching and – to our frankly great surprise – it does actually work. We walk the lanes along the edges of the canals and look at the carved chopsticks, the wooden tea sets and the printed cottons and silks in the rows of tiny shops.

More than anything else these days, Suzhou is famous for its gardens. On our first day in Suzhou we head straight for the Humble Administrator's Garden, probably the most celebrated garden in all of Suzhou.

It was created in 1513 for the retired official Wang Xianchen in a collaboration involving the artist and scholar Wen Zhengming. I would recommend searching out some of Wen Zhengming's pictures online or in person, because his art is a perfect example of the classical Chinese virtues of simplicity, balance and refinement. Wen typically chose to paint a single object or a small group of objects, a clump of grass, a cluster of saplings or a section of cliff face. In monochromatic inks he would render the most beautiful representations of nature in all her graceful asymmetry.

His garden design echoes the same values and aesthetics. It was a garden built for a man tired of politics, of scheming and machination and the slow whirring of sixteenth-century bureaucracy. It spoke to the idea that one might build a model of heaven on earth, a hymn to tranquillity and the simple delight in watching nature grow around you. Throughout his 88 years Wen celebrated both art and nature as one, combining poetry with calligraphy and painting. Here, in 1508, beside a curving and dynamic study of Tianping Mountain, Wen writes of a trip into the countryside with his friends:

Though we have not been called, we set out in the spring
Leaving the city behind, we travel for pure joy
The rivers have swelled high enough to carry our little
boat
The glorious mountains rise – like eyebrows – in surprise
The wind ruffles our hair and chills us in our spring clothes
The river is dark under the thick, green canopy of trees
Trees laden with peach blossoms fill my imagination
Our walking slows beside the Jiangcun River Bridge
Wen Zhengming
Wen Zhengming, *Travelling to Tianping Mountain*.
(c. 1508) Hanging scroll. Ink on paper.

In the Hall of Distant Fragrance, cold white light is reflected all around us from glazed panels in the screen walls that separate the spaces. Here and there pots of flowers sit on carved wooden tables, and the walls of the inner room are lined with ornately worked, low wooden chairs and stools. The glazed and fretted walls part to allow views to the south and to the north, where the wide pond is framed with weeping trees, pale stone bridges and nestling pavilions. The hall is named after the fragrance of the lotus flowers that drifts through the space in summer.

On the largest of the ponds float hundreds of lily pads, bigger than dinner plates and in a ringing, humming shade of cadmium green. We walk beneath the trees, drawn to a small pavilion, whose roof extends outward far beyond the walls. On each of its four sides are doorways cut like perfect circles and ringed with dark wood. Further still we find a stone wall with a rippling top dividing two parts of the garden. It also has an entrance cut into it that is perfectly circular, this one rimmed with slate. These circular entrances are very beautiful in their own right but they also serve to frame views of the garden, creating different pictures at different angles. To the sides of the pavilion grow lotus flowers in pots. The giant fuchsia-coloured buds strain towards the sun and the lotus when it opens is immense – the size of two adult hands cupped together. The fuchsia at the tip of the petals blends slowly into a soft shade of candy-coloured pink and then into white. At the heart of the flower is a cone-shaped, bright yellow seedpod surrounded by a little amber-coloured jungle of stamen. In another of the ponds, fat orange goldfish swim slowly beneath the green and murky surface and the stones of the pathways around the lake have been arranged into patterns and mosaic forms. Here a knot, looking almost Celtic. There a stork in flight. Sometimes the path curves from side to side or a bridge undulates in stone-built waves across a pond.

The most useful explanation I ever heard of Chinese opera was that it came from the same place as Chinese garden design. Both Kunqu – a classical form of opera – and garden design came to fruition in the city of Suzhou. To a Western ear Chinese opera is hard to appreciate, so full of trills, warbles and high fluting voices. But these are the sounds of the garden. The melodies of Chinese opera are trying to evoke the flapping of butterfly wings, the babbling of water over stone and the sound of bird song in the morning. The composer is working to achieve the same thing as the gardener: they are giving us a space to lose ourselves in contemplation.

Hours have passed in the garden and on the way out Chris grabs my hand and tells me he has to eat: 'Now!' Across the road from us a tiny one-room cafe is perched over a canal. The bamboo steamers in the window tell us that they serve dim sum.

We duck inside and sit at a table looking down on the canal, barely wide enough for a boat to pass down. I order soup and rice and Chris orders a double helping of *xiaolongbao* – a real standout Shanghai speciality. The tiny steamed buns are made by wrapping pork and crabmeat in a rich layer of aspic and then sealing that inside a twist of dough. The buns are then steamed and the aspic melts forming a little portion of delicious soup that fills your mouth as you bite into the bun. Chris proclaims them the best *xiaolongbao* he has ever tasted. It's definitely true that posh restaurants in China do not have the monopoly on good chefs. In fact, I have lost count of the times that we have had disappointing meals in upmarket establishments, only to discover cooking of pure technical brilliance in a shack or down a *hutong* or in an undecorated one-room cafe above a murky-brown canal.

That evening we take a boat ride around the outside of the city walls. Behind the ancient walls the tops of the trees in the great gardens gleam with green and white lights against a soft purple-black sky. Here and there, pagodas are lit in pink and red and green, their curved roofs picked out in strings of tiny yellow lights. We chug beneath a triple-arched bridge, lit red and orange like a sunset, holding hands quite tightly, just making sure that the other one is really there.

We've been discussing what to do about our visa renewal in June. Do we get another three months or another six? Things are not moving fast with our non-paying tenant. For some months now we have been offering her a reduced rent or a payment scheme but she ignores all communication. The agents go to the house every few days but she will not talk about the rent. Some weeks ago she dropped a hundred pounds into the office, which means we cannot start eviction proceedings against her until three months have passed with no rent paid.

Then – because things aren't quite difficult enough already – word spreads through the foreign community: China is not granting any new visas until after the Olympic Games in July. The protests against the Chinese presence in Tibet have made them nervous. The Olympic Games are about to bring an unprecedented number of foreign nationals into the capital city. The government is wary of Beijing being swamped by tens of thousands of foreigners on top of the tens of thousands already living there. Such large numbers will make it harder to keep order and monitor possible political protest. They can't stop foreign ticket holders coming to the Games: that would be financial madness. So they are issuing no new visas to current residents and all of us who need them renewed in the next two months will just have to leave the country or face being deported.

There is a mood of general panic. Many people live here on visas that have to be renewed every six months. People who have lived here for 20 years, who have businesses here, are going to have to decamp to Vietnam, Mongolia or Thailand. Business owners who had been counting on the Games for this year's profit won't even be here to see them happen. Thousands of us have just a few weeks to make new plans.

We can't go home to the UK. We have nowhere to live. We should be getting a small income from the house rental, but of course we are earning nothing and spending a considerable amount on solicitor's fees. Chris is interning with the Internet company unpaid. In his years as a corporate copywriter he worked for a large number of corporations and agencies, so he at least is well placed to pick up a little freelance marketing work, which he does in late spring. Between us we have a bit more than two thousand pounds in the bank. Our solicitor thinks we might be able to get our house back by the autumn, so we're banking on flying home three months earlier than planned in September, though we have no idea where we'll be flying from.

There's no point trying to resettle or work somewhere with so little time to play with. We're just going to travel. Throw on our rucksacks and go. I start to make a plan, a plan that will take us around Vietnam, Cambodia, Thailand and Malaysia. We need five hundreds pounds to buy our flights home. So that leaves us each eight pounds a day to cover travel, food and accommodation. Easy, I think. Easy.

We can only legally remain in China for another three weeks. So I set to work booking train tickets and cheap hostels and planning a route to take us south and then west, following the curves and bends of the South China Sea. Travelling overnight by train saves us a vast amount of money as train travel is very cheap and we don't have to buy accommodation for the nights we spend on the move.

We box up as much as we can and send it home to my parents in London and Chris's parents in Belfast. As the time to leave approaches we practise packing our rucksacks, carefully figuring what clothes and utensils we might need for three months of travel which will take in jungles and river rides, ferries and buses, a fair amount of hiking and lots and lots of trains.

It is our third anniversary of getting back together. I draw a card for Chris and wrap up the grumpy jade monkey I found in the market in Xi'an. He tells me that we're going out and that he'll be home early from work. I change into my only dress and put on my cleanest shoes and a necklace. When Chris gets home he pulls on his least torn shirt and we set out. We take a cab into town, but then we're caught in a snarl of traffic inside the second ring road so we get out and walk instead. The road is an unpromising tangle of building sites, American chain hotels and multi-storey car parks. We pick our way over the rubble and barriers with care. There, tucked back from the street, is a small white and black building with a single red banner hanging outside. The entrance is hidden from view but when we finally find it we walk into a dark lobby hung with red voile and lit with tiny lights, like stars in the sky. We are ushered through to a table that sits beneath a golden moon of beaten metal. Screens of fabric hide the other tables from our view. Our waiter arrives in a flowing robe of red and blue and hands us long jewel-coloured menus decorated with mystic symbols. I look at Chris.

'This,' I tell him, 'is very fancy.'

'Do you like it?'

'I do.'

'It's vegetarian. You can order anything on the menu!'

He has brought me to the fanciest vegetarian restaurant in Beijing. Bless his heart.

The city is full of five-star restaurants catering to the businessperson abroad and the well-heeled Beijinger but we do not have the budget to eat at them. Besides, they tend to offer Western food that we can find for a fraction of the price back home. Just last week on the subway I had the following conversation. I was approached by a beautifully coiffed Beijinger of about 15, a private schoolgirl judging by her uniform.

'Hello,' she said taking the seat beside me, 'can I practise my English with you?'

'Of course,' I told her, being quite used to such encounters. More than half of the children who you meet in Beijing will want to practise at least a few words with you. Normally you exchange pleasantries. Today is different.

'Where do you ski?' the elegant girl asks.

'Ski? I'm afraid I don't ski. I've never skied.'

'Then where do you winter?'

'I don't tend to take holidays in the winter. We took a road trip through Sweden last year.'

'We? Are you married?'

'No. I have a boyfriend.'

'Do you live together?'

'We do.'

Her eyebrows shoot up into her fringe and she looks both thrilled and shocked. She recovers herself. 'We winter in Chamonix. Have you been?'

'I'm afraid not,' I tell her, feeling considerably too low rent to even be in this conversation. She helpfully changes tack.

'How are you enjoying the food in Beijing?'

'Oh, it's wonderful. I'm learning as much as I can so I can cook some of the dishes at home.'

'What's your favourite restaurant?'

'Probably the restaurant at the Sichuan Regional Government Office though we're also fond of Yunteng Shifu. To be honest, the thing we get really excited about is the street food. Your street food is extraordinary,' I tell her, bursting with enthusiasm. Her face freezes.

'You eat street food?'

'Yes.'

'Why?'

'I think some of the best cooking in Beijing happens on the street. It's exciting. I love the honesty of it. And the drama. You can watch everything prepared. And it tastes... wonderful.'

'But we have many five-star restaurants. Don't you go and eat there?'

'Not really,' I confess, 'We're on a budget.'

The girl stands up and brushes down her maroon pleated skirt. She cannot bring herself to meet my eye. The doors open and she is gone.

Now here we are, in our last week in Beijing, and we're eating at a bona fide five-star restaurant. This is definitely not in the budget but neither is it the moment to mention that. Somewhere in a stone mansion in the suburbs I can feel a private school girl let out a little sigh of satisfaction. We have succumbed. We have forsaken the street.

I hand Chris the card and the little monkey, which he unwraps. 'It looks quite... angry,' he tells me. 'Is it supposed to be angry? Are you angry?'

'No! It was supposed to be a joke about how we've been grumpy so much lately. I thought it might make you laugh. These things are hard to judge.' I lean across and kiss him. 'Happy anniversary. We're both still here!'

'Happy anniversary,' he says. I feel a twinge in my stomach thinking of everything we've been through in the past few weeks.

We open the menus. I don't know what to choose. I'm used to ordering the least meaty thing I can find. In the end we settle for eight-treasure pancake from Yunnan, fake steampot chicken for Chris, fried water spinach, fragrant rice and a mint salad. Somewhere behind us water is flowing over pebbles and we become mesmerised by the darkness and sound of water. The restaurant is Buddhist and the interior is an oasis of calm refinement. The food when it comes is wonderful: the pancake of sticky rice is dotted with candied peel, the steampot chicken is juicy and well seasoned and the mint salad is sweet and tart by turns. For dessert they bring us a bowl of red-skinned dragonfruit – creamy white and dotted with seeds – sitting on top of a cauldron of dry ice. The steam pours over the top covering the table and our laps in a white mist. We reach through it and find each other's hands.

On our final day in Beijing, Chris goes to say goodbye to his friends at the Internet company and I get to take a last long look around Beijing. I ride the subway into town and walk down to Tiantan Park and the Temple of Heaven. The weather is beautiful and the temple complex is thronged with visitors. They walk the wide stone Danbi Bridge which links the southern part of the temple with the north; and climb up to the conical, three-roofed Hall of Prayer for Good Harvests with its dark-blue roof tiles symbolising heaven and its four giant pillars, heavily decorated with scrolling golden vines and representing the four seasons. Under the Ming and Qing dynasties, twice a year the emperor would leave the Forbidden City and travel to stay at the Temple of Heaven. In the great circular hall he would personally offer up prayers for a good harvest, symbolically representing all of China in his actions.

In the park beyond the temple a group of college kids are playing a game that is a bit like tennis. Six or eight of them each have a racket and run back and forth on the lawn, hitting the ball to one another. A petite Korean lady stands on the path dressed all in white, selling neatly cased racket sets to passers-by. I imagine Chris and I on a sunset beach somewhere – in Cambodia or Thailand – playing Korean tennis and laughing, free of care. So I buy a set and sling it over my shoulder.

From the Temple of Heaven I walk north, up towards Tiananmen Square. The walk should take me through a characterful little *hutong* district just south of the square itself. Full of ancient buildings and secret alleyways, it's a neighbourhood of family-run silk stores and grocery shops. A magical, if impoverished, neighbourhood that has changed little in the past few hundred years. I have walked through it often and I am sad that it's time to say goodbye.

But it isn't there. It's gone. A cluster of bulldozers and earth-moving machines sit on top of its ruins. As I walk around the building sites I can see that a selection of brand new shops and apartments are already half-built in its place. I walk on, into Tiananmen Square, where the customary smog obscures the government buildings. The metaphor implicit in this haze feels almost too much to bear.

Back home we pack our rucksacks, but we cannot fit everything in. We tip the excess into a giant shopping bag from our local Lotus, decorated – appropriately enough – with an electric pink lotus flower. The Korean tennis game will not fit into anything, so we take it separately.

We have said goodbye to Beijing and she has said goodbye to us.

After 27 hours on the train, we arrive in the town of Guilin – 2,000 kilometres south of Beijing – on a hot day at the end of June, lugging our rucksacks, Lotus bag and Korean tennis game down the main street and across the River Li.

Guilin is stunning, surrounded by high, verdant hills or more properly karsts. This is the same scenery we encountered in Ha Long Bay, but here it is transported from the water to the land. Over millions of years, limestone has slowly dissolved in places to leave tall, arching hills, little mountains covered with forest and topped with gently arched peaks. Karst formations tend to hide great caves within them and the hills themselves are fragile, making them unsuitable to be farmed or built upon. As a result they remain untouched, offering a home to hundreds of species of flora and fauna.

Colours really glow down here, the yellow wash on the city's walls warm like buttercream. Blue-roofed boats sail tourists up and down the river and at night a seemingly endless market is set up along Zhongshan Lu selling snacks, calligraphy sets, carved animals and jewellery.

In the heat of midsummer the city natives turn out in white and pastel dresses and shirts and carry jewel-bright umbrellas against the sun. The streets bustle with shiny new cars: city runabouts in citrus colours. Middle-aged men scoot about on mopeds, dressed in vests, chinos and espadrilles. Guilin is affluent, relaxed, likeable.

We find our hostel, which is bracingly rustic: up three tiled steps in the corner of the bedroom is a hole in the floor for a toilet. Lovely. We drop all our possessions and go out to enjoy the sunshine and the fact that you can actually see the sky.

Guilin is hugely popular as a tourist destination; it's one of China's most famously beautiful cities. It started as a trading post 2,100 years ago, aided by the two rivers that flow through it. Over the centuries, canals have been cut through the town to allow the movement of food from the Yangtze Plain to rivers flowing east and south. The whole city feels alive with lakes and rivers, parks, hills and mountains.

There are fast-food restaurants and pizza joints, smoothie stalls and DVD shops. The shopping streets are crowded with teenagers on school trips and sightseers from other parts of China.

We wander the streets the next day, and walk along the river. Late afternoon, we take a trip to Seven Star Park – one of Guilin's main attractions. The air is thick with heat and small insects and trees hang above us as we walk. The vegetation this far south gives off an almost jungle vibe. We stick our heads into the little zoo and I squeal happily (and quietly) at some shy red pandas. We tour the pathways again. Tiny cascades of water fall from rocky cliffs to our left as we loop through the gardens and up to the cave – Seven Star Cave with its kilometre-long walkway through.

We pay the entrance fee and climb the steps to the opening, high on the side of one of the hills. The tours all seem to be in Mandarin so we decide to wander through it on our own, not realising that the lights are only turned on – stage by stage – for the tours. We are soon picking our way through near-black chambers, lit only by tiny emergency lights nestled in the stone floor, completely alone, as bats swoop and squeal above our heads. We hold hands and laugh and joke about the darkness and the lack of other people, but all the same we walk faster and faster, willing the path to come to an end and for light to welcome us back out. Finally we reach the last chamber and spot a door. Chris reaches it first and pushes. Nothing. There's no handle. He rattles it as best he can.

'It's locked.'

'No.'

'No, really, it's locked.'

We squint at each other. It's the end of the day. We squeaked in under the line and now the last tour has left and they've locked the doors.

'They've only just closed them,' I say, 'We'll run back to the start.'

And so we're off. And the bats are swooping. Chris takes the lead, and now I'm slowing. One kilometre is a surprisingly long way to run when you a) don't really run and b) keep getting distracted by working out what you're meant to do if you find yourself locked in a giant bat-infested cave for the night.

I lollop along, listening to Chris get further away, his voice echoing:

'Miranda! Miranda? Are you still with me?'

I can't answer him because I'm sucking all the oxygen out of the space just to propel me the next few steps.

I staggerjog (believe me, if it isn't a word it should be) into the last chamber to see Chris hovering at the edge of the stone entrance. As soon as he catches sight of me he flies down the steps towards the little ticket office. I find him leaning against a low wall talking to a janitor in blue. The janitor casts an eye up at me, friendly but amused.

'Yeah... there was actually a bolt we had to open. We just panicked and missed it,' Chris tells me, slightly embarrassed.

'Can we go home now?' I ask.

'Back to Wales?'

'I'd settle for a hostel with a horrible toilet in the corner.'

Everything is damp here in the south. Our beds are damp. Our clothes feel damp. The contents of our rucksacks feel damp. Mosquitoes chew at our legs all night.

My black jeans, which I lived in during our time in Beijing, feel clammy in this new climate. I take some tiny scissors out of my sewing kit and hack them off just below the knees, hoping this will mean they're still suitable for visiting temples.

We pull on our clothes and step out into the morning heat, grumpy and silent. Chris makes a beeline for the food stalls at the end of the alley. We can't figure out the first one – there's a lot of meat and there's something doggy-looking about the shapes on the grill. The next one seems very popular. Bus drivers and travel agents in smart uniforms are queuing up to buy tiny bowls of noodles.

We watch a couple of them work the sequence. It's a bit like the shop by the train station in Nanning where the man pulled the noodles by hand.

You choose a two- or three-yuan dish depending if you want meat on top. The lady curls fresh white noodles into an enamelled bowl, and then she adds a ladle of stock from a giant, metre-tall metal vat that sits on the ground beside her. You then point to your toppings: two kinds of herb, chilli flakes, little chunks of pickled green bean and a few slices of meat if you've paid the extra.

Chris joins the queue. He gets to the front and holds up three fingers. Barely looking at him, the lady prepares his bowl. Her fingers hover over the chilli flakes and her eyes flick up again.

Chris nods enthusiastically: 'La! La! Shi de. Xie xie.' Hot! Hot! OK. Thanks.

We go and sit down on some squat plastic stools at a makeshift table.

Chris tastes the noodles. Then he tastes again. The bowl is gone in a minute.

He's on his feet already, 'I'm getting some more.'

'Were they amazing?'

'They were fantastic.'

'Shall I get some too?'

'I'll get you a bowl without meat.'

'OK.'

This time the lady smiles at Chris as he hands over our five yuan.

Back at the table I take a bite of the pickled vegetables; they are sharp and bitter, with a depth of flavour and just a little bit of sweetness. The nuts are toasted. I swirl the herbs into the noodles and taste.

Bloody hell. They taste amazing. The noodles are thick and white and slippery. They feel substantial as you eat them, but being made of rice flour they seem to disappear as you swallow. The stock is rich, salty and piquant. The flavour lingers in your mouth for more than a minute: now salt, now sweet, now rich dark *umami*. The pickles and the chilli soak into the stock, magnifying the flavours.

The stock is undoubtedly made with meat. What isn't around here? But it tastes amazing. And I'm being spared the slivers of... what is it that he's eating?

'What is that meat?' I ask Chris who has already finished his second bowl.

'No idea!' says Chris cheerfully. 'Didn't really care.'

We set off for our last day of walking around the city but we've lost a bit of love for Guilin. The countryside is beautiful but the city is so big and concrete and modern in the centre. I return to the hostel and spend the afternoon unpacking my bag and spreading everything out to air before we move on to Yangshuo tomorrow.

For our final meal in town, we sniff out a nice-looking Chinese restaurant, which seems to be filled with locals rather than tourists.

I order nun's noodles – the vegetarian counterpart to the dish of Guilin noodles we tried this morning. The rice noodles here are boiled and then added to a sweet, light stock with straw mushrooms, slivers of carrot and cabbage, locally made fermented tofu and pieces of scrambled egg. It's fresh and light and filling but it lacks a bit of kick. There's no chilli, no heat, no piquancy. I'm a hot and sour and bitter kind of girl. But mainly in the culinary sense.

Chris orders *pijiu yu* (beer fish), which is a famous Guilin speciality. Lying on two rivers, there's an abundance of freshwater fish available to the city's chefs and this dish is served everywhere, often made with local carp. The fish is cut into squares, then coated in flour and fried in oil. It's served in a sauce made from beer, chilli sauce, ginger, garlic, tomatoes, soy sauce and spring onions. It's served to the table sprinkled with fresh herbs in a dish surrounded by decorative leaves.

We finish our last meal in Guilin happy and sated and wander back down Zhongshan Lu where the stalls of the night market glow in the darkness, Chris squeezes my hand. 'Please don't buy any more crap,' he says. So I just buy calligraphy brushes, ink, paper, hair clips and a carved horse.

There's a Chinese saying: *Guilin shanshui tianxia mei, Yangshuo shanshui jia Guilin*, which translates as: Guilin's landscape is the most beautiful in the world, but Yangshuo's landscape is better than Guilin's.

Yangshuo is an easy 90-minute bus ride from Guilin. The journey from Guilin is comfortable if hair-raising. The roads are busy with coaches, lorries, cars, motorbikes, tractors and motorised rickshaws and the lanes – which are marked – seem nonetheless to be a fluid concept. Sometimes we travel on the left. Sometimes we travel on the right. Sometimes a line of cars comes driving straight towards us. Sometimes we arrive at a crossroads where the traffic lights show red and drive straight through. We spend so much time watching the traffic speeding towards our windscreen that we forget to look at the scenery.

We arrive late on a Tuesday morning and tumble out of the bus only to be wrapped in a blanket of sultry heat. Our hostel is a little trek away and we ate only dried jackfruit for breakfast, so we look around for a place where we can eat. In the corner of the bus station, a long line of white tiled steps lead up to a cafe which is little more than a brick box, open on one side to the elements. Bicycles are leaned, three deep, against its outer walls and the rickety folding tables inside are packed with bus drivers and cyclists and walkers, all Chinese. A large sign above the counter proclaims '2Y' – two yuan – and from the assortment of bowls on the counter and the giant metal vat of stock on the floor, it's clear that the shop serves some version of Guilin noodles.

I perch at the end of a table and Chris goes to order us two bowls. I watch the owner's ritual, as mesmerising as ever. The noodles fresh from the water, curled into metal bowls. The ladle full of stock. Chris asks her for a little shredded pork for his. Then she sprinkles on some crushed nuts, fresh herbs, flakes of dried chilli and heaps of shredded, pickled green beans.

He sits down opposite me and we smile at each other. We seem to have arrived in the most beautiful place on earth. Beyond the lines of buses, beyond the low-lying, pastel-coloured apartment blocks, there is a world of giants. The tiny low-lying town is surrounded by karsts, which break the skyline like deep-green camels' humps. The sky is hazy, but even on this greyish day we are struck by the fairy tale quality of this world. It's like going to New York for the first time – you can't stop looking up.

We wrestle our chopsticks into the slippery eel-like noodles and taste. Good God. We look at each other and taste again.

'Wow.'

A hundred layers of flavour are hitting my tongue as if at once. Sweet, salt, rich *umami* flavours hug the noodles. The dried chilli flakes and pickled vegetables crackle against the background. And the herbs are powerful, battering your taste buds into a kind of craven, and pleasantly confused, submission.

In this book full of noodles, I have to warn you, we've peaked. This was the single best bowl of noodles I ate in my entire time in Asia.

Why? Well, when I was researching recipes for this book I tried to get to the bottom of the extraordinary stock we tasted in Yangshuo. Readers of a vegetarian disposition may wish to look away now. Technically, this should include me, but I feel that at least one of us needs to keep typing.

The best stock in the world is typically cooked over a two-day period and consists of boiling the bones, innards and flesh of beef, pork and horse. Yes, gentle reader; this vegetarian is here to tell you that horse broth is bloody dynamite.

Throughout our week in Yangshuo we return to the cafe in the bus station again and again. The noodles do not pale with repetition. We know that we may never taste their like again, so we eat our fill. Each tiny bowl a completely perfect, sweetly satisfying experience.

Having tasted perfection that first time we haul on our rucksacks and trek through town towards our hostel. There we pore over a welter of leaflets for white water rafting, cycling, canoeing, walking and late-night theatre. Beautiful Yangshuo is one of the biggest tourist draws in China and a great favourite with residents of Hong Kong, who fly across for a day or more of lovely scenery and bracing walks.

The extremely hospitable owner warns us against white water rafting.

'So many accidents!' he says, shaking his head.

Instead we decide to book tickets for Impression Liu Sanjie, the spectacular outdoor production on the banks of the River Li that runs six days a week and boasts a cast of 800. We are quickly discovering that we can live on far less than eight pounds each per day, and this allows us to spend money on a few indulgences when the chance arises.

We eschew the travel companies offering expeditions and decide instead to hire bicycles when we need them and to put together our own River Li itinerary with walking, cycling and canoeing to explore the countryside down river.

In the evening, we wander into the centre of town, which is almost completely comprised of restaurants. Little tributaries from the mighty River Li flow gently through town and here and there small lakes and ponds are surrounded by pale grey rock, lush green willows and bonsai pines, and crossed by ornamental bridges. Long streets are crowded on either side with white-painted buildings, each one sporting the same bright blue shutters and blood-red iron balconies. Red paper lanterns hang above tables on the first floor and the eye is pulled in a hundred directions by the great, swagged restaurant signs, the brightly lit *hanzi* and the swirling, rainbow-coloured windmills of street sellers. It's barely 7.30 p.m. and the streets are filling up already. Bodies everywhere. Courtyards go from empty to full in the blink of an eye. We can't get a table at our first choice so we walk and read menus until we're exhausted.

At 9.00 p.m. we stand on an ornamental bridge over a little river and stare through the gathering darkness at the long strings of restaurants. It's all too much. Too many people. Too much choice. The heat is oppressive, even at this late hour. In desperation, I pull a guidebook out of my bag and start to look for smaller restaurants, something off the beaten track. There is one on the first floor of a small, darkened mall.

We drag ourselves up the stairs and are guided to a table and presented with a menu with pictures. We order Chinese white wine and a selection of dishes: noodles, green salads, something that looks like shredded lotus root in a bowl and soup. The waitress takes our order and disappears. The restaurant is empty except for one large group of young Chinese men and women celebrating a birthday. They're all pretty sozzled and their laughter and snatches of song at least imbue the restaurant with a little life. We finish a first glass of wine, then a second. No sign of the waitress.

I stare at the menu.

'What d'you think we ordered?' I ask Chris.

He pulls out his Mandarin-English dictionary. Nothing on the menu was very familiar and we were too tired to do more than point at the pretty pictures. He shuffles back and forth, trying to translate. I had my eye on the soup but when Chris finally figures out the last character it turns out we've ordered 'big organ broth'.

'Oh well,' I say, 'There's still the noodles and that salad of lotus roots.'

Finally, after nearly an hour, the waitress returns and fills the centre of the table with lots of little bowls. We are virtually falling asleep and I'm pretty drunk.

'Excuse me,' says Chris, before she disappears again, 'What's in the salad? Lotus root? White radish?'

'Ma,' she says and leaves again.

Chris pokes a chopstick into the bowl and swirls the white strands round.

'Funny,' he says, 'it doesn't look like horse.'

He takes an exploratory mouthful while I peer closely at the bowl of food. On closer inspection, the strands are more pink than white. Mmm. Blanched horse.

'It's nice,' he works on it a bit, 'chewy,' he chews some more, 'definitely not lotus root.'

We rent bicycles and cycle out of Yangshuo and around the mountains. The roads are mainly peaceful, though lorries carrying freight rush past every so often. The dark tunnels under the mountains are extremely nerve-racking, with no walkway or cycle lane and not much concession to cyclists by the passing van drivers. At one point I get stuck, literally clasping a wall for safety as a stream of taxis follows a tractor follows a lorry follows another lorry. I can feel them whoosh past my thighs, and just see Chris's little head peeking round from the other end of the tunnel. Outside the tunnel I swear never to attempt that again and Chris gamely suggests we try a 10-kilometre detour on the way back. He's actually lying. He fully intends to make me go through the tunnel again on the way home.

We arrive at a tumbledown village on the banks of the River Li and chain our bicycles to a flimsy-looking fence. We rent kayaks from a little hire shop and they give us basic instructions to get us from A to B.

'Always wear life vest. When you come to fork in river take right turning. When you see restaurant on the water stop and have lunch. They look after you.'

We pull on life vests, climb into our little orange kayaks and set off. Within five minutes we are alone in the world. The village has disappeared, out of sight behind us somewhere. It's incredibly peaceful. The sky is grey-blue, full of fat white clouds. The river before

201

us seems to flow into the mountains in the distance. The riverbanks are thick with squat, dark, shaggy trees and bushes. The air smells clean, with just a tang of wet grass.

The river curves gently and we follow it, paddling in a leisurely fashion, helped along by the flow. At some points the water is so still that we catch a near perfect reflection of the nearest mountain. The water-strafed image stacked neatly beneath the rocky tower like a Rorschach image or an optical illusion. We float for a while in silence, then paddle closer together and chat for a bit. I don't think I've felt this relaxed in months. As we near the fork in the river we catch sight of a pair of lean, brown, long-horned cows bathing in the shallows, and they watch as warily as we float by.

We drift further, past a bank of hills to our left and then at length we spot buildings and a little stone tower atop a hill. The tower, with its curved double roof and archway is the entrance to a village. Steps lead up from a little area of beach to the archway and a large, ramshackle shed stands to one side of it. On the river itself, moored to a jetty, is a cafe. A large wooden deck, sitting by the looks of things on some wooden legs and plastic oil drums. It has a straw roof, a plank to walk up and lots of folding chairs and tables. At the far end, a woman is cooking over a gas ring.

We paddle towards the jetty and a man comes down the plank to catch the boats so we can climb out. He welcomes us warmly and invites us to have lunch at the cafe. We're handed menus and order chow mein and bottles of water.

The man who helped us onto dry land has disappeared with our kayaks, but the whole atmosphere is so friendly and laid-back that we roll along with it. We eat in silence and look at the view. The woman cooking asks us if we liked it. We tell her 'yes'.

'Go and see the village,' she tells us, 'ruin village up the steps – then we help you get home.'

'OK!' we call back, happy to be taken in hand by people who seem to know what they're doing.

We walk up the steps and through the archway. On the far side of the tower is a space that feels as if it might have been the village square. Paths lead in all directions away from us. Cobbled streets are overgrown with grass. Here and there a wall of enamelled tiles stands out among the dusty white walls and chipped red bricks. Some of the houses are still intact, others lie in ruins. This – we later discover – is Liugong village. The houses date from the Ming and Qing dynasties and were constructed between 400 and 800 years ago. It was once the home of senators and wealthy landowners, but now the houses are abandoned and farmers use the pathways to move between their various plots of land. The grander houses sport beautiful circular windows and little diamond openings covered with carved wooden screens.

We turn a corner and find an old lady, sitting on a wooden stool with her back to us, preparing food over a bucket. So tiny are the alleys that she completely blocks the way. We try another alley, this one occupied only by chickens and a fat, brown rooster. One of the houses has an ornate tiled roof decorated with figures and roof charms, a style of architecture that denotes authority and officialdom. Here and there people have started to rebuild and use the empty spaces with tin for roofs or tarpaulin over windows.

The village is full of animals. Families of ducks wander past us, dogs play in circles with each other, here a cow is tethered to a tree, and there a calf runs down to the little beach. There are cats, a litter of puppies, a pig.

We emerge bewildered and intrigued to see the man who helped us ashore waving from a sleek engined boat, on to which he has tied our kayaks.

'I take you back?' he shouts.

And so he does. We sit on little benches on each side of the boat as he drives us back up the river, smoking a cigarette and looking at the view.

The next day, we set out to walk another section of the River Li. The guidebook promises a well-worn path and signage. The guidebook lies.

The number 11 boat drops us off at lunchtime some kilometres downriver and a very old map with peeling yellow and blue paint gently suggests a wiggly line that we may choose to walk. There are landmark hills on the map, but we can't understand their names and we're never going to remember all the shapes. The only other Westerners attempting the walk are a pair of very young Scandinavian women, wearing shorts and beads and pretty tops. As the boat pulls away they look at our trousers and trainers and rucksacks and ask:

'Are we meant to be dressed like that?'

'I don't think there are any rules,' I offer. The taller girl points at her feet. She is wearing paper-thin, beaded flip-flops. Then she points at her friend's feet. Platform espadrilles.

'Do you think we could get a bus instead?' her high-heeled friend asks.

I look around us. We are standing on an overgrown path that runs along the side of a mountain covered in jungle plants and trees. There are no houses in sight, no villages, no roads, no signs apart from the old map. We are a long way from Yangshuo.

'There is not going to be a bus,' her friend tells her, somewhat sharply.

The high-heeled girl is not happy. She stalks back to the river edge and sits pointedly on the bank: her back radiating anger like a cat's.

The tall girl looks at us and says very matter-of-factly: 'She is an idiot.' I sense they are not having the best time travelling together.

We leave them waiting for the late afternoon boat and set off down the path. At least we think it's a path. For a while it's a dusty road. Then we're just walking through a field. Then we pass along a line of bushes. We keep the river in our sights but we're at the mercy of a path that snakes its way higher and lower, and up and down the sides of the mountain. At times we get very high up and seem to be walking around the mountain, almost losing sight of the river. We scramble down a bank and then a ledge, then walk back a bit until we can climb down to a thin groove of brown along the edge of the river. Down on the bank again, we can see extraordinary butterflies flittering above the flowers. The wings of one sparkle and glimmer with iridescent teal and violet swirls. Another is striped black and emerald green, flashes of red weaving their way through the black. They are magical. Unreal.

As I try to photograph the butterflies, Chris stops, stretches and looks out along the river. The view is overwhelming. If you gave yourself all the time you wanted to look at it you'd never finish the walk. In the distance, a line of dark green peaks snake and curve just beneath the clouds. Nearer us, the cliffs are streaked white and black and crowned with great furry caps of forest. The plants along the edge of the river glow green in the bright blue sunlight and the river itself shimmers green with their reflection. It is a landscape out of a storybook. The kind of place where you expect to come upon a many-turreted castle, with a drawbridge and a moat and a fiery dragon. Instead, the only building we have passed in the last hour was a large white compound bearing a dark hammer and sickle and flying the red flag. China does have a way of sitting fatly on one's romantic notions.

A lady on a raft pulls up below us and shouts something to us.

'What does she want?' I ask.

'Probably trying to sell us snacks.'

'Let's just ignore her,' I say and we press on.

But she won't leave us alone. She is following us now down the river, pushing her raft along with a long pole as if she were punting. Beside her sits a basket of food.

We can't seem to outpace her but we try. Every minute or so she shouts something unintelligible up the bank at us.

We walk faster still but now the path is dipping lower and we are walking almost at river level. Finally her words become clear:

'You're on the wrong side. You need to cross over. You're going to run out of path.'

Oh.

We stare at her, still unsure.

'Look!' she says, pointing across the river to where a line of walkers can just be seen trailing along the other side.

Bugger.

'You meant to get boat across back there. You didn't get boat. I can help you cross river.'

'OK,' we say. 'Thanks.'

She doesn't ask for anything but we tip her five yuan, which is what we have on us. Feeling very silly we continue on our way. There is indeed a much better path on this side and we don't disappear round any mountains.

The path curves high above a grassy plain now, where skinny brown cattle graze in the sun and water buffalo lumber gently down to the water's edge. There are finally signs of habitation, beans staked in rows, a compound made of wood, a makeshift bridge over a stream. Now the fields are filling up with deep green maize and a little concrete aqueduct carries water across them. We pass a ruined village, its houses torn to pieces, roofs missing, walls missing, blue tarps billowing mysteriously in the windows. I guess the houses must still be occupied, squatted in perhaps. Now a village. Now a beach. Now a line of boats, a line of flags, a *paifang*. A mere 4 hours 30 minutes from start to finish and we are back in town.

It's twilight on the River Li and we take our seats for *Impression Liu Sanjie*. The sky darkens until we can no longer see the clouds above the tops of the karsts and the whole world seems veiled in a blue haze. Thousands have gathered on the banks as they do every night of the year to see the most extraordinary show in China. The tree-lined edges of the river are shrouded now and the mountains transformed into deep inky monsters, pyramids, camel humps against a watery night sky.

Liu Sanjie is a woman found in the oral traditions of the Zhuang people, a vast ethnic minority, mostly resident in Guangxi and second only to the Han people in their number. She is believed by many of the Zhuang to be a real person. In stories her name is given as Liu Shanhua; Liu Sanjie literally meaning third daughter of the Liu family. She is said to have been the re-incarnation of a lark and spoke in a whimsical and melodious tone of voice. In her teens she became famous among the Zhuang as a singer of folk songs. A local lord wished to take her as his concubine but Liu Sanjie rejected him. He plotted to murder her but with the help of her true love Liu Sanjie escaped, fleeing her village and finally finding freedom when she and her lover were transformed into a pair of larks.

The lights along the riverbank go out. We are plunged into near darkness. Liu Sanjie appears in the distance in a small boat that is lit from within. Her voice carries over the water. Lights come up on the 12 karsts that serve as a natural backdrop.

The film director Zhang Yimou worked for three and a half years to create this nightly production that utilises a cast of more than 600 and has been running continuously for ten years. It employs hundreds of Yangshuo men, women and children and many of the local fishermen perform in it each night on a stage that stretches for 2 kilometres along the River Li. I can't remember when I have encountered anything quite like it.

The story is told through a series of 'impressions', songs and tableaux. We start with Red Impression, an exultation of the work of fishermen on the River Li. Pushing themselves on rafts across the water, the fishermen appear before us in lines. They rise carefully to standing and unfurl great red silk banners that billow across the water, linking raft to raft to raft, and turning the whole scene red. I sense a subtle political message may be being played out. Suddenly the banners dip into the water and Liu Sanjie's boat skims across the top of them. Dozens of giant spotlights stream green light into the sky, ushering in a new impression.

In Green Impression, the far bank fills up with women washing clothes, birdsong echoes above our heads, cattle are herded home for the night and the sky fills with smoke from fires cooking evening meals. It is a rural idyll, the background to Liu Sanjie's childhood.

In Blue Impression, Liu Sanjie appears again, singing love songs in the classical Chinese style. Her pavilion floats on one boat, an island of trees on another. A crescent moon moves across the water towards us and on top of it a golden fairy – to the eyes of the audience naked but for her wings – dances. Fishermen in white-striped suits paddle rafts in long, snaking lines around the various tableaux. A young woman runs along the bank and kneels by the black water, staring into its depths.

Hundreds of Zhuang girls are snaking across the water now, their clothes studded with thousands of bright white lights, creating a galaxy of moving stars for Silver Impression. They join hands and dip and swirl before us in the darkness. Suddenly the lights are gone and the music echoes in absolute black. The audience holds its breath. Then the thousand white stars blaze again and the girls join hands to dance in swirling, dizzying circles of light.

Pijiu yu
Beer fish

The dish is true to many of the tastes of Guangxi province and borrows some of the heat and richness from neighbouring Hunan Province as well. The main flavours in the sauce are bitter and hot. It needs to be served with lots of steamed rice because the sweetness of the rice helps to balance the bitterness of the beer sauce. If you find the sauce is getting overpowering, try tossing it together with your rice as you eat to balance the two flavours.

Serves 2
Preparation and cooking time: 35 minutes

40 g plain white flour for coating
1 tsp salt
300 g white fish (ideally freshwater with a firm flesh), washed; or 300 g firm tofu, well pressed; cut fish or tofu into 5-cm cubes
5 tbsp groundnut oil for frying

Sauce:
5-cm piece of ginger, finely chopped
6 cloves garlic, finely chopped
1 red chilli, chopped
4 medium tomatoes, chopped
250 ml Chinese beer
1 tbsp light soy sauce
1 tsp Guilin Style Chilli Sauce (available in Asian grocery stories and some supermarkets under the Lee Kum Kee brand)

Garnish:
2 spring onions, topped, tailed and sliced
Handful of coriander, washed and roughly chopped

Put the flour and salt in a shallow dish and coat the fish or tofu. Heat the oil in the wok over a medium high heat and fry the fish or tofu until the flour is golden brown and crispy at the edges.

Using a slotted spoon remove the fish or tofu from the pan and retain roughly 3 tablespoons of oil in the wok for the sauce. With the wok over a medium heat add the ginger, garlic and chilli and fry for a scant minute. Now add the tomatoes. Turn the heat up to reduce the liquid from the tomatoes quickly. You don't want the tomatoes to be completely cooked; you're just boiling off the liquid. When the liquid is low, add the beer, soy sauce and chilli sauce.

Cook the sauce over a medium heat and add the fried fish or tofu. Don't stir too much or your fried pieces will disintegrate. When the fish or tofu is heated through, pile everything into a pretty bowl for the table and sprinkle over spring onions and coriander.

Guilin mi fen
Guilin noodles

The key ingredients here are really good stock, fresh noodles with bite and the pickled green beans. Take time to get this recipe right and it will become a lunchtime staple.

Serves 2
Preparation and cooking time: 25 minutes

150 g pork or beef
4 tbsp unsalted nuts (peanuts or pistachios are recommended – vegetarians should double this amount)
300 g fresh rice noodles (you can buy these in packets from most large supermarkets)
2 spring onions, finely chopped
4 long chives, chopped
2–4 tbsp pickled green beans (recipe follows below), chopped into short lengths
1 clove garlic, minced
1–2 tsp chilli flakes or fresh red chilli, chopped
400 ml stock (beef, pork, horse or vegetable – homemade ideally and as rich as possible)

If using meat, fry or grill to your preference and slice into thin strips. Set aside.

Dry fry the nuts then remove them from the pan and crush roughly.

Prepare the noodles according to the packet instructions. When ready, drain and put into two serving bowls. Gently heat your stock.

If using meat, lay the strips on top of the noodles and sprinkle over the 4-tablespoon quantity of dried fried nuts and the spring onions, chives, pickled beans, garlic and chilli.

For the vegetarian version, sprinkle over the 8 tablespoons of dried fried nuts and the other ingredients. Ladle the stock over everything. Some people prefer their Guilin noodles served quite dry, others like them covered in stock.

Notes on making a good stock

Much of the delight in the noodle dishes of Vietnam and China is down to the quality of the stock. A classic Chinese stock uses no herbs (these are all added later when you make the dish). The best stocks are made with a whole chicken but a carcass is acceptable as well. Pork bones, ham or duck may be added to this to increase the richness.

If you want to make your own stock, I would offer the following advice:

To make meat stock from leftovers collect and store the following: bones from meat, clean vegetable peelings, stalks from fresh herbs. If you never have leftover bones, ask your butcher if you can buy a bag of bones. You can also add in whole, peeled vegetables and fresh or dried herbs.

Beef, lamb, pork or horsemeat stock benefits from having the main ingredients roasted beforehand. Roast the bones and a couple of halved onions in a hot oven for an hour and then add these to your stockpot. Chicken stock benefits from being made with a whole chicken carcass in the pot.

Completely submerge all the ingredients in a large pot of water and cook at a gentle simmer for a couple of hours or until the stock has taken on the required taste. As it cooks remove the froth that floats to the top of the pan. If the stock seems too weak, give it more time. When you're happy with the taste, strain the stock through a sieve. You may also wish to chill it overnight and then remove the fat from the top of the stock.

Vegetarian stock benefits from using the same roasting method as the one for meat. Fill a roasting tin with halves of onions, cloves of garlic and perhaps some thyme or rosemary. Then roast in a hot oven for up to an hour. Now use this to start your stock and add plenty of vegetables or clean scraps to give it interest. Good vegetables and herbs for stock include: onions, celery, carrots, Chinese cabbage, mushrooms, daikon, lotus root, leeks, potatoes, fennel, parsnips, bay leaves, pepper, thyme, parsley, ginger, cloves and lemongrass.

Chinese fish stock is made using a whole fish that has been scaled, cleaned and gutted. Chunks of fish are then fried in oil until they are golden brown. Then the chunks are simmered with ginger and root vegetables for several hours to make a milky, sweet broth. To reduce the risk of bones making their way into the broth, you can tie the chunks of fish in muslin before they go into the pot. This stock is highly nutritious and excellent invalid food.

Pao jiangdou
Pickled green beans

These beans are an essential garnish to Guilin noodles. As well as being delicious in their own right, the brine they're pickled in helps to season broths, noodles, rice, meat and salad. I will happily sprinkle a handful over any bowl of Asian soup or noodles. Once you've opened a jar, you can also eat the pickled garlic cloves.

To make enough for two 227-g jars
Preparation time: 20 minutes
Pickling time: 2 weeks

400 g fresh green beans (you can buy the Chinese variety –
often called long beans – in Asian grocery stores)
300 ml white vinegar
2 tsp salt
4 cloves garlic
2 bay leaves
2 star anise
10 black peppercorns
½ tsp chilli flakes

Sterilise jars and lids (old, clean jam jars are fine) in boiling water.
Wash and trim ends off the beans.
To make the brine, mix vinegar with the salt with 150 ml water in a saucepan. Bring to a simmer.

Place 2 garlic cloves, 1 bay leaf, 1 star anise, 5 peppercorns and 1/4 tsp chilli flakes in each jar. Put the green beans into the jars. You may have to curl them into spirals to make them fit. Pour the brine over the beans until the jars are full. Put the lids on tightly.

Keep refrigerated and leave for two weeks before tasting. They will keep for a month in the fridge after opening.

Chapter 7

Stories from the Burial House

After ten days in Guilin and Yangshuo we get back on the train and head across the border to Vietnam, and back to lovely Hanoi with its cool French Imperial vibe, fine food and deadly traffic systems.

I'm still playing with ideas and characters for the play in my head – the one inspired by our visit to Banpo – so I'm keen to visit the Ethnology Museum in Hanoi. On our first full day back in town we gobble down a breakfast of baguette and scrambled eggs and rush to catch the bus from Hoan Kiem Lake. According to the guidebook the bus stops a few blocks short of the museum itself. Though the weather was sultry in Yangshuo, we are not prepared for the grizzly heat of Hanoi in midsummer. A misty morning evaporates to reveal a harsh, blue sky and angry sun. In the rush to leave we have forgotten both our sun hats and suncream. We are alone in getting off the bus at the given stop and as we stand in the large suburban street we realise we have no idea which way to go.

We walk. And we walk. Residential streets give way to more residential streets. In the unbearable heat of late morning, no one else is walking the streets and there are no shops where we can ask for directions. We walk for nearly 50 minutes, before reaching what seems to be the edge of the city and turn round. Finally, after nearly two hours we make it to the museum.

As Chris wanders from room to room, quiet and slightly stunned from the heat, I write and take notes and photographs of the clothes, the buildings and the artefacts. Chris goes to sit in a shady courtyard. There is a cafe but we have forgotten to bring sufficient money with us so we go without lunch. Truth be told, we're not that hungry and both feel oddly nauseous.

Inside the dark halls, I am madly writing – trying to understand multiple worlds all at once. Vietnam is home to 54 different ethnic groups, some so small that they occupy only a few villages and some numbering in the hundreds of thousands. They are a mixture of patriarchal and matriarchal societies and each has their own religion, mythologies, literature, art, industry and traditions.

The whole museum is arrayed like a temple to marriage, birth and death. As I walk from room to room I learn about the wedding practices of the Bo Y from northern Vietnam. On the day of marriage the bridegroom sends his younger sister with a horse to fetch the bride to him. The bride then emerges from her house carrying a pair of scissors – an item associated with ritual in Vietnam – and a small chicken that she releases into the forest when she is halfway to her new home. Romam women from central Vietnam no longer give birth in a hut in the woods – as is common among other Viet people. Instead birth happens at home. Strangers may not enter the house while the woman is in labour and if this rule is broken the stranger must be detained and prevented from leaving until the mother is ready to leave the house and present her child: who will then be named after the stranger.

Outside, in the grounds of the museum are replica tombs and burial houses representing the ways of death in Vietnam. Many groups will come together to build an intricate tomb, within which the burial will happen. This tomb – which looks rather like a single-room house – will be meticulously crafted and filled with statues, carvings and embellishments. The rituals of mourning will then happen within the tomb itself. People will gather together inside, eat fine food, drink alcohol or water and talk about the person they've lost. This concentrated mourning will last anywhere from a few days to a month.

After the first flush of mourning, the relatives and friends will leave the tomb and return to their lives. In some groups the tomb will be revisited for a meal on the anniversary of the loved one's death. But this tradition is normally limited to the first few years. Each group has a cut off point beyond which the tomb must not be visited and after which it will be left to fall into disrepair.

I can't help feeling that other cultures are much better at dealing with death than we are. The British tend to get the funeral out of the way and then attempt to pull themselves together as quickly as possible, which is an intensely practical way of doing things but not really respectful of the impact that death has on us.

I find myself sitting in a replica burial house in the garden thinking about my family and my own responses to death. So much about the museum speaks to the domestic and the female: all that is required of a woman, how she dresses, who she serves, who she loves, who she produces out of herself. As much as I want children and have always wanted children – endlessly drawing pictures of mothers with babies from the age of five or six – I also fear this next part of my life. When I look back at the women in my family I am reminded how fragile a woman's independence can be.

My maternal great-grandmother Eliza arrived in the UK in the 1890s, a French Jewish teenager sent over to London with only her younger sister, Juliette, for company. This was an age when many middle-class Jewish teens were sent away to avoid the anti-Semitic violence which was common on the continent but less so in the UK. Eliza and her sister met and married two young Jewish brothers from Poland: Victor and Daniel Luxemburg. Victor was a bright man, a grafter and an entrepreneur, who made a fortune and then lost it through unwise property speculation and gambling. Eliza and Victor had four children, my grandmother Iréne, Claude, Maximilian and Maurice and educated them at Roedean and St Paul's. But it was not a happy marriage. Eliza was a nicely-brought-up Jewish girl who cared about propriety and reputation. Victor shamed the family by investing in revue clubs in Soho and showed his utter disdain for Eliza's beloved religion when he came home drunk one evening and lit his cigar on the Friday night candles.

Iréne, born in 1905, was an intensely clever woman, as bright if not brighter than her brothers. But though she excelled at school Eliza and Victor denied her the opportunity to go to university. She had to watch as her brothers sailed off to Oxford and she stayed at home, teaching herself about music and literature and politics. A cousin of Rosa Luxemburg – who co-founded the German Communist Party and was murdered in 1919 for her political actions – Iréne had within her family the example of a woman who had lived the full expression of her intellect and beliefs. Rosa never had children, a fact which arguably left her free to take the considerable risks she did in pursuit of her beliefs.

In 1942 Iréne was 36, living in Cambridge and working in a left wing bookshop when she met Ted, a journalist ten years her junior who was doing his military training outside the town. She had had two significant relationships in her twenties, but neither had resulted in marriage. Then biology intervened. Iréne fell pregnant, which necessitated her marriage to Ted. From the very beginning the marriage was not a success. As a couple, Ted and Iréne had politics in common but little else. After the war their marriage slowly and painfully crumbled and Ted left. Iréne found herself a single parent, supporting two small girls and her impoverished parents. She worked numerous jobs, ploughing herself into keeping everything afloat. Her intellectual abilities were subjugated to her need to earn money, to support her children.

My other grandmother, though very different in some ways, found herself hamstrung by a similar set of conventions. My father's mother Cicely was born in 1908 and grew up in Ledbury, Herefordshire, an only child. Her parents' marriage was not a happy one and she became the go-between and the negotiator. She was dreamy and bookish, very fond of novels and history and she was sent away to a little boarding school where she did well and made plans to go on to university. But at the age of 17 Cicely was called home. Her father had had a breakdown and was unable to look after the family business. Cicely stepped into his place and proved herself a very able businesswoman, though her hair went completely white in the course of that year. When her father recovered she announced her plan to finish school and try for one of the few universities that accepted women students. Her parents told her no. They were ageing and she was their only child. She had to stay at home.

For eight long years Cicely lived at home, dreaming of a different life. Then, at the age of 26, she went to a party and met a schoolteacher – Robert, 15 years her senior – who was up from London visiting friends. Robert was Cicely's way to escape Ledbury and so they married, bought a house in the London suburbs and started a family. But even after her escape Cicely felt trapped by the life of a suburban housewife. She was bored staying at home. She worked for the local Conservative Party and raised money to send children living in poverty on holiday to the country. She never let go of the fact that she loved books and could have gone to university. I remember her talking of it often when I visited her: a bookish, only child myself.

Iréne was a secular Jew and a staunch socialist; Cicely was Church of England and a lifelong Tory. But they were women of the same generation: the only girls in their family; intellectuals who had been denied a university education because of their gender; women who were politically engaged and active and who felt conflicted about the tasks that domestic life required them to fulfil. How much different their lives might have been had they been allowed the opportunities of the men who were their brothers and contemporaries: the intellectual validation of a place at university and the hundred doors into the future that such a place provides.

Ted and Iréne had two daughters, my mother Jenny and my aunt Liz. Liz was the elder; tall, good looking and extremely academic. She was a scholarship girl who went on to study organisational psychology and gain three degrees. My mother, Jenny, was the creative in the family, dark and strikingly beautiful, gifted as an artist and actor. After school she studied first art and then drama and went on to work extensively in theatre and television, as well as writing poetry and plays.

Liz and Jenny's experience was in many ways typical of their generation of middle-class, female baby boomers. They studied the subjects they felt passionate about and launched themselves into the world of work in their twenties. They were economically independent, politically aware and sexually liberated. Both Liz and Jenny met their partners in their twenties and had their children as they went into their thirties. But the lives they had after marriage and children were not the lives they had had before. My mother continued to work as an actress for several years after I was born, but the demands of childcare and the need to settle somewhere so that I could go to school contributed to her withdrawing from that world. The needs of Liz's family, the breakdown of her marriage and ongoing illness combined to pull her away from her working life.

After their children left home, Iréne and Jenny both found a way back into their creative, intellectual lives. But a hiatus of 15 or 20 years is a long one. I feel as if I may be pausing at the edge of a two-decade-long interval in my own life. As if everything may come to a grinding halt when I have little people to care for. Or will it be different for me because I belong to a different generation? Has the world moved on? Or does your fate depend more on luck, money and personality?

My family was not a large one. My paternal grandfather Robert died before I was born; Ted died when I was eight. I knew only my parents, my grandmothers, my aunt and her two children. The year that I was 14 my aunt Liz died at the age of 46. That same year I lost my grandmother Cicely and three years later Iréne. By the age of 18 my close family consisted of my parents and my two lovely cousins. And we were a fragile bunch, riven with grief over the loss of too many people.

I dream of having a child. And I dream of having a child because we have been so few for so long. Death has left a deep impression on each of us. I long to bring new life into our family. To swell our numbers and bring us back to life and hope.

But as with so many things, while hope pulls me in one direction, fear pulls me in the other.

In my twenties I was single, economically independent, intellectually fulfilled: sometimes lonely but always free. As I move into my thirties, I wonder if I will be required to leave that all behind. I find myself financially dependent for the first time in my adult life, and that state will surely extend into the child-bearing years. My career as a writer is fragile, only just beginning. Chris – like many bright men of his generation – is a good feminist but as things stand economically I will be the one to stay home with the children. Many years ago, when I was still a very little girl, I came up with idea of being a writer because – don't laugh – that's what the mother in *The Railway Children* did. I looked at her, and later at her creator Edith Nesbit, and saw a model for economic freedom, intellectual fulfilment and motherhood.

I want to learn from the women who came before me. I want to avoid the traps they found themselves in. I want to live out the parts of their lives they were denied. Neither of my grandmothers were alive to see me pass the Oxford exam and make it to St Hilda's College to read English, which saddens me for it is what they dreamed of for themselves and I think it would have made them happy. But Cicely was mindful of my parents' variable income and she left me money in trust to help pay for my further education. I used it in part to pay for Oxford and after that to help me study playwriting at Birmingham. And with the interest earned on the money I started to travel.

We stumble back down the roads to catch the bus. As the boulevards flash past, Chris slumps forward onto his rucksack and starts to groan.

'What's wrong?' I ask him.

He just shakes his head. I don't feel all that good myself. The view outside the window comes and goes and my head is spinning. We get off at Hoan Kiem Lake and I lead Chris into a supermarket to find something to eat.

Neither of us can face the pastries or the sandwiches so we buy a packet of crackers to settle our stomachs and stagger back to the hostel. In the room we close the wooden shutters, drink water, eat a few crackers and lie down on the bed.

Chris groans quietly.

'Honey, what's wrong?' I ask him.

'Don't know,' he says.

I bring him a cold flannel.

'Sunstroke, I think,' he says.

Oh.

'Don't worry,' I say. 'Drink water. Eat crackers. Stay in bed.'

This is largely good advice and we would probably have been absolutely fine had we not contracted violent, violent food poisoning from the crackers. Or the water. We never do discover which.

It's a bonding experience having really horrendous food poisoning while sharing a bathroom with your other half. Not a bonding experience I care to repeat, but I dare say it adds a little something to the relationship.

Neither of us remembers anything about the day after but we emerged on the third day internally battered but with better-fitting jeans. We breakfast lightly and carefully and set out to find an artists' colony we have read about in Lonely Planet.

Once again, we catch a bus into the suburbs, but instead of the palatial cream-coloured mansions and tree-lined streets we find only an industrial wasteland and site after site filled with rubble and demolished warehouses. We get off the bus where the guidebook tells us to and cross a bridge over a sludge-coloured river filled with frothing pollution and rubbish. Across the road a dingy block of brick-built houses and courtyards marks the place where the artists live. We walk the edge of the river looking for signs or entrances. But the houses have closed their eyes to us: windowless, shuttered and seemingly derelict. A gate hangs off its hinges and we step briefly into a courtyard where the ground is piled with vast blocks of broken stone, and chickens step daintily in and out of a rundown stable. From a wary distance we peer through the windows of the neighbouring house, glazed and grimed and empty of life.

'Where is everyone?' we ask each other, pointlessly, as if we were C. S. Lewis's Polly and Digory wandering the streets of Charn before the ringing of the golden bell.

Back on the riverbank we pace back and forth, unable to decide what to do.

'Are you hungry?' Chris asks.

'Well, even if I was…'

'I can smell something.'

I stare into the foaming depths of the grey-black river. 'Sewage?'

'No. I smell something... barbecuing...'

'OK,' and we follow Chris's nose around the edge of the abandoned brick citadel.

As a teenager I had a weakness for a certain kind of posh, mid-century children's literature. The kind where girls called Maud ask girls called Phyllis if they're 'a dog person or a horse person'. Since coming to South-East Asia this has taken on quite another meaning.

On a far edge of this empty block a restaurant opens onto the riverside path. Hanging in rows from the awning are half-carcasses of roasted dog. A freshly killed brown and white dog lies in squared-off pieces on a huge wooden block under the shade of a little tent. Chris looks at me and I look at Chris. I wouldn't put it past him.

He shakes his head. 'Let's go and get the bus.'

Feeling a little wrung out we travel down the line into central Vietnam and to the sometime-capital Hue. We're slow in booking tickets and have to settle for seats on the sleeper train. When the lights go out we doze fitfully, then wake a little after 4.00 a.m. along with the rest of the carriage to watch the sky turn from purple to blue, from blue to orange before breaking apart into wild stripes of colour. The land below glows with a deep warm green. The fields stretch for kilometres, out to the mountains covered in thick forest. In the distance I spot a lone temple with a pineapple-shaped spire, glowing gold at the base of a mountain.

We're staying in the tourist-friendly South Bank district, east of the Imperial Enclosure and south of the Perfume River.

Central Vietnam is where fairy food starts to get its fire back. The cool climate of northern Vietnam is unsuitable for growing spices, but as you head down the tracks the days grow hotter and so does the food. Along with the familiar garnish of fresh herbs, salad leaves and bean sprouts comes chilli in all its forms. And here, as elsewhere, Vietnam observes the balancing of the five tastes: sweet, salty, sour, spicy and bitter. *Umami* is such a recently arrived concept that it doesn't make it into the traditional theory, but it is abundantly evident in the dishes we eat here.

The ubiquitous fish dipping sauce *nuoc cham* – one of the classic tastes of Vietnam – is prepared by balancing the five key tastes. So, the concentrated fish sauce provides the salt, ground pepper (or dried chilli) adds the heat, sugar gives us sweetness, lemon (or lime) zest give us bitterness, and the juice of the fruit rounds everything off with its sour notes.

Eating is as crucial a part of the culture in Vietnam as it is in China. As the saying goes: *Troi danh tranh bua an to*. Even God would not dare to disturb the Vietnamese at dinner.

We decide to sample Vietnamese Imperial cooking so we book a table for the seven-course treat and head out of town after dark in a taxi. It takes us down winding roads to a palatial nineteenth-century house whose lovely garden is filled with palms and orchids, little bridges and strange stone idols. A waiter leads us through an entrance hall tiled in shades of jade and emerald and cream, its windows draped with heavy, oyster-coloured velvet curtains. Above the iron and ceramic fireplace sit a pair of bronze peacocks with glinting jewelled eyes. The look is half Victorian stately home, half Buddhist temple.

The tables are set out in a stone courtyard, which is lit softly with glowing lanterns. Looking up all I can see is the night sky, a few stars gleaming here and there, and one solitary palm tree, its leaves stirring gently in the evening breeze. As we wait for our food a lizard climbs the wall beside us.

I already know that there will be almost nothing for me to eat, but I have come here for the spectacle and I am not disappointed. There is an ornate seafood cocktail with chilli peppers carved into tulips and giant prawns. A little sampling of the crêpe dish *banh xeo* with tomato roses and a ginger dipping sauce. And then crabmeat cooked with vegetables and served in fried shells of prawn batter and an edible phoenix constructed from a whole pineapple – lying on its side – with feathers, tail and head carved out of carrots and a feathered back made from tiny hand-shaped sausages on cocktail sticks. Just for a moment, I imagine Alison Steadman as Beverly fleeing from her ruined life at the end of *Abigail's Party* and opening a restaurant in central Vietnam: 'Little bit of Demis tonight, Binh Phan?' For dessert, a vase arrives filled with foliage and candied flowers on wire stalks, painted to look like succulent fruit. By this point Chris has eaten so much that he is ready to keel over. I have eaten... a lot of carved vegetables. In some respects I get the best of it, as the standard of the cooking is not exemplary. The experience on the other hand, the theatre of the whole thing, is intoxicating and we enjoy ourselves immensely: holding hands and drinking wine and giggling at the oohs and ahhs from the other tables as their phoenix land.

We rent bicycles and cycle out of town to the Imperial City. Set within a citadel 2 kilometres by 2 kilometres, and surrounded by a moat, the Imperial City was begun in 1804 for the Emperor Gia Long, who united what is now modern Vietnam after centuries of feudal warfare. Gia Long moved the capital from Hanoi down to Hue and arranged for his own version of Beijing's Forbidden City to be built in his new capital. Hue remained the capital of Vietnam until the establishment of a communist government in Hanoi in 1945. The Imperial City suffered a great deal of damage during the Tet Offensive of 1968 when it was bombed and shelled along with the rest of the city by the US and allied forces.

Today, parts of the city are intact while others lie in ruins. Most of the courtyards are overgrown now and the huge pools lie stagnant. Some of the lakes are almost completely covered in a lush carpet of green lily pads. Many of the walkways now carry you to... nothing. A building missing here, an absent gateway there, mysterious patches of dirt where people once lived and worked. By crumbling stone balustrades, dry leaves have piled up a metre deep.

A huge iron dragon roars alone in a field of wild flowers. A group of Vietnamese men sit and smoke weed by a three-tiered gateway that now leads to an earthwork. Under trees heavy with fruit and magnolia flowers a line of imperial courtiers stand, carved in stone. They present themselves to us along with an elephant and a horse, standing in a line, staring into space, as if waiting to observe a parade that never arrives. Walking the walls of one compound, covered in blue and white mosaics, we come upon a flesh-and-blood cow just standing on the path, eating grass.

Here and there the splendour shines through. Mythical beasts and scrolling clouds are fashioned on a wall out of fragments of blue and white pottery: the jumble of differently shaped pieces cemented into the outlines of a scene from fantasy. A vast wall down one side of a garden is made out of ceramic blocks, fretted with graphic patterns

like airbricks, and stained amber, olive, indigo and black. In a room inside one of the gateways a painted panel shows a day of ceremony at the court: a line of flags flying in the breeze, men on the backs of elephants, courtiers thronging the courtyards in robes of mint and jade and white, lakes scattered with pink lotus blossom.

We're near the coast and the weather is sizzling, so we decide a day at the beach is in order. I haven't swum since we've been here so I go shopping for a swimsuit in the market. Taste in swimwear is conservative to say the least and swimdresses seem to be the item most available. I buy a cream one covered in 1950s-style red roses and bright green leaves.

The beach is a bit too far to cycle so we take a cab and find, when we get there, a sea intensely green and acres of soft, pale brown sand. Families sit in little groups, most of them fully dressed, and watch the waves break against the steeply sloping beach. Gangs of teenagers, mostly boys, splash about in the sea, often swimming quite far out until you can barely see their heads against the choppy surface of the water. Ladies in pink shirts and pink jeans walk the beach with little boxes full of Coke cans and bags of dried jackfruit. Rows of beach umbrellas proclaim Pepsi in several languages. Further up the beach, away from the sea, large blue huts are available for hire. Set up from the hot sand on stilted legs, they have a bamboo floor, fabric walls and a pitched fabric roof. Inside these spacious blue rooms, middle-class families lounge and eat and play games; the ladies wearing (probably-not-really) Gucci sunglasses, the men dangling heavy Rolex look-alikes from their wrists.

We swim and read and drink and swim and read and catch another cab home as the last of the daylight fades, a little sunburnt, a little sand sore, full of salt and Coke, and slippery with suncream.

We judder down from Hue to Nha Trang on an overnight train, in the relative comfort of a soft-class sleeping compartment. Chris is snoring happily by 10.00 p.m. but I can't sleep. The train bumps and bangs. I feel dislocated, homesick for Beijing, homesick for China and Chinese trains and a country I had just settled into. I feel worn out by this constant movement. I speak no Vietnamese, and French seems to be of almost no use at all. I just want to stop moving.

I climb down and watch the dark rice fields and the shadows of mountains fly past against a grey-black, blue-black sky. Hours pass. No one stirs. Unlike the Chinese trains we've come to know so well, there are no midnight suppers or late-night card games. On the sleeper everyone sleeps and I am alone in this strange, dark country.

I have the sense of things slipping away from me. I have lost a handle on why we're here. After all, since we had to leave China we are only here because we can't go home. Home itself no longer seems to exist. The house may or may not still be ours. Our possessions may be there or they may be gone. I have a recurring nightmare. A fire in the house consuming everything. Sometimes we are trapped inside and sometimes we are outside, unable to stop it, unable to help.

I have said goodbye to my possessions. They are just things. I'm sad about the writing. All those plays. My half–finished epic historical romance. Notebooks crammed with poetry, sketches and tiny watercolours. One or two things from my grandmothers that I would have wanted to keep. But I have let it go. Things are not people. In my growing years I lost too many people. I know the worth of human life.

Chris is my home now and he is here. So, what is my problem? I'm home, aren't I? Why do I feel so lost?

I think about that night in Beijing. That driving certainty that it was my time to leave. That overwhelming need to run. I've always been quick to say goodbye. I've walked out on jobs, gone missing from friendships, walked away from relationships, moved home, moved town, moved country. I am always on the lookout for the next possible loss, the next possible rejection. I leave before I can be pushed. Sometimes I just leave before I get too close, too dependent.

In part, it's just that I'm a bit of a loner. An only child, bookish and a bit dreamy. I like my own company, I'm never bored, my mind whirs constantly, interested in a million different things at once.

And in part it's that too many people left when I was young. At points in my teens I felt that everyone I loved would leave, everyone I loved would die. Even now, in my thirties I find it hard to believe that the people I love won't just disappear one day. It seems so inevitable.

In truth, it's just easier to run away.

Bun thit nuong
Grilled pork or aubergine on noodles

Like a lot of Vietnamese food this dish is quite delicate in its seasoning. It's sweet and sharp and fresh: a perfect, summer supper.

Serves 2
Preparation and cooking time: 2 hours 30 minutes

300 g pork, sliced or 1 large aubergine, quartered then sliced
2–6 tbsp unsalted peanuts (use more in the vegetarian version because this is your protein)
300 g rice vermicelli
Half a handful of fresh mint leaves
5-cm piece of cucumber, unpeeled and cut into matchsticks
1 tbsp pickled vegetables (or see *do chua* recipe in Chapter 8)

Marinade:
50 g minced lemongrass
50 g sugar
2 tbsp fish sauce (for vegetarians: 1 tbsp dark soy sauce and 1 tbsp light soy sauce)
1 tbsp ground black pepper
3 cloves garlic, crushed
2 shallots, minced
3 tbsp groundnut oil

Nuoc cham **dipping sauce:**
6 tbsp of a solution of 1 part sugar to 3 parts water
2 tbsp fresh lime juice
1 tsp fresh lime zest

2 tbsp fish sauce (for vegetarians: 1 tbsp light soy sauce)
1 clove garlic, crushed or minced
½ tsp crushed dried chilli

Combine everything needed for the marinade. Toss the pork or aubergine slices in it and leave to marinate for 2 hours.

Dry fry the peanuts in a pan until slightly browned. Remove from heat, crush roughly and set aside.

Prepare the *nuoc cham* by combining everything and decanting into dipping bowls.

When the 2 hours marinating time are up, heat a griddle pan until hot. Remove the aubergine or pork from the marinade and griddle until well cooked. Remove from heat.

Boil a large saucepan of water and cook the rice vermicelli for 6 minutes. Eat a strand to check it's cooked through. Drain and refresh in cold water.

Place the noodles in a bowl and top with the pork or aubergine. Sprinkle over the mint, cucumber, pickled vegetables and reserved fried peanuts. Serve to table with *nuoc cham* on the side.

Chapter 8

The Little Red Book of Diving

The sun shines citrus-bright on whitewashed buildings and dusty grey-brown streets. We walk down the middle of the quiet road with our rucksacks, Lotus bag and Korean tennis game. Past the little white tower blocks, open-air cafes and dozens of wrought-iron-clad patios lies an endless sweep of pale, golden sand and lines of fluttering palm trees. The esplanade is clean and modern and banks of sunloungers cling to the edges of the beach waiting for the holidaymakers to arrive.

Chris reminds me of that moment in *Back to the Future II* when Marty visits 2015 and walks past a poster enjoining people to 'Surf Vietnam', an idea so wildly unimaginable in 1989 – 14 years after the end of the devastating war – that it felt worthy of a jokey prediction in a major film. But now the prediction is made real, here in Nha Trang, home to surfers, scuba divers, spa lovers and sun seekers.

After a string of cheap hostels of variable quality, we're treating ourselves to a B&B – the Perfume Grass Inn – for our few nights here. Three days on the beach, we reckon, and then we'll set off to Ho Chi Minh City (formerly Saigon) refreshed.

We drop our bags at the hotel, where they're serving departing guests breakfast, and set out to get our bearings. Two roads down from us we spot a sign proclaiming 'Book Exchange' in English. We step into a large, light interior. Wooden tables and cushioned chairs wait for us and a cat wanders from table to table. As a young Vietnamese woman feeds her noisy, exuberant toddler in the back garden we melt into little cups of sweet, thick Vietnamese coffee and Chris prowls the bookcases like a strangely cerebral wolf, plucking volumes from the shelves and cramming them beneath his arms.

The sun is up and heat and light bounce through the glassless windows from the surface of the road. I invite the cat onto my lap but she prefers to swaddle my legs. Too hot to be cuddling cats anyway. We order more coffee. I open a Kate Atkinson and read.

High on coffee we head out again into the sweltering heat. The sun seems to be sitting 20 metres above our heads. We make it down a few roads and pause again by the posters outside the Rainbow Divers building: a PADI centre taking bookings for try dives.

In this throbbing, pounding heat I cannot think of anywhere that I'd rather be than in the sea. We've been hoarding the money left over from our eight-pounds-a-day budget for moments such as this. We head in and book two places for tomorrow's dive.

The dusty roads are barely busier than they were this morning. We lope up and down the roads until we are hit full on by the heady and unexpected smell of cumin, coriander and curry leaf on a quiet cross road.

Under an awning and at the top of a series of white tiled steps, sits a dark, quiet Indian restaurant, as barely furnished as a theatre set: just walls and floor and tables and chairs. We order big bottles of Kingfisher and a waiter brings us poppadums and lime pickle. I haven't tasted Indian food in more than six months and I am immediately transported home. Home to south London, home to Oxford, home to Birmingham, home to Wales. Indian food tastes like every home I've ever had. From Haweli in St Margarets to Swagat in Richmond; to Lal Quila in Lyme Regis and the many wonders to be found on Balti Row in Birmingham; to Shezan in Oxford where Belfast-born Chris had his first taste of Indian food and nearly passed out from the heat; and Vegetarian Food Studio in Cardiff with its little homemade pots of sun-hot chutney.

If I shut my eyes, I'm back in Brixton, eating curry and drinking beer and laughing with Chris. The Chris who was and is my friend. The Chris who I loved and who left me. The Chris who never really went away. The Chris who has become a part of the fabric of my life. Who is so woven into who I am that I can't imagine saying goodbye. The icy cold Kingfishers sweat drops of ice water over our fingers. We break the poppadums and pass them back and forth with the comforting familiarity of religious ritual.

The waiter brings us copper-brown bowls of ghee-shined, turmeric-bright balti and white bowls of fragrant pilau rice. Every wonderful mouthful is infused with nostalgia and the passion for a home I can't leave any more than I can leave the man I love.

Nha Trang is a relatively new city. Until the 1920s the area was a tropical expanse of jungle and scrubland, dotted with a few fishing villages along the coast and inhabited by tigers, parrots, eagles and rare deer. Under French rule a town was established on one of the larger bays and Nha Trang quickly grew into a thriving municipality funded by shipbuilding, tourism and fishing. Today, it's one of Vietnam's principle tourist destinations and home to more than 400,000.

Much of Nha Trang cuisine centres on locally caught seafood, but marinated and grilled pork and beef is also a local speciality. The meat is soaked overnight in a mixture of fish sauce, sugar, salt, pepper, starch and sweet annatto oil, deep red like henna and peppery on the tongue. It's pressed onto wooden skewers to make a kind of mini kebab and grilled until crisp on the outside. Key to the rich seduction of the dish is the dipping sauce that is served with the meat. There are various versions, but it can include sticky rice, prawns, minced pork, pig's liver, soy sauce, red onion, annatto oil, sugar, salt and pepper, roast peanuts and red chillies. The meat and sauce are served with fresh salad vegetables, boiled rice noodles and rice paper. You break off pieces of meat and arrange your table-made spring roll with green vegetables and light white noodles, before dipping the whole lot into the extraordinary sauce.

In the evening we wander down Tran Phu – the long, curving beachside road – home to many restaurants and bars. We choose a restaurant with a pretty balcony and drink beer and cocktails as the dark descends on the lovely beach and the communist-themed illuminations spring to life. We walk drunkenly back to the hotel, stopping to admire the illuminated Lenin and the mighty, glowing presence of Ho Chi Minh in statue form.

We breakfast on bananas, jackfruit, butter and brioche and roll up to Rainbow Divers just as the bus is leaving. Having read and signed the slightly terrifying safety disclaimer we scramble aboard and join multiple pairs of girl travellers from Australia, Sweden, South Africa, Germany and France.

On board the boat we sit through a fairly intensive class on what we'll be wearing, how we'll be staying safe and what you have to remember getting in and out of the water. It's a bit of a shock to the system, suddenly finding myself in a classroom again; but I have a healthy fear of drowning so I drag my attention to where it needs to be.

The boat takes us out to sea and we change into our suits, weight belts, masks and fins (those long rubber shoes that help to propel you through the water). Then they fit us with a scuba unit and we attempt to walk down the metal ladders in fins, staggering and tottering like baby penguins drunk on freedom and sake. I concentrate on not falling over my own feet, which is harder than it looks. Wearing the suit out of water, you feel disabled, as if you've grown extra limbs overnight and are now expected to use them.

Once in the water, an experienced diver helps us to get accustomed to breathing through the regulator and when we're comfortable and have practised the underwater signs we go gently down, down, down. We stretch out flat in the water and our instructor swims above us, looping his arms around us and using tiny delicate movements to point out the coral and fish. Held like this, the underwater world feels safe and comfortable. We do no swimming ourselves, just watch how the light moves above us near the surface, how the water swims with grit and sand: like motes in a shaft of light. The water above is blue and green, streaked with white.

White coral springs from the rocks like soft bonsai pines; every tendril tipped with a firework burst of red and orange. Two rocks on and a great orange octopus of coral drapes itself over the craggy grey, a thousand white daisies riding its limbs. We swim lower and a forest of white/grey coral makes way for purple and brown where the rocks are hidden from the light. Tiny fish swim calmly past. Occasionally our instructor stills us to allow a creature to pass untouched. We are under strict instructions to touch nothing living: no fish, no crabs, no seahorses, no coral. A tiny orangey-brown crab spotted with black, scuttles across the rocks carrying something between two pincers. I am entranced. I feel as if I've gone to space or entered a mythical world. How can a world like this exist so close to our own and yet remain a virtual secret?

Back on the boat we breathlessly compare notes. We cannot bear the thought of leaving without diving at least once more. Back at the offices we look at our options. We can do more try dives but everything else is barred to us because we haven't taken our PADI certificates – we aren't trained, we aren't safe. We look wistfully at the PADI courses running for the rest of the week. We're meant to be moving on to Ho Chi Minh City (HCMC) in less than two days.

We can't really afford it. We have two thousand pounds to last us three to four months and get us home. Of course, there is our contingency fund...

In the end we spend our contingency on a full PADI course, rebook our hotel in HCMC and pay for extra nights in the now inconveniently expensive B&B.

Our instructor is Grant Martin, a Brit, and one of the most experienced dive instructors in Vietnam. Grant is completely assured; he's also funny, plain-spoken and not above ripping into someone if he or she is not taking things seriously.

The next few days pass in a whirlwind of practice dives in a swimming pool, practical exams in open water and written exams back at the offices. The written exams scare me almost more than the diving. I find memorising anything incredibly difficult – it may be an aspect of the dyslexia or it may just be me. Relaxing at the end of the day with a few beers seems to be the done thing but I quickly discover that diving with a hangover is torture. I stop drinking.

It's meant to be a beach holiday but all I do is revise. And not drink. Sounds deadly but the diving more than makes up for it. From the outside, diving looks like it comes with a lot of stuff: endless pieces of kit that you surround yourself with. But the experience of diving is of being stripped down. Your senses are blunted. Sound travels in odd ways, so you can't trust your ears. You can smell and taste nothing helpful inside your mask. The lower down you go the more visibility fades and currents sometimes carry great slow-moving swirls of sand into your path taking away any sense of where you are and where you're headed. You can touch, but the water and its pressure alters sensation. There's no talking, only the bare bones of communication. Under the sea you have only your equipment, your body, your memory and your wits. It's a great leveller.

I freak out once, just once, but it's once too many. We are sitting on the bottom of the deep end of a swimming pool with Grant, practising taking our regulators – the things divers hold in their mouths to allow them to breathe in oxygen – out and putting them back in. I mistime this and take a great mouthful of water by mistake. Suddenly I am choking. I can't breathe and I can't remember what to do. I look up at the light lying like a sheet above me and all I want is to be there now. So I swim up, much quicker than I should, shooting up into the light to gulp air. Grant comes up after me, shaken by my panic. If I were to ascend that quickly in open water I could give myself decompression sickness that is potentially fatal. I can feel him losing confidence in me.

He's responsible for keeping us alive, and we can't continue if I'm not together enough to follow the basic rules of safety. We talk about it on the edge of the pool and I try to assure him that I won't make the same mistake twice.

But back in the hotel that night I lose confidence. It's one thing telling someone else that something won't happen again. But it's quite another actually making good on that. What if I can't do this? The next time I try this we'll be sitting on the seabed and much further underwater. Panicking out there is not a safe option. I lie in our dark room and listen to the mosquitoes moan against the shutters. The hours pass and I cannot sleep. I sit up in bed, my heart pounding against my chest.

I have to calm down. I have to calm down. I slow my breathing. Counting my way from one to ten in long, deep breaths. One deep breath. Hold. Two deep breath. Hold. Three deep breath. This is how I'll do it. When I panic underwater, I'll just breathe like this. I'm not going to give up. I came out here to get me back to me. I came out here so I wouldn't go into motherhood as a frightened wreck. I know I have the strength of will. I have been through harder things than this.

In the morning we arrive on the quay for our hardest exams yet. Grant is sitting on a pile of lifebelts looking gloomy.

'I didn't sleep last night and I feel like shit. Right. Let's go and do this.'

We follow him quietly onto the boat and are driven out to open water. In time, we descend and join Grant, sitting cross-legged in a circle on the gritty seabed. We have to remove our masks – which normally cover our eyes and our nose, keeping them dry and comfortable – and show that we can swim from one point to another without their protection. This is my favourite bit. Growing up I loved to swim underwater in the sea – off the coast in Hove or Lyme Regis or St Ives. This is part of the appeal to me. Returning to this silent underwater world where I always felt safe as a child: weightless and untouchable, cocooned by the water pressure and the silence. Chris of the cold-North-Sea childhood is terrified of removing his mask. He has never swum underwater without goggles and the feel of the seawater on his eyeballs confuses and scares him. I signal that I will happily go first. I take off my mask and blink as my eyes adjust to the murky depths, the gentle swirls of dirt and sand and my natural short-sightedness turning the world into a tangle of smudged colours and impressions. I swim slowly from the first point to the second, relishing the absolute peace of the world down here.

I replace my mask and glance towards Chris. I can see the tension in his body. I shoot him a smile. He removes his mask and for a moment he flails, arms moving up and down, eyes tight shut. I will him not to panic. He presses his finned feet down into the dirt and sets off, weaving a tentative course towards the stopping point. As soon as he's there he pulls his mask firmly back over his eyes and clears it of water. I shoot him a sneaky OK sign and our eyes wrinkle in a collaborative smile of relief.

Now we have arrived at the part I'm dreading. Removing our regulator and breathing into our mask without it. Grant moves us to the edge of a large underwater rock and leaves us for a minute as he swims to the surface. When he returns, Chris signals that he will go first. He removes his regulator, blows bubbles from his mouth, waits for the signal and replaces it. Simple. But my chest and my shoulders are tight. I look up towards the surface but it's so far away that it registers only as a distant change of light. Chris looks across at me and he holds my gaze. His look is so full of kindness and compassion that for a moment I forget what it is that I'm about to do. He holds my gaze and his eyes shine with love.

Grant signals to check I feel OK. I nod. I take my time. I breathe. 1 2 3 4 5 6 7 8 9 10. I feel my whole body grow calm. I remove the regulator and blow out. 1 2 3 4 5 6 7 8 9 10. As I count I look across to Chris and he looks across at me. His gaze holds mine, his eyes suggesting a slight smile as we wait. Grant nods and I replace the regulator. Chris beams at me and we move off together.

For our final test we have to swim to the surface without our regulator. We must follow the rope of a buoy that floats far away on the surface. The ascent must be done slowly, using a single breath, and controlled movements. I'm up first. I take a long deep breath from the regulator and remove it. I swim, slowly, slowly upwards, bubbling a tiny piece of air from my lips. I pause. I feel different now. I feel in control. Grant is a metre away from me, watching. A second movement of the feet. Slowly, slowly upwards. Not rushing towards the light. Pacing myself.

I distract myself by the beauty of this ascent. Looking up, I am alone in the silent ocean. I am leaving the earthy gloom of the sea floor. The light is flashing and playing above my head. With each tiny kick, I get a little closer to the bright world of the surface. I repeat the process five times. Then six. As I reach the seventh, I can feel the pressure squeezing at my chest, the overwhelming desire to take a breath. Pain is starting to tickle at me. I count in my head. Slowly, slowly up. Bubble, bubble. The surface arrives like a kiss and I am blinking in the glaring sun of midday Khanh Hoa.

Grant's head appears beside me. He removes his regulator.

'Well done. I'll be back with your better half.' And he disappears.

I swim to the next buoy and tread water as I wait. Below me I see the figures of Chris and Grant appear out of the gloom. Then they stop. There are hand movements. And then they're gone again. I wait and I tread water. The sun beats down on my head. Once more Chris and Grant appear from the darkness, only to stop. Signal, signal. Chris replaces his regulator and they disappear again. I sigh gently. Though he has now quit, many years of smoking have left Chris with the lung capacity of a flounder. I stare across the surface of the ocean towards the distant green line of coast. I think about his eyes watching me as I counted. I think about all that may lie before us. Trying to conceive, pregnancy, childbirth, the wild strangeness of a life with children. I think about the hard things we will go through together and the hard things we have faced already. I think about him holding my hand as we stood in line at Brixton Police Station on the morning I was attacked, all that time ago in London. I think about the nights we have sat up and talked. Not just as lovers but as friends. He knows everything about me and I about him.

And then I think about China and how lonely I was and how much I wanted to leave. And I realise something with great clarity. We are each of us independent beings with a lifetime of coping skills deeply ingrained within us. And we are trying to come together. We are trying to learn to cope together: as a unit, not just as two separate beings. And sometimes we are managing it and sometimes we aren't. We both have a tendency to retreat within ourselves and it's hard to move beyond that. But not impossible. I think of Chris's eyes watching me as I tried not to panic and I know with absolute certainty that this is the person I want beside me in the delivery room in some future moment, when I am afraid and in pain and I need to focus on something other than my fear.

I know that these are the eyes I want to look into when the hard moments come. In times of grief. When things go wrong. Because I believe in Chris. I believe in his commitment and his kindness and his love. We are still here, after all the ups and downs: still trying to help each other, trying to reach out.

On his fifth attempt, Chris makes it to the surface and clings to the buoy, winded, unable to speak. I swim over to him.

'You made it,' I say. Chris just rests his head against the buoy and nods soundlessly.

Four exams and two dives later we graduate. We are officially allowed to dive. We toast Grant with a lemonade at the Rainbow Cafe and stagger out into the heat of the evening.

Our legs are stiff and aching, my back is killing me from shouldering the equipment out of the water, we are covered in mosquito bites and my shoulders are horribly sunburnt from the one morning I forgot to apply suncream. But we're going to celebrate, God damn it. Celebrate if it kills us.

We change into our least painful clothes and stagger down to Tran Phu. Cocktails on the balcony, noodles, Vietnamese fried rice, grilled beef with prawn sauce, squid broth. The illuminated hammers and sickles twinkle red in the gathering dark.

One of the odd coincidences of our childhoods is that Chris and I both spent summer holidays in Stratford-upon-Avon. Me because my father worked for the Royal Shakespeare Company on and off through my childhood, and Chris because his father had grown up there and his family would make a yearly crossing from Northern Ireland to visit Chris's grandparents, Alan and Bertha.

Since there were only a handful of things for small people to do in early-1980s Stratford we undoubtedly crossed paths, down by the river, on the lawns outside the theatre, at the Nine Men's Morris, making brass rubbings.

We failed to meet again in the early 1990s, when we both travelled to the Soviet Union – Moscow and then Leningrad – in the last months of its existence. And had my mother not bridled at the idea of me leaving to study in Northern Ireland (The plane rides! The bombs!) I might, as I had planned, have followed my passion for philosophy to Queen's University, where I would have come to know his mother Mary whose job it was to look after the philosophy students. As it was, my mother begged me to take Queen's off my UCAS form and I relented, ending up instead at Oxford studying English and meeting Chris one strange, hot summer in the mid-1990s.

We sat up night after night, talking about Lermontov and Dostoevsky and left-wing politics and theatre and drinking and relationships, sitting on the mattress in Chris's bare room as cars thundered down the Cowley Road, drinking tea and smoking cigarettes. And I thought perhaps that I had never met anyone in my life who I liked talking to more than Chris. But then it was time for me to leave for the Edinburgh Festival and when I returned Chris had left for his year teaching in St Petersburg. On my desk I found a note from him, wishing me luck in his spider scrawl, and a little white china bowl shaped like a lotus flower and filled with presents. And I didn't know quite what to do with the things I felt for Chris, just as I didn't know what to do with so many things at 19.

On our last morning in Nha Trang I sit on a stone wall between the beach and Tran Phu and stare at the unlit illuminations and wonder how I'm meant to feel about this remnant of Communism in this not-really-Communist, not-yet-democratic country. The politics of the countries we're visiting have been pulling at me, tugging at my mind and memory for many months.

As I child I would sit around in basement rooms in Hove listening to my grandmother and her friends talk. They were in their seventies and eighties then. Old Communists. Cerebral. Jewish for the most part, sometimes Quaker. Around Christmas (which we did and didn't celebrate) there would be a sing-song in a house with a piano. 'The Internationale'. 'The Red Flag'. They all knew the words and I would try to follow, a little dazed by the noise of it all and my distance from their very particular history. Their houses were decorated with mementos of foreign lands and posters depicting the unjust pyramid of capitalism. They went on fact-finding holidays to Cuba. They sat in their cool, dark living rooms on fiercely-hot July days and talked about what could be done about the party, what was happening in South Africa, whether the coal miners could hold out and for how long. They talked about Karl Marx and George Bernard Shaw and Charles Dickens and William Morris.

We ate lunches of cold meat and salad around huge dining tables and I stared at the strings of birds from South America and the carved giraffes from Africa, unable to follow the conversation. Politics was everything. Politics was our religion.

The world of the left in the 1980s was a strange and intense one. I remember an awful lot of achingly serious conversations, which in accordance with Section 3 Subsection 8 of the Left-Winger's Handbook, could last no less than 5 hours and 15 minutes and would sometimes stretch to 14 or 16 hours. I remember a lot of hand wringing. People crying at unvarnished wooden dining tables over bottles of cheap wine, ostensibly about apartheid or the destruction of the unions, though in reality – I suspect – about something else entirely.

I remember music, lots of music. I remember singing 'Little Boxes' and other grown-up anti-establishment anthems at Woodcraft Folk and not having a bloody clue what they meant. Woodcraft Folk was to the alternative set what Brownies were to Middle England: where children were sent on a Saturday morning. We learned about campfires and woodcarving and nobody asked us to show allegiance to either God or the queen. Everything seemed to have a special version, a left-wing alternative edition. We read feminist fairy stories in which girls rejected their princess dresses and killed dragons or went into business with them as organic farmers. My colouring books featured happy men and women exploring their sexuality. Since the books were surprisingly vague as to what this entailed, I believed for many years that bisexuals mainly spent their time picnicking together in groups of three and all lesbians rode around on tandems.

On Friday nights in our flat in south-west London my mother hosted a women's group. My father and I, banished to the front room with a television, watched *Cheers* instead, occasionally interrupted by howls, shrieks, cackling, giggling, shouting, sobs from the living room. My mother belonged to many groups over the years: writers' groups, theatre groups, unions, women's support groups. At times she was too unconventional: knitting and offering opinions from the chair at meetings, refusing to observe the conventions of... just about everything really. At other times she was too conventional: guilty of the crime of having a partner who stayed by her side after 1980, when a special resolution sent from an unknown height seemed to decree that 'all the fathers should leave'.

But there was a community, a community to which we belonged, a big, thriving, diverse community of communists; republicans; pseudo anarchists; socialists; liberals; feminists; anti-apartheid campaigners; gay rights' campaigners; trade unionists; rich, bohemian Marxists from leafy Hampstead; and shaven-headed animals-rights' campaigners from tower blocks in Bethnal Green.

Our politics had a soundtrack and a menu. I honestly don't know what people played at parties before 1986 but in August of that year Paul Simon, perhaps responding to a request from the left, kindly produced *Graceland* and forever after all parties chuntered to the sound of 'The Boy in the Bubble' and 'Under African Skies'. Labour Party fundraisers tasted like underdressed rice salad until the introduction of hummus in the late 1980s. Thereafter, everything, even the tea, tasted of hummus. Old communist sing-songs tasted like Garibaldi biscuits and marzipan. Women's groups tasted like Pinot Grigio and chocolate digestives. Greenham Common tasted like tangerines and cold tea. CND marches tasted like Salt 'n' Shake crisps and Rose's lime cordial. Left-wing dinner parties looked like lamb, mash and rocket salad but tasted entirely of olive oil.

A great swarm of ideologies jostled against each other. We were utopian communists, democratic socialists and pacifists: pacifists whose forebears had volunteered to fight in World War Two because, of course, we were anti fascists too. We believed in human rights and women's rights and gay rights and race equality. There were a lot of ideologies to contend with. Great tracts of thought and theory to yoke together. And into the midst of this great mass of abstract thought and practical deed, came the much-heralded death of Communism. I'm too young to remember the exact trajectory of feeling and thought; perhaps it was different for everyone. But I remember a kind of scattering of belief. A defensive movement as points of treasured belief became unsayable, tied as they were to the shadow of tyranny and murder.

'But it was a part of the struggle...'

'Of course, no-one wants these things to happen but when you look at the bigger picture...'

'But millions were lifted out of poverty. We have to remember the good that the party has done...'

The Soviet Union, Vietnam, China, Laos, Cuba: these were still countries where the left had won. The great experiment was at work. Many tried to hide themselves from the truth, so painful was the reality of totalitarian rule. Others ran from the word communism and into the friendly embrace of socialism with its comforting overtones of Clement Attlee, Aneurin Bevan and democratic mandates. Still others withdrew from thoughts of practical solutions and into a dream-like world of theory and utopianism.

For people as young as myself, the stripping away of belief in the great Communist states was not so great a shock. At the beginning of my political life, not yet eligible to vote, I refashioned my beliefs around those parts of the vast ideological landscape which seemed to survive the test of rational thought and history: a cast-iron respect for human life and dignity, the undeniable importance of democracy, the right to free speech and political thought. I was still a humanist, still a feminist, still believed in gay rights and racial equality. I did not feel the loss of Marx, I didn't mourn Lenin or Mao: but I witnessed those who did.

Are ideologies inherently dangerous? If so we have to throw out all the major religions, for millions upon millions have died in the name of their protection.

There is no simple answer. In fact I would go further and say that simple answers are the problem. The world is not a Ladybird book. Communism, Capitalism, Christianity, Judaism, Islam, Hinduism, Sikhism, Buddhism. None of these hold the secret and the truth. They have things to say about morality and things to say about social organisation. They are all part of the conversation. But we shall never pinpoint the perfect way to organise our world or ourselves. Because there is no magic formula. There is no shining light of truth that some of us see and some of us don't. There is no elect.

It is 7.00 a.m. We scrape our belongings together, repacking our rucksacks with the violence of the seasoned backpacker. We fill the Lotus bag with towels and souvenirs. Chris slings the Korean tennis game over his shoulder. We throw cups of black coffee in the direction of our mouths and then we are off. A coach waits outside the little travel office, holding a handful of other travellers and our garrulous guide: Mr Hồ.

The coach rumbles slowly out of HCMC and into the countryside. Fields flash by. Mr Hồ chats happily away, dipping in and out of Vietnamese history and tradition.

Mekong culture is river culture. The Mekong River's system of tributaries covers 39,000 square kilometres, covering the southern tip of Vietnam and providing a winding, watery path into Cambodia. Around 17 million people live in villages and towns along the rivers and the coast, most of them ethnic Viet, though some Khmer (of Cambodian origin). With its oft-flooded low-lying plains, the area is well suited to rice production, and tens of millions of tonnes flow out of the Delta and across Vietnam every year. And so strongly entrenched is river travel as a means of transport that many areas do without any kind of developed road system. It is extraordinarily beautiful. Lush, green and heavy with the sounds of jungle life: home to tens of thousands of different insects, birds, mammals and fish.

We climb onto a river barge and chug slowly down a tributary, hung thickly with giant ferns, palms and a plethora of small, fiercely green trees. Along the sides of the river small boys are cutting the bark from trees while their elder brother climbs a palm to remove the largest leaves. When the river narrows too much for the barge to continue, we climb out, put on our rucksacks and hike along the sides of the river. So dense is the vegetation that barely five centimetres of sky can be seen and the air is close and prickly with wet heat. Strange purple fruit with leaves like red lotus petals hang from the tree above my head. I want to ask Mr Hồ what they are, but I can no longer see him. I have a feeling we have been sent down this path alone.

We arrive at a village. Well, village is stretching it. We arrive at a piece of road. About 30 metres of it is tarmacked; before and after the tarmac it is dirt. Along it are six or seven wooden shacks, painted green and thatched with dry palm leaves. And a concrete box, which appears to be a garage and a shop. The concrete box is also partially thatched with palm, and the fronds hang down all around the edges like a dense and badly cut fringe giving it the odd appearance of a building wearing a wig. A motorcycle and a pile of oil drums are stacked outside and half a dozen lines

of washing are strung between its awning and the fruit trees that surround it. Mr Hồ appears as if from nowhere, waving hello and drinking a Coke.

'Twenty minutes this way!' he shouts. 'Lunch at a honey farm.' We troop obediently after him.

The honey farm turns out to be a sizable wooden farmhouse, with rows of white hives lined up under fruit trees in a shady orchard. On the far side of the house the farmer has built a large pergola where he and his wife and daughters serve us lunch. There is bread and honey (naturally) and bowls filled with chunks of dragonfruit, jackfruit and pineapple. There are dishes of longans and lychees in their dark red skins. We're offered glasses of local wine – which taste like pure alcohol – and then cups of tea laced heavily with honey. All the sweetness is a little overwhelming but it also serves to highlight the sharp and sour notes of the fruit.

After lunch Chris strolls off with a Danish couple to look around the orchard and I sit in the shade of the pergola and sketch. I look around at my fellow travellers, lolling on the grass or the steps of the pergola swigging from bottles of water. We have disappeared inside our travellers' uniforms. Here we all sit in our scruffy trainers and long shorts and T-shirts. You can guess at nationality from our features. And you can guess at income from the fact that we are backpacking in Asia. But the subtleties of class or country are for the most part erased by the practicalities of travel. We are dirty, sweaty, clothed for tropical heat, unmade-up. Until the person beside you opens his or her mouth to speak you cannot guess what language, accent, education, status or views will emerge from it.

Late in the day, over cups of sweet coffee, I discover a little about them all. The beautiful young Asian woman who I imagined to be perhaps from India is a trainee GP from Birmingham. The tall, fair-skinned man sitting beside her in a world of his own is her husband: a strangely dreamy PE teacher. The blonde lady with deeply tanned skin and her diminutive friend with the spiky haircut are a couple: gay South African accountants. The Danish couple are an investment banker (him) and an ancient languages doctoral student (her). The attractive WASPs are from Boston. They met at Stanford. Despite their achingly expensive travel wear and attachment to their currently useless iPhones they're actually rather nice, laid-back and good-humoured.

The subject of money comes up. Not salaries of course, God forbid. But rather the cost of the trip. The Danish couple are telling the WASPs that they paid two hundred US dollars per person in Denmark for this three-day excursion. Mr and Mrs WASP exchange a look and laugh slightly uncomfortably. They paid sixty US dollars more per person to a US travel agent they confess, and thought it cheap. But now they know! Chris's eyebrows have disappeared up behind his fringe. He looks at me and I look at him. We booked our trip from a little travel stand in HCMC and paid twenty-one US dollars each. We decide everyone will enjoy their holiday more if we pretend this isn't true.

It's so very beautiful here. The light glows warmly through the tangle and canopy of leaves. The food grown in the rivers and the orchards and the paddy fields is full of flavour and goodness. In the villages we pass through extended families live and work together in double-storeyed homes made out of bamboo and wood. The grandparents keep an eye on the children, who play in the reeds by the riverbank or feed the animals. The mothers seem mostly to work in the home, weaving and making baskets. The fathers are invisible in the villages we pass through, away from the house working on the land or selling their produce at market.

I'm thinking about the place we live in Wales. And I'm thinking about the Mekong Delta. What really signifies when you try to judge quality of life? Is it economics? Or social structure? Does the beauty of the place you live in matter more or less than your right to vote? Chris and I left London because the economic disparity between the classes and all that that entails had made it a stressful and expensive place to live. We chose somewhere greener and quieter with a big sandy beach for the future children to play on. We chose to live in a town where no one asks what you do for a living but complete strangers will come up to you in the street and ask you how you are today, do you have any children, are your parents keeping well? We chose a different set of values and a gentler, less monied way of life.

I think of the faces of the factory workers in Beijing who climbed above our heads to get a seat in the bus. I think about the stress and the years of grinding effort required to work your way out of poverty in a developing nation. I think about the choking pollution in Beijing and the hundreds of thousands of workers walking and cycling through it every day to make good in the capital city. I think about the silence imposed upon billions of people by the one-party system, the millions starved and beaten and executed in the name of progress. Is it frivolous to talk about quality of life and beauty in the face of so much political and economic turmoil? Is it bourgeois to think that the good people of China and Vietnam might need nature, a social system that supports family ties, jobs which satisfy the soul, in addition to an economic system that works and the right to live in a democracy?

Many people argue that if you sort out money and democracy then all good things follow as the night the day. But I don't believe that for a second. We come from a wealthy country with a long history of democratic freedom, but we still do not place enough value on our environment, on the family, on the purpose of our working lives. Maybe this argument belongs to a particular moment in a country's history: a post-industrial, post-imperial moment in time. But there is a crisis that we face – beyond our choice of economic or political system – and that is a crisis of value. What have we failed to assign value to? What have we sacrificed along the way? Placing value upon the environment, upon the family and upon the worth of our work will require economic sacrifices to be made by us all; and we don't seem ready yet to make them.

Do chua
Vietnamese pickled carrots and daikon

Daikon is also known as mooli, Chinese radish and Japanese radish. It can be found in most Asian grocers and some supermarkets. I've given you this recipe partly because pickled vegetables used in a few of the recipes in this book, and partly because pickled vegetables are such a simple but effective way of adding interest and layers of flavour to South-East Asian food. Sprinkle them on noodles, add them to soup when serving, toss them into a salad or roll them in crêpes or spring rolls. They have a crunch and piquancy that sets off other vegetables beautifully and complements most meat.

To make enough for two 227-g jars
Preparation time: 20 minutes
Pickling time: 24 hours or more

1 large carrot, cut into matchsticks
12-cm piece of daikon, cut into matchsticks
½ tsp salt
55 g sugar
150 ml white vinegar
125 ml warm water

Sterilise the jars and lids (old, clean jam jars are fine) in boiling water.

Put the carrot and daikon matchsticks in a bowl and sprinkle over the salt and 1 tsp of the sugar. Toss the matchsticks in the salt and sugar, gently kneading them for several minutes to reduce their water content. When ready the daikon should be very flexible. Drain and rinse in cold water then divide them between the two jars.

Mix the remaining sugar, vinegar and water in a bowl and stir until the sugar has completely dissolved. Pour into the jars until full and put the lids on. Store the jars in the fridge. The pickles can be used after 24 hours but will taste better after a week. They are best eaten in the first month of making. After this they become a little soft and tasteless.

Banh xeo
Sizzling crêpes

This lovely dish gets its name from the sizzling sound the rice batter makes when it hits the hot fat. I've given you the southern version, which is a little richer than the northern and central varieties where the coconut milk and/or the turmeric are omitted. It's somewhat more fatty than your average Vietnamese dish, so it's seen as a treat and served mainly in winter to provide warmth and energy to the cold, hungry and tired.

In some parts of Vietnam this dish is made in a wok, in other parts a very large frying pan. You need to cover the food briefly so, if possible, use a wok or frying pan that comes with a lid. If you don't have such a thing, don't worry. In Vietnam, many cooks use a large saucepan lid (smaller than their frying pan) and just cover the centre of the crêpe, where the main ingredients tend to congregate.

This is a great dish to make for a dinner party or a celebration meal. There is a feeling of ritual about the tearing of the pancake, the assembling of the leaf and garnishes and the dipping of the roll.

Serves 2
Preparation and cooking time: 50 minutes

Crêpe batter:
50 g rice flour
¼ tsp turmeric powder
Pinch of salt
125 ml water
60 ml coconut milk

1 spring onion, finely chopped

Filling for meat eaters:

6 tbsp groundnut or peanut oil

50 g small uncooked shrimps, peeled

50 g pork, cut into thin slices

Pinch of salt

Half a medium white onion, sliced finely

1 medium chilli, deseeded and sliced

2–3 mushrooms, finely sliced

60 g bean sprouts, washed and trimmed

Filling for vegetarians:

6 tbsp groundnut or peanut oil

80 g tofu skin or strips of dry-fried firm tofu

3–6 mushrooms, finely sliced

Pinch of salt

Half a medium white onion, sliced finely

1 medium chilli, deseeded and sliced

60 g bean sprouts, washed and trimmed

Nuoc cham **dipping sauce:**

6 tbsp of a solution of 1 part sugar to 3 parts water

2 tbsp fresh lime juice

1 tsp fresh lime zest

2 tbsp fish sauce (for vegetarians: 1 tbsp light soy sauce)

1 clove garlic, crushed or minced

½ tsp crushed dried chilli
Salad:
Large lettuce leaves, washed
Handful of fresh coriander leaves
1 carrot, grated
8-cm piece of cucumber, unpeeled and thinly sliced
Handful of fresh mint leaves

Mix together the rice flour, turmeric and salt. Now add the wet ingredients and whisk to a batter. Leave to stand for 30 minutes.

While you're waiting for the batter to thicken prepare the nuoc cham dipping sauce (mix all the ingredients together and decant into dipping bowls) and the salad vegetables and herbs.

When the batter is ready, cook crêpes. This recipe makes two *banh xeo* so remember to reserve half the filling ingredients and batter for the second crêpe.

Place a large frying pan on a high heat and add 2 tbsp of the oil. When the oil is hot, add your filling ingredients with the exception of the bean sprouts. Meat eaters should make sure that the pork and shrimps are half-cooked before adding the batter. Some people like to make a little path in their pan through the middle of the ingredients. This makes the crêpe easier to fold at the end. When the ingredients are lightly cooked add the batter and swirl to coat the bottom of the pan. Place a handful of bean sprouts on top of one half of the crêpe and turn the heat down to a medium flame. Drizzle a little oil around the edges of the crêpe.

Now cover your pan (or as much of the crêpe as you can) and allow the ingredients to steam for 1 minute. Remove lid and when the edges of the crêpe are going brown and crispy, loosen and check to see if nicely browned on underside. When happy with colour underneath, fold the crêpe in two – the side without bean sprouts folds to the top. Slide the whole thing onto a plate and make your next crêpe.

The crêpes are traditionally eaten by tearing off pieces and then placing a piece inside a large lettuce leaf sprinkled with cucumber, carrot and coriander and mint. Then the lettuce leaf is rolled up, dipped into the *nuoc cham* and eaten like a spring roll.

If you have some *do chua* in the fridge, it's nice added to the salad and herb mix in the lettuce leaves.

Chapter 9

Mournful and Homely

It's our second day on the Mekong Delta and we are getting nearer to Cambodia. In the morning we travel by boat to a huge market on the banks of one of the main tributaries. People come from all around to sell fruit and vegetables and trade with each other. The more established stalls sit under a makeshift tarpaulin awning in the centre of the quay while the smaller sellers spread their wares out on the ground at their feet. These smaller sellers, mainly women, squat or sit on the ground in brightly coloured trousers, jackets and conical bamboo hats. In front of them are piled fifteen giant bundles of coriander or twenty bunches of freshly cut lemongrass. One woman is just selling bitter melons from a basket.

On the far side of the quay a young woman perches on a stool behind a low table. She is filling banana leaves with noodles to sell to the traders. Her jacket makes her look almost clown like, a riot of lime green and yellow dancing pineapples, but her face betrays an intense level of concentration. Hands moving over her multiple ingredients like a magician, she soaks her noodles, then beats up

a fresh batch of dressing with chopsticks in an old jam jar. The soaked noodles are dressed and tossed with shredded lettuce. She pulls a banana leaf from a plastic bag held between her knees and deftly makes a parcel, wrapping the ingredients many times so nothing will be lost until the buyer is ready to eat.

Beside her on the kerb a woman draws up and hops lightly from a moped. She is wearing a bright blue crash helmet and a handkerchief masks her face against the dusty roads. The back of her moped is stacked with crates of food and she starts to unpack these: slabs of tofu, curled balls of dried noodles, a crate of mushrooms and another of water spinach and then some bitter melon and rambutans. She loads herself up with crates so that her face disappears behind the stack and scurries across the quay, deftly dodging shoppers, until she is lost among the crowd gathered around the floating sellers on the river.

Back out on the water we pass barges and speedboats piled with fruit and vegetables. One woman is rowing a small dinghy downstream. It is piled so high with melons that the tower of fruit is higher than her head. Along the sides of the river are moored numerous narrow boats and small fishing boats and as she rows slowly past each of these she calls out softly, so softly that I cannot imagine how anyone hears her over the sounds of the motors and the sloshing river. Now and again a hand will shoot out of the round porthole of a narrow boat and she will take a note from the fingers and place a melon in the palm. Many of the sellers know each other and their voices ring out as their motorboats or punts pass in the centre of the river, exchanging jokes and silly insults.

Cambodian and Vietnamese cuisines have a lot in common but you won't find the relationship readily acknowledged in either country. Despite, or perhaps because of, the large number of Cambodians who fled to Vietnam and the Vietnamese who fled to Cambodia over the course of the twentieth century the two countries share a tense relationship. The Mekong Delta once belonged to Cambodia but is now controlled by Vietnam and the land and sea borders have been pushed and pulled by both sides.

Under the Khmer Rouge, Cambodians were encouraged to hate their Vietnamese neighbours who had committed the grievous crime of 'stealing' the Mekong Delta and who had been guilty of war crimes against the Vietnamese over many centuries. Of course it served the Khmer Rouge well to demonise the Vietnamese given that a feeling of nationalism served their 'great project' and dissuaded their citizens from fleeing east across the border.

In reality, both nations have used the Mekong waterways for food and transport. Families and villages have moved backwards and forwards over the border. And the border has moved backwards and forwards over them.

We travel through the afternoon, sometimes on foot and sometimes in little boats which chug chug chug down the great brown rivers, past alligator farms and tiny factories given over to making sweets or rice paper wrappers, past villages where the shady lower floor of every stilted wooden house hums softly with the sound of looms. Past fish farms where the fish live under the stilted river houses, fenced in with netted walls under the water, and are fed via trapdoors in the patio. Past a floating petrol station, built onto an old barge, where petrol is pumped straight from giant barrels on the deck. Children wave from every bank and bathe together in the brown waters.

In the evening we stop in a small town on the coast where the rest of our party disappears for dinner and we go in search of the only computer within striking distance that has an Internet connection.

Back in central Vietnam we learnt that our solicitors had served an eviction order against our non-paying tenant. Despite everything, I feel sick at the thought of somebody being forcibly removed from our house.

We queue up in a tiny office where dozens of mosquitoes seem to hum all at once, waiting for the local Viet men in front of us to send their emails. Finally it is our turn and Chris checks his account. He looks at me. He doesn't speak. He points at the screen.

I bend down and read an email from the house agent telling us that the day before the eviction she turned up to find that our tenant had packed everything and left. The agent has been down to the storeroom and our boxes all seem to be there. The house is dirty and the furniture all over the place but all in all it seems to be basically intact.

I can't really think what to say. I just feel numb. We pay our 8,000 dong (twenty-five pence) and walk out into the darkness. We're in a seaside town that has a promenade and palm trees. A gigantic statue of Ho Chi Minh stands at one end of the prom and waves to visitors. We're too tired to celebrate. Actually, we don't feel like celebrating. We're just exhausted. Relieved and exhausted. Much like the feeling you get at the end of food poisoning or a migraine. Thank goodness that's over. Now I just want to go to sleep.

We can't really take on board what this means for us now. The more we have travelled the more unreal the whole thing has become. Like a nightmare that we keep remembering but can't quite reconcile with fact.

On day three we climb the sides of a mountain to a beautiful Buddhist temple, built in layers or stages into the sides of the mountain. Each layer includes a little garden, a small temple or a pergola. The main buildings are painted a shade of deep, oxblood red. Rather like the structures in the Humble Administrator's Garden, the little pergolas and single rooms afford many beautifully framed views. Circular doors and windows frame statues of the Buddha. And all around us, trees and mountain plants hug the complex tightly. As we reach the top layer Mr Hồ points down the mountain, across flood plains to a different section of the river.

'That's where we're going,' he tells us. 'That's Cambodia.'

After a border transfer that seems to involve a lot of climbing up muddy banks while wearing our packs, we are deposited on the banks of the Mekong just inside Phnom Penh.

Home to two million Cambodians, Phnom Penh is at first glance a carbon copy of the big, modern cities of Vietnam. The roads are crowded with motorised rickshaws, buses, vans and scooters; the noise of horns is intimidating in its ferocity; and you'll struggle to spot the French Colonial buildings among the 1960s office blocks and under the layers of red-brown dust.

We're planning to travel to the imperial beach resort of Kep on Cambodia's sprawling south-west coast. After a week on the beach, we will travel back up to Phnom Penh and then along the north shore of Tonle Sap Lake to Siem Riep and Angkor Wat.

We have been warned about the bus ride from Phnom Penh to Kep. Cambodia doesn't have many decent roads. Years of civil war have left the country with a tattered infrastructure and a depleted and impoverished population. The country is rebounding at an extraordinary rate but the roads aren't keeping up.

We get to the bus station at 6.00 a.m., where we board a large and ancient coach. Its side still bears the name of a US travel company, suggesting that it's somehow hitchhiked here from a past life in Reagan-era Kentucky. We scramble over piles of food supplies and boxes of toys stacked in the aisle, dragging our rucksacks behind us. Chris throws me the Lotus bag and I find us two seats. Chris pulls out his book on Genghis Khan and I my knitting and we make ourselves as comfortable as we can given the badly sprung green and pink velour seats.

We set off. The skyline of Phnom Penh melts into the dust of shabby industry and then into the green of rain-soaked fields and hills. We watch children tending chickens and pigs, and women treading the borders of rice fields, vast baskets balanced on one hip. Cambodia is lush with plant life. It is lush generally. It is lush because it rains a lot.

About an hour into our 5-hour journey the rain starts. And it does not stop. The sky closes grey above our heads and a mist of rain and fog envelops the bus. We speed and slow often. The driver uses the brakes a lot. Now and again we hear shouts of anger and alarm from outside the coach and crane our necks to see drenched cyclists standing over their bikes at the side of the road.

After 3 hours the coach stops for fuel in a small town whose sole economy seems to be providing services to the bus from Phnom Penh. The driver stands up.

'Everybody off! All bags off! Nothing left here! Food and toilet stop.'

There is a moment of disbelief. Then we all start to pack up our stuff.

A tall, blond American – travelling with a group of tall, blond Americans – stands up, 'Er, how long?'

The driver ignores him.

'Erm, how long have we got? How do we know when to come back?'

The driver doesn't meet his eye. 'I tell you when to come back.'

We drag our angry bones into the rain and carry our possessions to the Traveler's Caffe where noodles with onions, tomatoes, pineapple and chicken can be bought for the extraordinarily high price of thirty thousand riel (four pounds and twenty pence). The food is not nice. The coffee is horrible. The bathroom is so full of spiders I cannot bring myself to pee.

The driver sits on the steps of the coach and spends the break chatting to a young mechanic who is checking the tyres. They chain-smoke and drink soda and show each other their phones in the shelter of the bus. The rain pours on; we slouch deeper into our plastic chairs in the humid air of the transport cafe. Some people are already asleep when we hear shouting.

Somewhere outside, behind sheets of rain, a man is shouting: 'Quick! Quick!'

It's our driver. He is standing inside the bus shouting at us.

'Leaving now!'

We grab our bags and stumble out of the cafe. He turns on the engine.

'Closing doors!'

The group of tall, blond Americans throw themselves at the bus and block the doors with their backpacks. We struggle past them, hauling our stuff. Then it's over the sacks of rice and grain and the

273

boxes of noodles and the tins of tomatoes and the boxes of toy cars and spacemen and guns. Back to the green and pink velour and the springs. We huddle in our seats, the rucksacks and the Lotus bag and the Korean tennis game piled on top of us. All around us people are crashing into their seats and bags are flying above our heads. The bus pulls out. Through the white and grey haze I see the Traveler's Caffe slide away behind us.

Then all of a sudden someone is shouting: 'Charlie! Charlie! Stop the bus.' It is the group of tall, blond Americans and they are all standing, or attempting to stand in a coach where the floor is covered in provisions. They try to struggle forward. The driver doesn't turn.

'Stop the bus. Our friend's back there. Stop the f---ing bus!'

The driver drives on through the pounding rain. Two Swedes and a Finn on the back seat start a running commentary.

'He's coming after us. He's thirty...'

'Maybe forty metres away.'

'He's keeping up.'

'Ohhh.'

'What? What's that?' cry the tall Americans.

'He fell over,' the Finnish girl says sadly.

'Stop the f---ing bus!' the tall Americans are screaming at the driver.

The bus lurches suddenly to one side and comes to rest at an angle. The gears scream. The driver is swearing in Cambodian. This is not an intentional stop.

I look at Chris. Chris looks past me out the window. We have a worryingly close-up view of somebody's front garden. The gears scream and the bus judders and the wheels sink further into the mud. We all start to lean in the opposite direction to compensate.

The driver stands up and breathes hard. Without looking or speaking to the tall Americans he gestures to them to follow him off the bus. They throw down their bags and climb off with him. Everybody looks murderous. They disappear behind the bus.

An angry conversation can be heard over the din of the rain. Suddenly a young Chinese woman gets up and starts to pick her way over the rice and the noodles and the toy guns.

A German traveller leans across to her boyfriend: 'I don't think she should go out there.'

Her boyfriend shrugs, 'She has to pee.' He watches as she descends from the coach and walks up the garden path to the house whose wall we are threatening to demolish. He looks at the German and shrugs again, 'There were spiders.'

The young Chinese woman disappears inside the house. More shouting can be heard from behind the bus. The driver climbs back on and starts the engine. The unseen tall Americans are trying to hoist the bus out of the ditch. The rain continues to pour. The sky gets darker. Cambodia has disappeared behind a wall of grey.

The bus sways occasionally, passengers start to climb to the higher side, and the driver runs a tense hand through his hair. In the middle of all of this a red-faced and muddy young man climbs aboard and deposits his bags in a seat. He flashes an embarrassed grin at the occupants of the bus and gets out again. This, one imagines, is Charlie.

The rocking gets more violent. Bags start to fall from ceiling racks. We hold on tightly to our green and pink velour seats. Then a splutter and a judder and the bus lurches forward. The driver presses down hard and we are upright once again. Six very wet and muddy, tall Americans drag themselves back up the stairs and fall on top of the piles of rice, exhausted. The doors close and we move off.

The young Chinese man stands up, 'Ah, no...' he starts, 'Sorry! No! My girlfriend is in the house.'

The bus moves forward. Once again we press our noses to the glass. The young Chinese woman is running down the garden path of the house we didn't crush. She is holding her jacket and a roll of toilet paper and waving at us. The bus is crawling forward through the mud.

The Chinese woman is gaining on us. She can't reach the windows but she does start knocking on the glass with the roll of toilet paper. Her boyfriend continues to implore the driver to stop. You can read the driver's frustration in his hunched shoulders. He now has both hands running through his wet hair and we're still moving. The roll of toilet paper moves towards the doors. Eventually, a human-shaped shadow appears by the driver's door. We keep moving and the doors open. The young woman pulls herself in, thanks the driver and starts to climb over the bags of rice and spacemen. She is caked in mud and her flies are open. Someone takes the toilet roll away from her so she can move faster. When she is close enough to reach, her boyfriend scoops her up and deposits her in her seat. She is crying and laughing all at once.

We move on through the rain.

Two hours later we reach the coast. The clouds have broken and the dark has lifted. Up on the hillside, the burnt-out remains of French Colonial mansions can be seen, surrounded by overgrown gardens and tumbling stone walls. Down by the roadside, vast, hand-painted hoardings implore women to take control of their sexual and economic destiny. Paintings show happy women with one child outside family planning clinics. Discreet pictures of condom packets and diaphragms can be seen in the bottom corner.

We have been warned by guidebooks that Kep is a request stop and that the request needs to be a firm one.

As we enter Kep, seasoned travellers start to climb over the noodles and toy guns. An esplanade stretches before us, a giant statue of a crab faces away from the sea, towards town.

'Kep, please,' the Americans chorus. The bus does not slow down.

The Finnish girl and her Swedish friends are climbing down from the back.

'Kep,' they chorus, 'Kep! Stop the bus, please.'

We do not slow down. The bus is now alive with cries of 'Kep! Kep, please!'

We move along the esplanade, past the town square, past the crab market and join the winding road out of town. The cries become roars.

'KEP!'

'KEP, PLEASE!'

'STOP THE F---ING BUS AND LET US OFF!'

The bus screams to a stop and we all fall forwards. A tall, muddy, blond American yanks the door open and holds it while we stagger off one by one. The driver stares ahead of him, thunderous with rage. When we are all off, standing in the road with our bags, the doors close and the bus screeches on to Kampot and Sihanoukville. We blink at each other in the cold, grey light. No one says anything. We put on our rucksacks, pick up our Lotus bag and our Korean tennis game and head back into town.

If you choose Cambodia for your next beach holiday – and I recommend you do – remember to check when rainy season starts. And when it ends.

We are booked into a chic, beachfront hotel for a week of sun, sand and cheap Cambodian beer. On day one, it rains. On day two, it rains. On day three... You can see where this is going. I eye the Korean tennis game sadly as it sits unused in its blue and white cover. We have carried it 3,400 kilometres. Is one day of sun-filled beach action too much to ask for?

Infrastructure in general is a little lacking on the coast. The electrical supply comes and goes. There's no television. No Internet. No phones.

On day four, the weather breaks early and we take our one and only proper excursion: to Rabbit Island.

Mournful is the saddest dog in the world. His eyes gaze up at you like black pools of liquid ennui. His tail flollops slowly from side to side. He keeps his nose slightly bowed as if to say: it's OK I'm not expecting you to stroke it. Is there a reason for Mournful's sadness, you ask?

Well. Not really. Mournful lives... in paradise.

Beaches of white sand ring his island. Its few inhabitants (including Mournful's loving owners) live in long, wooden shacks, work the land, keep cattle and cook for the visitors. The isle is thick with lush vegetation, flowering bushes and palm trees. It looks out over a seascape of turquoise and teal, cresting white and aquamarine. If someone asks you to imagine a desert island: this is what you see.

Boats don't land at Rabbit Island. They get as close as possible and then you throw yourself over the side. Braced for a cold landing, you find instead that you're up to your thighs in warm, bright water – clear as glass. You wade ashore and there waiting for you is Eeyore's dog-line descendant.

'Ahhh,' the assembled girls chorus, 'Look at the lovely dog.' Mournful is immediately surrounded by adoring fans, who stroke him and pat him and ruffle the soft yellow fur on his chest. Mournful does not seem to mind this. Eventually, he turns and leads us up the beach towards a line of palm trees and a clearing where a collection of huts stand. Inside the huts the islanders play host to their daily visitors and supplement their small and fragile income. Cats and dogs trot in and out of the huts and sit watching from the wooden picnic tables.

For five thousand riel (about seventy pence) you can hire loungers and cushions for the day and sprawl in the sun on the perfect white beach. Chris has brought his customary pile of books, I have brought drawing things. Inevitably, we have forgotten the Korean tennis game. We lie, melting gently in the heat, on our bamboo and wicker sunloungers and I draw the palm trees up above me. The island is very quiet. Occasionally you hear a bird shriek, or the sound of one woman calling to another between the huts. But for the most part there is only silence. I sketch the bushes and the scrub and the line of sand as it leads the eye away.

Presently, something wet pokes my arm. It is Mournful. For a depressed animal, he's quite forward. Mournful has been sitting under a tree, watching me. Fair enough I think, that's what dogs do. Well, that's what depressed dogs do.

But no. Mournful wants to play. A little grudgingly, I put down my pen and paper and tickle Mournful under the chin. He throws himself down in the sand and presents his belly to me. I roll off the sunlounger and tickle his belly. He waggles his paws at me and I tickle him... do dogs have armpits? I tickle him under his armpits.

His doggy body contorts with pleasure but his face remains static, staring at me with the big, sad eyes.

I am determined to make this dog happy.

I get up and we chase each other around the nearest tree. We play catch with my drawing pens. I attempt to nuzzle him into submission. Mournful stares at me with his drooping and unhappy mouth. I start to feel slightly annoyed. 'What's wrong with you?' I think. 'You live in the most beautiful place I've ever seen. You are showered with love and attention. Cheer up, dog. CHEER UP!'

At lunchtime we are called to one of the wooden huts, which is open to the elements on one side. A kitchen has been constructed from many ancient devices and tables spill out from the hut and into the clearing. We are presented with a can of Coke and get to choose our food from plastic gingham menus. There is an extremely long list of dishes. On closer inspection they are all prepared from the same five ingredients: noodles, tomatoes, pineapple, onion, chicken.

Chris makes a face at me. He doesn't think pineapple belongs on savoury food. He regards my love of pineapple on pizza as a freakish aberration alongside my otherwise exquisite taste in international cuisine. Unfortunately for Chris, everything in this part of Cambodia comes with tomato and pineapple.

We're distracted by a rattling, scratching noise and look up. Above our heads, cats are scampering across an upper floor of the hut. I didn't know huts could have two floors. But this one does. Tucked into the roof is a large sleeping platform covered with thin, threadbare duvets. From the edge of this, cats crane over and watch the tourists eat their lunch. Mournful drifts over to us as Chris mutters into his can of Coke: denigrating Hawaiian pizzas and sweet and sour chicken under his breath. Mournful is soon joined by two other dogs. We are entirely surrounded by animals.

'D'you think we're meant to feed them?' I ask.

'No.' says Chris firmly.

'But look at them.'

'They're animals,' Chris says. 'They're built to look hungry.'

'I want to take Mournful home,' I say, gazing into Mournful's big, black eyes.

Chris looks at me and then at Mournful. 'You are only the latest in a very, very long line of women who have wanted to take Mournful home.'

'But...' I begin, as noodles with pineapple, onions, tomatoes and chicken arrive in front of us.

'Eat your lunch,' says Chris.

On our fifth day we encounter Tam, the heavy metal rickshaw owner. We've heard about a public bar with wi-fi in a luxury resort on top of the mountain behind our hotel. The resort is best reached by car, but failing that you can attempt a treacherous, muddy climb.

The mountain behind us is a rugged mess of scrubland, pasture, dirt paths, cottages, ransacked colonial villas and overgrown gardens. We march purposefully through the town square and start up the nearest path. The path leads us round in a circle and back to the town square again. We try again and find ourselves in a cul-de-sac of charred colonial remains. Something putters up behind us.

'Want a ride?' We turn to see a mass of curls and a bandana. A tall Cambodian man is squinting at us through giant sunglasses.

He's dressed like a sixth-form deadhead and he's riding a bright red motorised rickshaw – with flames painted on it. 'Where you going?'

'There's a bar at the top of the mountain and they have Internet...' Chris waves his hand above his head in the direction he thinks the bar might be.

'Yeah,' says Tam. 'Get in.'

The rickshaw grinds and squeals its way up the mountain, and over the noise of the engine Tam introduces himself and gives us a stark and unemotional guide to Kep's history.

Founded in 1908, Kep-sur-mer was the playground of French Colonial society throughout the 1920s and 1930s. When Norodom Sihanouk won his country's independence in 1953, Kep enjoyed a renaissance as a fashionable resort for Cambodia's new financial and intellectual elite. But when the war in Vietnam spilt across the border, life in Kep spiralled into chaos. Many of the owners of Kep's mansions died at the hands of the Khmer Rouge. The buildings were defaced, looted, torched. Kep was hollowed out and abandoned.

Tam's narrative grinds to a halt. He stares ahead of him as though absorbing the fact of it once again.

'So what now?' shouts Chris over the noise of the engine.

Tam bobs his head, weighing up his prospects along with those of Kep.

'It gets better. We have a bit of money. We need more electricity.'

'Do you think you'll leave?'

'Maybe. But my family's here. If tourists come...' Tam trails off. He points up the road to a sign to the resort. The engine cuts out. We scramble out of the rickshaw carriage. Chris gives Tam ten thousand riel and he putters off, waving a goodbye at once cheery and nonchalant.

We step carefully into the well-trimmed gardens of the luxury resort. Hand-carved signs direct us to a bar, which spreads itself over a huge wooden deck overlooking the sea. Somewhere far, far below, Kep is lost behind thickets of brambles and a tangle of trees. When the weather closes in, clouds will form below the platform and the whole world will disappear in white and grey. It's awe inspiring – a tree house for the gods. Chris orders a beer and chips and attempts to email home. I cannot tear my eyes from the view.

Kep is known for its wonderful seafood and the crabs and shrimp come in daily before being shipped off to Sihanoukville and Phnom Penh and beyond. At little stalls near the water's edge you can buy a freshly caught and cooked crab or a plate of shrimp for fifteen thousand riel – about two pounds. It's a pittance to us but extremely pricey by Cambodian standards. Chris claims this is the best shrimp he has ever tasted and if nothing else I can attest to the fact that the man has eaten a lot of shrimp.

There is no meat on the menu here. Fish has completely taken its place. Small fish come deep fried with rice and salad leaves. Larger fish come stewed in stock or coconut milk. Soups come flavoured with prahok or kapi, Cambodian varieties of fermented fish paste that lend a sour salty tang to everything they touch.

Some evenings we eat in an open-air cafe by the sea, where they serve sweet and sharp noodle dishes and soups heavy with pepper. Kampot pepper – which comes from just down the coast – is one of the finest peppers in the world and was for many decades the pepper of choice for top chefs in Paris. It is milder than many peppers, with a gentle heat and a savoury, herbal quality. It smells like incense, like a floral kind of unlit tobacco, and this beautiful smell seems to perfume the table over dinner and add a subtle bite to all the other dishes.

On day six we explore the mountainside, a superabundant land of ruins and children and animals. It's one part dystopia and two parts garden of Eden. Strange and beguiling, with an edge of horror.

All along the sides of the paths run walls and fences, entrances to long-dismantled villas. The gates and the gateposts still stand, untouched – hardly weathered at all. Some of the villas are almost gone; here and there a wall still stands, covered in rain-soaked whitewash. The grass grows 30-centimetres high and orchards threaten to swallow each other up. Cows and goats graze freely in the abandoned gardens.

We pass a house where only the front wall is gone. Like a giant doll's house, it has been opened to the elements. The weather has cleaned the colour from the walls; the staircase is intact apart from the bottom flight. The floor of the living room is gone and vegetables have been planted there instead. Two motorbikes and a bicycle are parked in the old kitchen. One of the upper rooms holds a bright purple, plastic dining set... and a shiny, red cement mixer. We surmise that the house has squatters. And that they're planning to rebuild. A skinny cow – the colour of milky coffee – crops the grass at the side of the path. A hammock and a washing line are hung between the trees.

Further up the track, rebuilding is in full swing. The skeleton of a mansion finds new bones in the form of freshly planed timber. A cement floor has been recently laid, extending one wing by 10 metres. Young trees have been planted in rows beside the dirt drive and mounds of sand and earth are waiting to be moved.

We trek on, as the houses disappear and the trees block the sky above our heads. Cambodia is aggressively verdant and the whole landscape is soaked in deep, dark, saturated greens and browns.

Chris spots a young boy in bright blue football shorts and a stripy button-down shirt kneeling beside one of the stained concrete gateposts.

We approach him slowly and quietly, in case he's praying. But no. His hands are moving with great care over the dark grey, mottled surface. He holds a tiny stick of chalk the colour of saffron and he is drawing a god.

The god is taller than the young boy, dressed in armour and densely draped finery. He sports a tall, pointed hat and M. C. Hammer trousers, his feet look like the roots of a tree and he wears golden anklets.

The boy turns, startled at first, then he smiles brightly. We gesture to tell him we like his picture of the god. He looks delighted – and a little bashful. Then he returns to drawing the pleats on the god's billowing trousers.

After seven strange and extremely damp days we return to Phnom Penh and make arrangements for the trip to Siem Riep.

The story of human life in South-East Asia is the story of a force and a foodstuff: water and rice. So densely forested was this region that for many centuries the only possible settlements lay along the coast where hunter-gatherers lived for the most part on foraged plants, wild cattle and fish. Trade was possible by sea, but the complex system of rivers and lakes that criss-cross Cambodia were of little use because the land on their banks was so hard to settle. China's cultivation of rice between 8,000 and 13,000 years ago had given her the means to settle much of her challenging terrain. But civilisation arrived relatively late to Cambodia.

Rice cultivation is demanding. It is well suited to the monsoon-heavy, tropical climate of the area but the techniques of farming have to be carefully studied. It requires a grasp of maths and the means and ability to flood fields and calculate the time to harvest. By contrast, wheat is a strikingly easy crop to farm, one which follows the seasons of the year and where the time of harvest can be judged by eye. Rice is responsible for a fifth of all the calories consumed on the planet every day and is the staple food of much of Asia, Africa and South America. Part of the reason for this is the nutritional value of rice. Gram for gram rice provides more carbohydrates, protein and calories than wheat. A hectare of land given over to farming rice will feed more adults than a hectare given over to farming wheat. And so rice remains popular in countries which are highly populated and where many adults are forced to survive on a single foodstuff.

While flatbread represents (or becomes) the host in the taking of Christian communion, rice is worshipped and celebrated as the bringer of life in South-East Asia. Bowls of rice are a common offering to the gods and spirits. Sacks, bowls and boxes of rice are typically found as grave goods. In parts of Vietnam, grains of sticky rice are placed on every object at the birth of a baby, thereby blessing the tools that will nurture the child and after death the mouth of the deceased will be left open so that visiting mourners may place a grain of rice inside. In scripture, the Buddha was nourished with rice cooked in milk and the Prophet Muhammed with rice cooked in ghee. In many parts of the region offerings to a female rice deity are still practised and rice as a sacred object has come to symbolise fecundity and wealth.

Four thousand, three hundred years ago the knowledge required for rice cultivation was brought to Cambodia by travellers from the north and east. Suddenly native Cambodians had a reason to clear the great flood plains around the Mekong River and Tonle Sap Lake and move away from the coast. Since you cannot rely on the flooding of the plains to coincide with your water needs, farmers were forced to build reservoirs to store water and to earth-wall fields on higher ground. Cambodia's many waterways allowed for movement and trade within the country and into (modern-day) Vietnam and Laos. Cambodia entered her Iron Age around 500 BC and within a hundred years she had established several major trading routes, crucially including those with India.

In the following centuries, the state of Funan sprang up in the Mekong Delta and benefited massively from trade with the Roman, Greek, Persian, Indian and Chinese empires. Funan was the first great economy of South-East Asia and imported many of its ideas and cultural practices from India. Sanskrit was the language of the court, while Hinduism and then later Buddhism were the advocated religions.

The coastal power of Funan was superseded by the inland kingdom of Chenla. The kingdom was built on the wealth of a trade in iron, salt and rice, and enjoyed a reasonable level of stability in part because of her tradition of dynastic succession. Over the years Chenla society slowly separated into an upper and a lower class divided by language, with the upper class speaking Sanskrit and the lower speaking Khmer. Chenla temples were plentiful and ornate, built of brick and stone and often featuring a stone lintel decorated with gods, spirits or monsters. As impressive as they were, the temples of the Chenla period were to be dwarfed by what came next...

We are standing in a field. It is 5.00 a.m. The night blue sky is still closed above our heads. There is just a suggestion of light on the horizon and slowly, slowly, three towers are emerging from the gloom. It is chilly this morning, a long time since coffee; we pull our hoodies round us. Looking for all the world like three giant pine cones, readying themselves for a launch into space, the towers of Angkor Wat are growing more distinct.

Next we spot a cluster of Cambodian and Chinese visitors, squatting by a giant pool, their white shirts glowing a pale electric blue. They point their cameras at the temple before us. We are all here for the same reason. To see the sun rise over Angkor Wat. The silhouette of the temple towers has been joined by other silhouettes: palm trees, mango trees, banyan trees, horses... We watch the horses wander slowly past the temple, cropping the lush grass as they go. Flickers of white appear in the sky. No yellow sun this morning, only pale blue clouds. The temple is coming into focus before us.

In 800 a new king, Jayavarman II, established his reign on the northern banks of the Great Lake. He renamed his kingdom Kambujadesa – Cambodia – and had himself crowned king of kings and representative of heaven on earth. His court was situated close to the site of Angkor, but since most of the structures were made of wood, little of it survives. Jayavarman's empire flourished – principally upon the production of a rice surplus – and his descendants ruled for the next 200 years.

By the twelfth century the unity of the nation was weakening. Rival factions were laying claim to the throne. Then in 1113 Suryavarman II was crowned king and made it his mission to strengthen the national bonds. He tried – unsuccessfully – to annex parts of neighbouring countries. He re-established relations with China allowing for greater trade between the countries. And he commissioned the building of Angkor Wat to celebrate the god Vishnu. After Suryavarman II came Jayavarman VII, who responded to a devastating attack on the city, by building a new walled city – Angkor Thom – on top of the ruins left by the Cham. Jayavarman VII was a Buddhist and under his highly successful rule Angkor transitioned from being a place of Hindu to one of Buddhist worship. Today it is both.

We walk through the fields, past the pool and horses, and mount the steps that lead to the first gallery. The world is growing brighter by the second. Greys and greens are sharpening, the shadows of the temple lifting. Somewhere inside, in a small room filled with golden candles, a monk is lighting incense in front of a statue of the Buddha that has been dressed in a saffron robe, and pilgrims are arriving to pray.

Angkor Wat is the most famous of the temples – its picture can be found on the Cambodian flag – and the one that nature has least invaded. It is surrounded by moats and the forest has not made its way through the walls or the roof as it has elsewhere. We walk the open stone galleries gazing in wonder at the bas-reliefs. Huge stone carvings, metres high and the length of a corridor, they illustrate scenes from Hindu legend and Angkor life.

We see a king being carried through the trees on a palanquin – a covered sedan chair – borne by many servants. Visitors riding on elephants join a procession alongside dignitaries on horseback, whose heads are shaded by servants carrying umbrellas which reach right to the tops of the trees. Further on a battle rages; arrows are fired from elephant-back, and soldiers dressed only in loincloths and chains squat in preparation to throw spears. Now we find scenes from the life of Vishnu; the churning of the sea of milk shows gods and demons working together to release the nectar of immortal life from the primeval ocean.

Looking at them, I'm reminded of the Bayeux Tapestry, which was made in England roughly 70 years before the bas-reliefs at Angkor Wat. These are novels by other means: graphic novels telling stories to the literate and illiterate alike; commemorating battles, glorifying kings; littered with topical references lost on a modern audience. Beautiful. Humorous. Robustly narrative.

Thinking about medieval Britain helps to put the city of Angkor in context. In the early twelfth century the population of London was 18,000. By 1300 it had 80,000 inhabitants and was one of the most important cities in Europe. In this same period the city of Angkor was home to around 750,000 people and covered an area of up to 1,000 square kilometres – making it the largest pre-industrial settlement in history. Angkor was, for a time, the greatest civilisation on earth. And yet in 1431 the city was abandoned and the capital moved to Phnom Penh. Bit by bit the wooden buildings rotted away and disappeared into the jungle floor. Trees and grass covered the streets. Nature reclaimed everything but the temples and parts of the palaces made of stone.

Imagine London turned overnight into a forest. Squirrels nesting in the facade of St Paul's. Crumbling cream-coloured walls marking the edges of an ivy-filled Buckingham Palace. Deer grazing around the paws of one solitary bronze lion in the field where once the fountains played at the base of Nelson's Column. That is Angkor today. It is a city out of science fiction. A lost world from fantasy.

No one knows definitively how Angkor came to fall apart so quickly. It fought a long drawn-out war with Siam (the former name for Thailand), which hit the populace hard. Some historians believe that when Buddhism became the prevalent religion it undermined the status of the king by denying the cult of worldly personality. Others site the extended drought that Cambodia experienced between the fourteenth and fifteenth centuries. Without sufficient rain the rice farmers could not continue to flood their fields and so overpopulated was Angkor that any major fall in farming yields could well have led to famine. The latter explanation is perhaps the most convincing one on offer and further proof, if any were needed, of the way in which water and rice have shaped this country's path through history.

We buy souvenirs and gifts from local sellers, families who have lived on this land for hundreds of years but are no longer allowed to farm it now that it's a protected area. They rely on making and selling handicrafts and we see stalls and sellers where ever we go.

The next day we hire bikes and cycle out of Siem Riep and back to magical, crumbling Angkor. We pass Angkor Wat and cycle on, heading for Angkor Thom and Bayon, a temple topped with 54 towers – 37 of which remain – each of them encircled by four huge carved faces. There's some argument as to whom the faces are meant to represent. It could be that they're meant to be bodhisattvas, Buddhism's enlightened beings of compassion. Or they may be the Buddha himself, or King Jayavarman VII in a Buddha-like form. Certainly the faces are not obviously of one gender or another. They are rounded, plump, smiling, beneficent. They make us smile and lend this strange airy ruin a humanity and a kindness that causes us to linger, sitting on the upper levels, gazing through the sea of faces out over the trees.

We cycle on to the elephant terrace where life-size stone elephants – their trunks weathered and flattened – hold up a viewing platform from where the King once watched his battalions returning from war.

It's incredibly peaceful here, almost silent as you cycle through the jungle. There is an extraordinary sense of freedom as well, to leave the crowds at Angkor Wat and cycle out along the many kilometres of paths, under the shade of the trees, listening to birdsong. We cycle in silence and then stop and look at each other and share the wonder of the place. We want to stay here forever, in the beauty and the quiet. Since we found out that we have our house back, the change has been gradual. It's taken us a couple of weeks to absorb the fact that this particular battle is over. But cycling along the paths here now I can feel the weight that has been lifted from my shoulders. I feel freer. My feelings towards Chris and motherhood are somehow less complicated. As if the invasion of our house and the fight to get it back acted like a kind of spell to distort everything else around me. My natural sense of trust is beginning to return. The world seems a less scary place than it did a few weeks ago.

A little further on we spot a Cambodian family piled onto a moped. The children are bending down to feed bananas to a small crowd of monkeys. The baby monkeys are climbing up the backs of their parents to get the fruit. The larger monkeys place a firm hand on the face of the little ones and push them down, then slope off to consume the rest of the fruit. Their bananas gone, the family rides on and we stop to watch the baby monkeys playing by the side of the road. On the lookout for more food, monkeys are now appearing from everywhere. Down from the tops of the trees and out of the darkness of the forest. There are 30 or 40 of them now, macaques with pale brown fur, skinny limbs, delicate hands and long, wizened faces, eating or watching us beadily. I get off my bike to take photos and gingerly cross the road to where the small ones are playing. I snap happily away until I feel something tugging at my shirt. At first I think it's Chris, but he's 5 metres away. Now there's something on my head.

'Oh my God! Monkey! Monkey! Monkey!' I scream, flapping my arms wildly and pointlessly and running towards Chris. 'Get them off me!'

The monkeys are already dropping down – there were three of them – and one of the little buggers has my hat. Quick as a flash a group of monkeys gathers in a circle near the tree line and starts gnawing at the edges of my brown cotton sun hat.

I recover from my shock and run towards them shouting 'Shoo! Shoo!' and wishing I didn't sound so English and incompetent. What does one say to a monkey who has stolen one's hat? The monkeys ignore me. They have spotted the wooden beads on the string round the brim and are trying to chew them off.

'Get off my hat!' I scream at them, feeling a bit of a bully. A large monkey is now choking on half a bead. It spits it out in disgust and abandons the hat, running back into the jungle. I stuff my poor chewed hat back onto my head and get back onto my bicycle as Chris laughs. A lot.

We pass one of Angkor Thom's four gates – which lie at each point of the compass – where more giant godheads sit atop the stone and wooden gateway. As we stop to admire the scene a Cambodian boy cycles through wearing jeans and a T-shirt, his tiny size throwing into relief the immensity of these monuments. I think of those hundreds of thousands of people ebbing and flowing through this great city and the awe in which they must have held the giant carvings, and the might which was attached to their city and their kings. Did they feel empowered by that might? Did it inspire pride in them or fear?

Many of the temples show scenes from everyday life. Here a
woman in labour attended by midwives, there a cockfight and a
game of chess. Fishermen draw in their catch. Farmers transport
their grain to market. Trees are cut down and planed to make a
new palace. A Chinese trading junk arrives on the banks of Tonle
Sap. On the walls of the Bayon we see servants preparing a feast

in a forest. They boil rice in a pot and grill fish over open flames. A whole pig is being tipped into a cauldron as their masters wait, sitting on the ground under trees full of monkeys and birds.

We cycle on and on, never wanting this day to end. Near some of the more inhabited parts of the forest live groups of dogs with yellow fur: skinny mongrels that scavenge for food among the tourist waste and food stalls. As the light starts to fade we circle round past the edge of Angkor Wat and one of these dogs breaks away from his group and attaches himself to us. He follows us along the paths and waits by the bicycles when we get out to explore temples. I tickle him under the chin and rub his ears. Chris eyes him beadily.

'I don't think you should encourage him,' he says.

The light is fading fast now. It's too dark to make our way round unlit temples. We turn around and cycle towards Siem Riep. The dog follows us. We pass through the exit. The dog is still following us. We cycle faster. The dog runs happily after us. As if it's a game.

'What do we do with him?' I shout to Chris.

'I don't know. But don't stop. It'll be dark soon and we don't have lights.'

Night falls fast. On the road towards Siem Riep we find ourselves cycling in the pitch black. Now and then a car passes, briefly lighting the road around us. I am scared. Scared of cycling when I can't see. Scared of cycling down the steep bank and into the trees on either side of the road. I can hear panting and I shout to Chris. We both stop. It's not as if it can get any darker now. We grope our way towards each other in the darkness.

'The dog's still here,' I say. 'I can hear it. Homely! Homely!' I have given it a name. Homely. Because it is sweetly ugly, and obviously wants a new home. Homely pads up and breathes happily against my leg. I can feel his tail wagging.

'We'll just ignore him. He'll give up in a bit.'

We get back on our bikes and cycle on, slowly, trying to keep in a straight line so we don't dive off the side of the road. But now Homely is running beside me. And into my front wheel. I can't see him so I can't avoid him. And he, obviously, can't avoid me.

'Go home, Homely!' I shout. 'Go away! You'll get yourself run over!' I run into him. Again. I get off my bike and shout at him. He nuzzles my leg.

We cycle on and into Siem Riep. To my great relief where the town starts, so do the street lights. Homely runs beside me down the main roads, dodging vans and motorbikes, occasionally letting out a yelp of terror. We are exhausted now and longing to be back in the bar, sitting down, ordering noodles. We arrive at the hostel. Homely tries to come inside the reception with us. I appeal to the hostel owner for help. He squints out of the window and nods.

'He has followed you a long way. It happens. I will tell him to go home.'

We go upstairs to shower. Back in our room, I gaze out of the window. There is Homely, sitting on the pavement, his tail wagging happily and there is the hostel owner pointing in the direction of Angkor and shouting at him in Cambodian. But Homely doesn't leave.

We eat dinner and he is still there. We undress for bed and he is still there. We lie in bed and have the inevitable 'but can't we take him home' conversation. But we can't. We just can't.

In the morning Homely is gone. I hope that he's OK. He had a kindly soul.

Sach moan cari ang chomkak
Grilled chicken or tofu kebabs

This recipe is popular in the Chau Doc region of Cambodia. The kebabs are normally served with tirk salouk swai (mango salsa), the recipe for which you can find below. The spicing is very delicate and quite fragrant and sweet, so this is a good place to start if you don't like spicy food. The kebabs can be served as a starter, or as a main meal with rice.

Serves 2
Preparation and cooking time: 40 minutes plus 2–24 hours marinating time

Meat kebabs:
250 g chicken, cut into chunks
8–10 30-cm bamboo skewers

Vegetarian kebabs:
150 g firm tofu, pressed well to release water and cut into 3-cm cubes
Half a red pepper, deseeded and cut into 3-cm squares
Half an aubergine, cut into 3-cm cubes
8–10 30-cm bamboo skewers

Marinade:
4 cloves garlic, crushed
2 tbsp minced lemongrass

2 tbsp medium curry powder

½ tbsp soy sauce (1 tbsp if omitting fish sauce)

½ tbsp fish sauce

1 tbsp honey

1 tbsp lime juice

1 tsp paprika

60 ml water

2 tbsp peanut or other mild oil

Several grinds black pepper

Mix the marinade in a shallow bowl. Add the chicken or tofu and vegetables and toss thoroughly. Cover the bowl and leave to marinate in the fridge. The vegetarian version should be left for 2–4 hours and the meat version for a minimum of 4 hours and ideally overnight.

When marinating time finished, skewer the kebab ingredients on the wooden skewers and cook on a preheated grill, griddle pan or barbeque until crispy on edges.

Tirk salouk swai
Mango salsa

This is a hot salsa. If you're wary of heat, use only a quarter of a chilli. I made this in a blender the first few times and it became inedibly hot, so stick to chopping and mixing by hand.

Serves 2–4
Preparation time: 15 minutes

  1 ripe mango
  2 spring onions, finely sliced
  1 green chilli, deseeded and finely sliced
  4 tsp lime juice
  Handful of fresh coriander leaves
  Generous pinch of salt

Peel the mango and remove the stone. Chop the flesh into small pieces. Toss with the other ingredients. Taste and add extra salt if wished.

  If you make this in advance it will allow the flavours to develop. Serve with grilled meat, fish or tofu.

Chapter 10

Your Hat of Many Memories

I'm not sure which was the worst part of the journey from Siem Riep to Bangkok: the bumpy bus ride; the 30-minute trudge through mud and driving rain trying to find a passport control office; the hour waiting in a steaming line while the officials watched their country compete in the weight-lifting; or the fact that we were left to find buses which were parked almost a kilometre away and then had to draw all the curtains on the bus and keep our heads down so we could drive through a 'restricted area'. What was it with the restricted area? Who knew that Thailand loved a weight lifter? Why hadn't we sprung for a luxury transfer?

By the time we get to Bangkok we are in pieces. We stagger through the city, catching bus after bus with the rucksacks and the Lotus bag and the Korean tennis game. In the hostel we eat horrible French fries, balk at the communal showers and fall – sweaty, smelly, wet and weary – into bed.

The following morning we set off to explore, taking a boat down the Chao Phraya, the main river that runs through Bangkok. We pass temples painted in a myriad of crayon-bright colours and giant golden Buddhas reclining on lawns; palatial riverside houses with steepled roofs like Swiss cuckoo clocks and waterside verandas groaning with vast potted plants, palm trees and wooden altars. Later we wind down smaller canals lined with flags and sumptuous many-storeyed homes. Past a temple with rows of white pillars topped with gold, and a stack of roofs patterned with rows and rows of terracotta and emerald-coloured tiles. Past water markets, where sellers pass sacks of pumpkin and melon from boat to boat, the money whisked from hand to hand, each transaction finished in the blink of an eye. Past cargo ships with great blue hulls, their anchors sunk deep in the dark grey, murky water.

Bangkok started as a small trading post on the Chao Phraya in the fifteenth century. By the eighteenth century it was the capital of Siam and since the 1980s it has been home to the offices of dozens of multinational corporations, drawn in by the Asian economic boom at the end of the twentieth century. The city is booming but parts of the infrastructure are lagging behind.

Heading away from the river we try to navigate our way back across town on foot. In Cambodia, a road is a rare and precious thing. Not so in Thailand. My first impression of Bangkok is that it consists of one enormous road that had somehow become tangled. The city resembles a giant tarmac-covered ball of wool. Motorways and main roads and flyovers and bridges and underpasses: they curl and stack and loop together to form a kind of dystopian vision of a future in which the roads themselves have decided to rise up and strangle us. As we wait a small eternity to cross the road motorcycles crawl past us, two riders apiece; then rickshaws; bicycles; buses; more buses; and then hundreds of cars – no – thousands of cars in white and black and sweetie-coloured pink and blue and orange.

Travelling on foot around Bangkok involves crossing and re-crossing this traffic carbonara. Or you can take a bus and sit in it instead. After a couple of hours I grind to a weary halt outside a giant mall called the Siam Paragon. Chris marches on to do something virtuous and cultural involving a temple and we agree to meet again at 5.00 p.m.

Everything sold in the Siam Paragon is wildly out of my price range; its marble floors shine cleanly; beautifully dressed Thai, Chinese, Australian and American women click neatly and quietly from Marc Jacobs to Gucci and from Hermès to Escada. Creamy mannequins model suits for autumn, trench coats, evening dresses in jade and turquoise and glittering beaded black. From the windows of the stores black-and-white pictures of models and actresses stare vacantly out at me, 6 metres high, 3 metres wide. Their lips are painted and still, their mouths unspeaking, their hair shines like a halo, their eyes are painted thickly and blackly with the markings of their sex.

I catch a glimpse of myself in a mirrored surface. My hair is long and unkempt. I am wearing my black New Look jeans, now hacked off below the knee, a green and black baseball shirt, my half-chewed sun hat and chunky black trainers. My legs haven't been shaved in more than a week and I look... grubby. I mean, I shower daily but something about my whole appearance is just grubby. I am the least kempt thing in the whole of the Siam Paragon.

I find my way down to a chemist's shop on a lower floor and I wander up and down the aisles of shiny creams and potions. I can't really afford any of these and I have a bar of soap back at the hostel. Does it matter how filthy I am? I haven't really minded in months. Not since we left Beijing. Not since we started living out of packs. Why do I care now? Because the damned shops reminded me of what I was meant to be aspiring to.

In my old life I wanted to be glossy, well dressed and cool. Living in London, you are surrounded by the chic and the street. You can sit and style-watch all day and never grow bored. And there is a buzz, a visceral buzz, to walking down the road in London in a 1950s dress and Doc Martens, or an ankle-length opera coat and heels, and being a part of that scene. But now... I haven't looked in a full-length mirror in months, my hair was last cut a year ago, I have been wearing the same pair of jeans, the same bra, and the same trainers – pretty much solidly – for seven months.

The Siam Paragon has confused me. What am I meant to want right now? Am I meant to want to look polished? I'd forgotten, actually forgotten, that this thirst could exist. I haven't had to look any particular way for many months. In China, I grew used to looking quite different to the general populace. I was surrounded by examples of Chinese femininity, but since I was so much taller and bigger and paler than every model on every poster they held no power to inspire or exhort me. I was comfortable looking different, uninterested in attracting the male gaze. I was living out of a single rucksack of clothes and vanity had become a pointless burden that I happily threw aside. Once on the road, I was rarely even aware of how I looked. I went days at a time without looking in a mirror. My beauty regime consisted of showering and brushing my teeth. It was too hot to keep make up in place, so I stopped using it at all. I was tanned from the many days walking in the sun and up until today felt quite pleased with how I looked. When I did catch a glimpse of myself in a mirror I decided I looked healthy, with uncharacteristically dark skin and blonde streaks in my hair. I had forgotten that healthy was not the point. I am meant to look thin and groomed, well dressed and seductively made up. I am none of these things.

I'm having possibly the shallowest existential crisis in the history of the mind. A crisis from which I am disturbed – and we shall tread carefully here, for male readers can be a delicate lot – by the realisation that I require a packet of ladies' necessaries. Which solves my problem of what to do with the seventy baht (one pound twenty pence) burning a hole in my pocket. Frankly, ladies' necessaries are a luxury on this trip. I have been improvising without them for some time now. I purchase said necessaries and leave the lovely chemists' shop hiding them in my sun hat. Really: could I feel any grubbier right now?

I can no longer handle the glare of the black-and-white tyrants. I run away and hide in the ladies' toilets until it's 5.00 p.m. and I can go looking for Chris. I find him wandering in the foyer with the kind of dazed look that malls engender in the non-shopper.

'Can we eat?' he asks.

'Well, I don't have any money. But if you fancy it there's a lovely restaurant on a higher floor called the Orangery. I mean, it'd be a treat but...'

'Does it look nice?'

'It looks lovely,' I tell him. The tables are placed around the edge of a huge curving window that looks out over the city. And the view is topped by curtains of tiny lights that glow like stars. There is a maître d' and piano music. It is everything we aren't used to.

Chris smiles. 'Let's have a treat.'

So we ride the escalators to the Orangery where the maître d' duly shows us to a table by the window. We sit beneath the fairy lights, ignoring the massive concrete flyover that dominates the view. I am once again deeply aware of how messy we look but there's no one else eating here this early. I have no bag in which to put my ladies' necessaries, so I wrap them in my sun hat and hide them on a little ledge under the table.

We carefully peruse the menu, which offers food from a range of countries. *Pad Thai* and *khao mok* from Thailand. Sizzling beef and mapo tofu from China. Spicy *rendang* stew and *laksa* from Malaysia. *Bun bo hue* and *goi cuon* from Vietnam. Rainbow sushi and miso soup from Japan. *Gejang* and *kimchi* from Korea.

I lean across the table towards Chris and whisper: 'What can we afford?'

Chris leans towards me and we pretend to be having a romantic moment. 'One dish and a small wine,' he mutters, his face craning lovingly towards my ear.

I pull him closer, 'Let's skip the wine.'

He smiles lovingly into my eyes: 'Let's not.'

The maitre d' stands by the bar chatting to the barman and watching us with an amused but benign eye. We eat *goi cuon* and sizzling beef and giggle into our small glasses of wine in the stillness of the empty restaurant. The fairy lights above us seem to blur gently as evening slips into night and we take each other's hand and start the long walk home.

The next day we visit the temple of Wat Pho, where a 46-metre-long golden Buddha reclines, his head resting gently on one raised hand. The soles of his huge feet are covered with mother-of-pearl inlay illustrating the symbols by which Buddha can be identified. Laid into the centre of ornate squares are muscular animals prowling on the ground, lean herons cutting through the sky and turbulent, fish-filled rivers surging through the countryside. As we make our way out past a grinning stone giant that is said to be an image of Marco Polo we spot a poster for a one-day vegetarian

Thai cookery class. I have become so used to pulling apart whatever is on our plates in order to reverse engineer a recipe that the thought of an actual cookery class fills me with glee. We book places for the following day.

We go out for dinner, slipping round the corner to a little cafe, open on three sides, where they serve the most glorious *pad Thai*. The noodles are salty and sweet and slippery, the tofu fatty and crunchy on the outside, and the coriander leaves and slivers of chilli crunch into little angry bursts between your teeth. It's a hot, greasy, moreish plate of comfort.

Mai Kaidee is standing in her eponymous restaurant, telling us the story of her life and her philosophy of food. As a young woman she came to Bangkok to work and found herself seduced by the all the rich food that the city had to offer. She soon found that she was gaining weight and however much she moderated her diet she couldn't seem to eat the food she loved and lose kilos. So she educated herself about nutrition and came up with her rules for healthy eating in Thai cuisine. Replace white rice with brown. Use coconut milk sparingly. Make everything fresh and use plenty of vegetables. Mai herself is a picture of health. Despite being in her forties, she looks 20. She is very petite and bubbly, extremely articulate and really quite beautiful. She is a canny and charismatic businesswoman who now owns a string of restaurants and a cookery school where she teaches her course twice a day, most days of the week.

Mai is taking us to the market to buy some of the food we'll be cooking with this morning. She walks purposefully along the edge of the stalls by a small canal, handling fruit and veg, squeezing papayas to judge their freshness and introducing us to the local fish sauce seller. Called *nam pla* in Thailand, *nuoc mam* in Vietnam and *teuk trei* in Cambodia, South-East Asian fish sauce is made by packing anchovies and salt into wooden boxes and then pressing them as they ferment. It has a pungent smell and a sour, salty, *umami* flavour. Versions of fish sauce are found all over the world, in the UK we consume it as Worcestershire sauce, in Malaysia *belacan* made from fermented krill adds a sour note to curry pastes, and in ancient Rome cooks made a variety called *garum* which was typically mixed with wine, vinegar or honey. Mai tells us how to replace this ubiquitous ingredient with a combination of light and dark soy sauces. She picks up onions, garlic, fresh galangal (a sort of Thai version of ginger) along with handfuls of chillies and some fresh stalks of lemongrass. Then she leads us back to the little cooking workshop she's built in the back yard of her cafe.

We're supplied with aprons and dozens of little bowls of ingredients that have been assiduously peeled and deseeded and chopped by her assistants. The gas is lit on a line of burners, gigantic woks appear and Mai sets to teaching us ten dishes in less than 2 hours. She walks behind us, adjusting our posture, leaning in to swirl the fat round the wok, guiding our hands between the bowls of ingredients, telling us to slacken here and increase the heat there. It is a virtuoso performance and one built on teaching thousands of travellers to cook over many, many years. Almost every dish is complete within 10 minutes, we then have a couple of minutes to taste and note the seasoning and we're off again. We make *tom yum* soup, heavy with spice and fragrant with coriander leaves. In giant black mortars we pound together kaffir lime leaves, galangal, lemongrass, cumin, coriander, chillies, shallots, garlic and oil to make Thai curry paste, creating a perfume so heady that you can't stop yourself burying your nose into the bowl and breathing it all in. We learn how to make Thai green curry and Thai red curry, frying our spice mix in oil and then slowly adding coconut milk to make a paste in which to cook our vegetables. Having filled our wok with vegetables and tofu we make the sauce from coconut milk mixed with water. Everything is cooked for only a few minutes, to retain the nutritional value and the bite of the vegetables and when the sauce has thickened you taste and adjust the seasoning with sugar for sweetness, lime juice for sourness and soy sauce for salt and *umami* flavours. We learn how to adapt this recipe to make *massaman* curry by frying our paste first with Indian spices and fresh tomatoes. The spices of Thailand mix with the spices of India creating a great burst of warmth in the finished dish that lingers on the tongue as you eat. We peel fresh green papaya and pound peanuts with chilli and coriander to make a salad. We fry noodles with tofu, peppers, chilli, garlic and bean sprouts to make a quick *pad Thai*.

After 2 hours we gather together in the restaurant to eat the lunch we've just prepared and to chat about the food we've come from and the food we've found. Our fellow students are from Australia, Germany, Sweden and France. Some of them are vegetarian but most of them aren't; Mai's course comes so highly recommended that even meat eaters find themselves drawn here.

The German girl sitting next to me explains that she grew up in a commune where everyone was a vegetarian and she cannot imagine eating meat. She tells me with horror of the butcher's shops she passed on the way here and how she cannot bring herself to look at the poor animals hanging up in the window.

'Have you ever eaten meat?' she asks me.

'Oh yes,' I tell her, 'I didn't even start becoming a vegetarian until I was 12. My parents and most of my friends and my boyfriends have always eaten meat.'

'Don't you mind?' she asks.

I think about this for a moment. 'Not really,' I tell her. 'My attitude is to live and let live and I extend that to my nearest and dearest. If they want to eat meat, that's their choice.'

'But if no one in your family was a vegetarian, then why would you become one?'

So I give her the official story of how I became a vegetarian, though like all official stories it is not a complete truth.

'Twenty years ago, when I was 12 I went on holiday with my school to the Isle of Wight and we visited a pig farm as part of a geography project on farming. As we toured the farm buildings a young worker beckoned us into one of the barns. There, in a small sty full of straw and under bright lights a large pink pig lay half awake. At her teats there suckled a little tangle of pink and brown piglets. They had been born that morning and like their mother were quite exhausted. We watched them for some time as they snuffled and burrowed and drank and lay down in the straw to sleep. After a while the mother pig woke and opened a single eye. She bent her head to lick the head of the nearest sleeping piglet, nuzzling it gently to check that it was actually alive.

'The same employee then led us through to another barn to see the piglets in their various stages of growth: at six weeks, at six months, at one year. Here and there we noticed small chalkboards hung up on the wall with numbers written on them. As the pigs grew larger the numbers counted down. "Why?" asked one of the boys. "What are you counting down to?" The employee nodded his head towards the barn on the other side of the large farmyard. "Slaughter," he said.

'That night at dinner the hotel served us ham salad and five of us – all girls – refused to eat it. We had been given a glimpse of the realities of farming and could not reconcile the wonder of birth with the gruesome reality of why the piglets had been bred at all.'

'Goodness,' says the intense and friendly German girl. 'Was your geography teacher a vegetarian?'

'I don't know. But you do have to wonder...'

Chris smiles across at me. He has heard this story before. There is a larger story which remains unsaid; a more complicated story that is perhaps more pertinent.

For as long as I can remember I have assigned human frailty and need to animals and objects that cannot speak. I have projected my emotions onto things that cannot possibly have the same emotions as myself. As a small child I would hesitate to pick a flower from a field for fear that I might hurt the feelings of the other flowers. I would whisper to dolls in a toyshop if they weren't the ones I chose to take home that I still loved them and I was sorry. I couldn't bear the thought of anyone or anything being hurt because of my actions. I wanted to make peace with everything around me.

I wasn't a perfect child. I was kind most of the time but I could be unkind as well. I was not beyond making jokes at other people's expense but I would suffer fits of terrible squirming guilt after the fact: guilt which would tie me up in knots of physical pain as I lay in bed at night. I wanted to mend everything. To harm nothing. And this unrealisable desire would sometimes paralyse me. The thought that an animal might die so I could eat so appalled me that I became a vegetarian out of a sense of horror. At my mother's insistence I kept eating fish until I left home, but as I soon as I moved out I gave this up as well.

I still remember keenly how much I loved eating meat and fish. Growing up in a foodie family I had tried dozens of strange and interesting dishes while I was still a child: steak tartare, octopus and sushi, guinea fowl and swordfish, and I relished the taste of raw meat and fish, the cold, slippery bite of flesh and fat and sinew. In the 20 years before I came out here to Asia I never intentionally ate a piece of meat. And yet in the past seven months I have eaten horse broth noodles, rice fried in pork fat, slivers of every type of meat imaginable mixed in with virtually every dish I've ordered or picked over. I've twice ordered and eaten sea cucumber thinking it was a kind of rubbery seaweed. As with so many other things I feel pulled in two directions. The foodie in me misses the opportunity to eat anything and everything, to cook every dish in the world and learn its secrets. But I am still in part that small child who wants to mend everything and harm nothing. I feel a responsibility that extends far beyond what I can reasonably be responsible for. A ridiculous and impossible desire to care for the whole world.

On our final day in Bangkok as I pack my rucksack, I realise that my hat is missing. My battered brown cloth sun hat. The one I wore through China and Vietnam and Cambodia. The one I fought the monkeys of Angkor to regain. I am distraught. We have three hours until we have to be on a train. But I know where I left it. It is sitting on a little ledge below the table at the Orangery restaurant in the Siam Paragon, hiding a packet of ladies' necessaries. I get in a taxi and set off for the Siam Paragon. But the traffic is solid. I scrutinise my map: can I walk there and back, pick up my rucksack and still get to the train? Probably not. And I cannot make us miss the train. So, after an hour sitting in steamy, honking traffic, I give up the ghost, pay my driver and walk the couple of kilometres back to the hostel.

I've never been averse to heaping meaning into inanimate objects, and my battered brown hat had come to represent this trip. It represented a kind of mission. A desire to travel and explore. To regain a sense of myself. Despite the little wooden beads, it is a thing of practical purpose: a means of not getting fried in sweaty jungles or on palm-lined rivers; of not succumbing to sunstroke on the sides of mountains or as I walked on searing tropical beaches. And now it was lying on a shiny marble floor, underneath the twinkling fairy lights, coyly hiding my decadent packet of necessaries.

Five months from now I will be back in the UK and still gently mourning the loss of my battered brown sun hat. So I will send a pointlessly optimistic email to the Siam Paragon, explaining that the previous year I left a hat in their restaurant and telling them briefly what I had gone through in that hat, all the things that made it so very special and that I would happily pay the postage for its return. I received a very courteous reply from a young lady saying that she would look into it. And then I heard nothing more. Weeks passed and I decided that it was too late. Some things stay with us only briefly, and perhaps I shouldn't be too attached to anything that wasn't human. Then one grey February morning the postman knocks on the door and hands me a large brown box, so light that I can't believe there's anything in it. The stamps show it has come from Thailand and my heart leaps a little as I tear off the packing tape and find inside my battered brown hat, with its wooden beads half-chewed by monkeys. A compliment slip from the Siam Paragon holds just one sentence in a beautiful, looping cursive: Your hat of many memories.

My battered brown hat hangs in my study now. And when I take the time to look at it... really look at it... I feel a rush of warmth. Yes, it holds the memory of kayaking on the Li, climbing the Great Wall, circling Ha Long Bay and cycling to the Imperial City in Vietnam. Yes, I wore it on Rabbit Island and grappled a troop of monkeys for it in Angkor Wat. But more than that it reminds me that a young woman in Thailand, who I never met, did me a wonderful kindness. Her kindness has suffused this flimsy cotton object; it has made it mean something else. What once stood for adventure now stands for love: in the greatest sense of the word.

For travelling is, in the end, an exploration of love. The human love of the world, the victory of hope over fear and a belief in the kindness of strangers.

When someone commits a crime against you, when someone steals from you or hurts you or destroys the things you have, it is as if your world shrinks. Faith, hope and love: each of these shrivel to a small and withered thing, hiding somewhere in the pit of your stomach. You become hyper-aware, neurotic. You become someone who stays to lock the apartment door even as an earthquake shakes you to the floor. And if too many of these things come together they can destroy the greater part of who you are. For without hope or love or belief in the possibility of kindness, your world shrivels into a dark hole. Life outside your little corner of the world becomes a fearful thing, impossible for some.

This is a book about love. But it's not just a book about romantic love. It's a book about love in its wider sense. The love of other humans, which is the same thing as hope. It's about learning to regain trust. It's about taking the moments of kindness – the goodness in the world – and letting them shine brighter than the stupidity and the cruelty, the desperation and the destruction.

We climb aboard the International Express, a second-class sleeper train that will take us from Bangkok to Butterworth in Malaysia, the jumping off point for the island of Penang. Second-class sleepers are retro space-age – think Woody Allen's *Sleeper* or *The Jetsons*. By day, Chris and I sit opposite each other in two vast armchairs beside a curtained window. At night the armchairs slide together to make a lower bunk and the great curved ceiling above your head descends to make the upper. An attendant arrives with fresh sheets and makes up the beds.

Each bunk comes with its own set of curtains that hang between you and the aisle and the whole set up and experience reminds me of school camping trips. You remember that moment when the grown ups leave you alone for the night and you zip yourselves into your own little plastic world? Far away from parents and several plastic walls away from teachers you are suddenly invisible to the adult world and anything is possible. Tonight I feel about eight, and so intrigued by the experience of life in my little curtained bubble that I cannot sleep. Chris is safely snoring above my head, but I lie awake all night, reading books, listening to podcasts and watching a still, dark Thailand fly by past the windows.

A little past 4.00 a.m. the sky begins to crack open. The solid canopy of night slides over the roof of the train to reveal a watery grey sky, shot through with dazzling tendrils of sunlit cloud. The sun is rising from behind the mountains, making black silhouettes of the trees and hedges beside the railway line. Suddenly the white light catches on the flooded fields and the world outside the window lights up like a paper lantern. The edge of night's grey canopy is still visible as each point of light gains a golden halo and the gleam behind the trees slips from grey to white to yellow, then to orange.

The orange grows, ebbing across the sky, lighting new clouds: pink and orange and red, steel-grey-blue in shadow. Now the flooded fields take up the orange and the red and the whole landscape seems to catch fire. The mountain peaks in the distance are burning, the fields are like fiery pits and the sky is an angry fireball coursing above our head. The world burns brightly for 15 astonishing minutes and then it's gone, flushing away into a grey day of damp, tropical weather.

Khao mok
Thai biryani

This fabulous rice dish has borrowed many elements from Indian cuisine. It is intensely rich but the accompanying sauce has enough hot and sour notes to freshen the palate.

Serves 4
Preparation and cooking time: 1 hour 15 minutes

8 chicken thighs or 2 large aubergines, cut into long, thick strips
6 tbsp oil for frying
1 onion, peeled and chopped
2 garlic cloves, finely chopped 2 tsp turmeric
8-cm piece of cinnamon
2 bay leaves
300 g long grain rice, washed
350 ml chicken or vegetable stock
200 ml coconut milk
10-cm piece of cucumber, unpeeled and sliced
4 tomatoes, sliced
Salt and pepper to taste

Spice rub:
1 tbsp curry powder
1 tbsp turmeric powder

Sauce:
80 g sugar
2 tbsp water

80 ml clear vinegar

2 green Thai chillies, stalks removed and finely chopped

5-cm piece of ginger, peeled and finely chopped

Half a handful of coriander, chopped

4 spring onions, heads removed and finely chopped

Pinch of salt

Start by rubbing the chicken or aubergine with the spice rub. Set aside.

Now make the sauce. Heat the sugar and water in a saucepan. After a minute add the vinegar. Take off the heat and add the other ingredients. Adjust to taste with sugar, salt or vinegar. Decant into individual dishes.

Heat half the oil in a large frying pan. Cook the chicken or aubergine, and then set aside.

Heat the remaining oil in the pan. Fry onion and garlic until golden then add turmeric, cinnamon and bay leaves. Add in the uncooked rice and fry gently for a couple of minutes, coating the rice.

In a large lidded pot combine chicken or aubergine with the rice mixture. Add the stock and coconut milk and simmer, covered, over a medium heat. When rice has absorbed all the liquid it is ready. Serve with slices of cucumber and tomato on each plate and a dish of sauce.

Chapter 11

August is the Month of Hungry Ghosts

We arrive at Butterworth station early one morning and take the ferry across to Penang's capital George Town. As we hum across the water, the city's skyline comes in to view: Georgian clock towers and red-roofed resorts, glass-walled office buildings and far in the distance an undulating line of blue-green forested hills.

Equipped with only a tiny map we walk looking for the street – or *jalan* – our hostel sits on. Most of the shops are still shut, but by the side of the road and behind hatches in shopfronts men and women in white aprons offer omelettes, Indian roti bread stuffed with curry, and paper plates of brown fried noodles for breakfast. In front of one cart a long line of workers in shorts and T-shirts chat quietly as they queue for bowls of *congee* which the seller ladles on top of pungent century eggs – those shiny black Chinese delicacies made by preserving eggs for weeks in ash, quicklime, salt, clay and rice. I stand and watch the chef at work as he plucks a slippery black egg from a metal vat and places it in a tiny clear bowl. Blindly his other hand reaches for the ladle of chalky-white rice porridge and the egg disappears like buried treasure beneath a dune of sand. Chris calls my attention away from this to the far end of the street that is filling up with smoke.

'What is it? A bonfire?' We edge closer.

Great puffs of grey and white vapour are blooming from one side of the long *jalan*, swirling together and wisping their way up into the blue morning. We approach with caution as the smell of cloves, sandalwood, star anise and cinnamon reaches us.

'What is that smell? Curry?'

'No. It's stronger than curry. I think it's incense.'

The heady scents come and go with the breeze that swirls the smoke into the street and up over our heads. We wait for a gap between the grey clouds and move on, finding ourselves in front of a square courtyard, open on one side to the road. Dotted about the square like statues, middle-aged men and women stand facing away from us. Above their heads, their hands are held together in prayer and each of them clasps a great bundle of lit incense sticks. As we watch, a stooped man in a grey sweater and worn trousers bows his head, drops his hands and steps forward to place his bundle of smoking sticks into a large metal vessel decorated with dragons and clouds. We can see now that most of the smoke is coming from a line of three-legged copper cauldrons which sit to one side of the courtyard heaped with black balls of incense. Behind the clouds of smoke and the standing worshippers we can see a small but colourful temple. Its steeply raked roof is covered with bright terracotta tiles and green dragons leap and play along the ridge at the top. Behind a delicate screen of wrought iron the walls of the temple glow with lacquered surfaces in shades of crimson red, sky blue and emerald green. Just visible inside the open doors are tables covered with plates of oranges, bowls of rice, pastries, mooncakes, melons and nuts. For this is August. And August is the month of hungry ghosts.

It is the seventh month of the lunar calendar – seven months since fireworks and New Year dumplings – and the moment in Buddhist and Taoist belief when the gates of heaven and hell open and the hungry ghosts walk the earth. In a culture devoted to ancestor worship the spiritual and symbolic feeding of those who have gone before is a central duty for every observant man and woman. And August is the month when those ghosts who have not been fed return so that their inattentive relatives can make amends and offer them food and prayers to ease their journey in the afterlife. Yesterday was the fifteenth of the month, the Buddha's joyful day and the high point of the festival of hungry ghosts. As I lay awake on the train watching the fields and mountains flash past, tens of millions of people flocked to temples across China, Korea, Japan, Vietnam, Singapore and Malaysia to light incense, offer food, share meals and pray for their dear-departed parents, aunts, uncles, grandparents and great-grandparents.

Of all the narratives we live with – the history of our nation, the story of our faith or politics – the most potent of all narratives is the story of our family. Humans have a burning desire to fit inside their own unique history. Scarred as it might be with great wrongs and tragedies, we feel a very basic desire to own and understand our origin story. This is why those who are forced from their early lives and homes by war or domestic strife will fight to discover who they are and where they came from. This is why the story of a family will be told and retold, transforming itself as it goes, sometimes by design and sometimes by mistake. One of religion's greatest appeals is that it has offered the human race a series of grand origin stories of which to be a part. It is no coincidence that the decline of theist belief in the West followed Charles Darwin's publication of a new and radically alternative origin story. Humans feel marooned without a sense of where they came from, as if they cannot decide how to finish the story unless they know how it started. Sharing your origin story is an act of bonding around the globe. After all, what is it that you do in those long first sleepless nights with a new love? You share your origin story, you share your body and you share your dreams. Where you came from, who you are now and where you want to go.

However far it is we think we've moved on, our past will always call us back from time to time. Back to the side of graves or a temple filled with fruit and incense. Back to our native country or the town we were born in. Back to our origin story and the remnants of our past. Back to who we were long ago before the compromises of adult life transformed us from our first fragile selves.

George Town is packed to the brim with tiny, distinct areas, often no larger than a single street. Chinatown sits cheek by jowl with Little India. To the west these neighbourhoods are bounded by the faceless modern shopping district with its 65-storey Komtar Tower, which stands like a stiff-necked statue staring blindly over the heads of the more interesting offerings grouped around its knees.

To the east lie the sea and a disjointed smattering of Georgian officialdom: a fort, a barracks, several churches. We spend the afternoon wandering listlessly around the eighteenth-century Fort Cornwallis, which seems remarkably well preserved until you consider that it's never been involved in any kind of military engagement. It was built by the incoming British forces in 1799 and in the absence of any conflict ended up serving as a kind of unofficial town hall, a group of offices from which the British officers could rearrange George Town to their liking. These days a solitary chestnut horse crops the grass beside the disused prison cells.

The view from the walls is stunning. A great blanket of blue sea – tingeing towards jade green where it meets mainland Malaysia – serving as a backdrop to the huge cannon that noses its way over Cornwallis's walls. What was it like, I wonder, to travel thousands of kilometres from a comfortable life in London or the home counties, to a little island in the Strait of Malacca where every colour you've ever known seems different? When they built the great neo-classical facades of St George's Church or the Church of the Assumption did they think these buildings looked foolish in their tropical surrounds?

One of the ironies of the British colonists importing Palladian architecture to Asia is the fact that this style of building looks considerably better in a sunny, bright environment than it does in drab grey England. In the hazy heat of a Malaysian summer, the temple edifice of St George's shines like a sheet-white beacon amid the tropical greens and browns. Much as I love St Martin-in-the-Fields, it has a tendency to look as if stuck in a permanent state of grief, sitting sadly by the side of Trafalgar Square in a cloudy London spring, counting the music lovers in and out. Of course, this is hardly surprising since the Palladian style was imported to England from Italy, another land of soft, warm light and vivid colour. I imagine the soaring white columns and clean-lined cornices marching stiffly from central Italy, stopping briefly and expensively for lunch in central London before hopping, refreshed, aboard a boat for Malaysia where they get to live out a never-ending retirement surrounded by palm trees.

So successful was the transplant of Palladian architecture that the British continued to build official buildings in this style well into the twentieth century. George Town fairly bristles with wedding cake town halls and clock towers, neo-classical schools and railway stations. Penang State Museum is another double-deckered pastry of a building, one that we visit the next morning.

We linger longest in the rooms given over to the Peranakan culture. Peranakan is here used to mean 'descendant' and the descendants in question are the Chinese who arrived in Malaysia and Indonesia in the late fifteenth and sixteenth centuries. The culture is perhaps better known as Baba Nyonya, and is most identifiable to Western visitors by the proliferation of Nyonya cuisine across Malaysia.

Inside the museum they have recreated whole rooms evoking Peranakan houses of the past few centuries. The artistry is breathtaking. Carved wooden lamps covered with scrollwork, and shining from inside etched, frosted glass. Every colour and shade of wood imaginable is carved and smoothed and polished to a mirrored gleam. Doorways framed with golden dragons and curling leaves. Four-poster beds hung with drapes of eye-searing red and canopied with fat embroidered roses looping across silk of duck-egg blue. Every millimetre of furniture is decorated, every piece of fabric exquisitely dyed, printed and embroidered. The rooms sing with colour and opulence.

The reason this is particularly striking is that it represents traditional Chinese culture without the interruption of the revolution. Baba Nyonya have long prided themselves on being 'more Chinese than the Chinese'. While the Cultural Revolution was tearing apart lives, buildings and artefacts in the homeland, Peranakan society pottered on.

Chinese traders predated the British in the Strait of Malacca by many centuries and the trading communities of Malacca had, by the fifteenth century, established a practice of paying tribute to the incumbent Chinese emperor. In 1459 the emperor sent one of his daughters to the Sultan of Malacca as a way of strengthening the bond between the two countries. Hundreds of courtiers and servants travelled with the princess and settled in Malaysia, forming the first large, stable Chinese community. Penang bristled with trading possibilities and wealth. During periods of economic hardship, waves of Chinese immigrants would arrive in Malaysia, strengthening the community here.

The Baba Nyonya speak a Creole language (Baba Malay) that melds together aspects of Malay with Hokkien Chinese and borrows from the languages of many of the nations who colonised the area over the past millennia. The name of the group comes from *baba* (man) and *nyonya* (woman); *nyonya* most likely finding its origins in the Italian *nona* or the Portuguese *dona*, and *baba* a Persian honorific which arrived via Malay. Also from Malay, the Peranakans borrowed a strong tradition of oral poetry and hundreds of rhymes were passed down detailing Baba life and culture.

> On the First and Fifteenth Day the lamps they are lit
> And what do we see but a bride making ready.
> Is the lady tall or is she slight?
> Light incense for your father's ancestors.
> Father is not in his ceremonial dress.

Light incense to honour your mother's ancestors.
Mother is not in her ceremonial robes.
Light incense to honour the dragon boat now coming
The dragon boat which flies on the water now.
Two lads dry a tea urn, making ready
The urn tumbles to the ground
As the two boys wrestle on the table.
Now the table breaks and falls,
Leaving the boys dangling in the air.
Chee, Johny *A Tapestry of Baba Poetry*. Verse translation
in English by Lim Poh Keng (2007, Areca Books).

With their long-established cultural arrangements, wealth and influence the Brits – who arrived in 1799 – saw the Peranakan as natural allies and as time passed the Peranakan borrowed heavily from various aspects of British culture, most notably the British education system. In Singapore and Kuala Lumpur, so heavily was the Baba Nyonya associated with the British that they went by the nickname of the King's Chinese.

But over the course of the 1940s, 1950s and 1960s the community suffered a number of serious blows. The Japanese executed many influential Peranakans during the war, and most of their land and property was seized. A sizeable group of Perakanan left Malaysia out of choice after Mao called on Chinese citizens throughout the world to help him rebuild the nation. The majority of those who left were wealthy intellectuals and having returned to China they found themselves the target of myriad abuses during the Cultural Revolution.

On the edge of Little India stands the Penang Peranakan Mansion, built by Kapitan Cina Chung Keng Kwee, a nineteenth-century tin mine owner. Outside, the walls are painted a brilliant mint green; and white and gold columns support an improbably curlicued balcony that hangs over the pavement. To the front of the steps a line of rickshaws queue for tourists beside a bright-red British phone box. Inside, pots of orange orchids and lacquered screens sit alongside Art Deco drinks cabinets and High Victorian Gothic bevelled mirrors. Red paper lanterns light the way up the mahogany staircase and bonsai trees in ebony pots share a hallway with a selection of stags' heads. One of the salons shines copper-brown as the light glances off a dazzlingly ornate parquet floor, a sea of musk-brown diamonds and teak-lined stars. On the wall a scene of a stag on moorland is rendered unreal in monochrome mirrored pieces of glass: black, gold and silver. In a pleasing act of cultural recycling the Peranakans, having a love for all things English, imported vast numbers of decorative Victorian tiles. These tiles typically bore the influence of British artists' obsession with Eastern art. And so lotus blossoms and curling vines made their way from east to west and back again.

We are whizzing through the Penang countryside in a small grey minivan. In the seats behind us sit a well-dressed Chinese mother and her two sons, four and six. Younger son is crouching in the foot well, seeing how far he can throw coloured erasers under the front seats. Older son is a ball of black mood, trainered feet firmly planted on the seat, ignoring his mother's exhausted entreaties to put his feet down. His mother's eyes are large black seas of pity, her whole body telegraphing a kind of surrender.

Chris and I watch her, fascinated. Is this our future? Is this what it's going to be like? Two children in a minivan and no hope? We nobly ignore her children's delinquency and try to make morale-boosting conversation with her. She's bright, well educated and fluent in multiple languages. Once she was a professional, now she's a professional wife, following her husband and his company around south-east Asia: Hong Kong, Taiwan, Singapore, Indonesia, Malaysia. We don't ask but I assume that her non-resident status accounts for the two boys (for many months we've barely seen a Chinese mother with more than one child). Her husband is on Penang for a big meeting and she and the boys are doing what they always do, trying to find things to fill their days.

We have come together for a tour of cultural Penang: temples, giant Buddhas, batik workshops. As the children canter noisily in front of us we climb the walkways of the Kek Lok Si Buddhist temple, which sits like a white and shining city on the hills above the sea. It has been under construction since 1890 and if you're lucky enough to visit it, you're bound to find yet another temple building or giant statue covered in scaffolding and waving plastic sheets. The temple has been built to embrace many traditions within Buddhism. The main pagoda of 10,000 Buddhas has an octagonal cream-coloured Chinese base with tiered roofs above the gateways. Above this sits a central section made from tiers of white archways with swooping highly-decorated roofs, representing the temples of Thailand. On the very top is an undulating Burmese crown of rich yellow, pointing its stacked domes towards the sky.

A 30-metre-high bronze statue of Kuan Yin, the Buddhist goddess of compassion, peers out from behind great towers of ironwork. They are building her a canopy. She smiles beatifically

across the hills to the sea and her many visitors. We pay for a red ceramic roof tile and write our names on its crest in black marker pen.

We travel down the mountain where we're deposited outside a Chinese restaurant by our guide and the driver, who leave to eat burgers closer into town. We make our way cautiously inside. The restaurant is deserted. All around us chairs are stacked upside down on tables. There are no other patrons. There are no waiters. No cooks. No cleaners. I know this because at one point we chase the delinquent six-year-old out the back of the restaurant, as his mother attempts to lasso his brother who is literally trying to climb the walls, and the kitchens and back yard are empty of life. It is the ghost ship of Chinese restaurants. Maybe there's something wrong with it.

An invisible force has placed a selection of plates on our table: noodles, spring rolls, rice with pork, dumplings, spiced chicken wings. We search in vain in the drawers and cupboards for chopsticks, then give up and eat with our hands. The four-year-old sits next to me helping himself to food, often out of my hand. He chatters away incessantly in Mandarin. I understand about one word in ten. But he doesn't really care. It's a preschooler's monologue, driven by an unselfconscious place at the centre of the universe and an unfaltering well of quasi-demonic energy.

Eventually I apologise and explain (in Mandarin) that my Mandarin is awful and I can't manage much more than songs.

'*Hao. Chang ni de ge,*' he says. OK. Sing your song.

Both the mother and Chris nod at me encouragingly so I launch into my thousandth rendition of '*Liang Zhi Laohu*'. '*Liang Zhi Laohu*' – sung to the tune of '*Frère Jacques*' – is a real Chinese nursery standard. I memorised it early on as someone recommended it as a way of ingratiating yourself to small children, and their parents, on long train journeys.

> *Liang zhi laohu, liang zhi laohu,*
> *Pao de kuai, pao de kuai,*
> *Yi zhi meiyou yanjing,*
> *Yi zhi meiyou erdou,*
> *Zhen qi guai! Zhen qi guai!*

> Two tigers, two tigers,
> Running fast, running fast,
> One of them has no eyes,
> One of them has no ears,
> How very strange! How very strange!

Both boys stop eating and stare at me intently as I sing. This is rather unnerving. When I finish the mother smiles at me politely and the six-year-old leans across the table and in perfect English says:

'Your pronunciation is awful.'

My gaze flicks briefly to his mother, but she is closing her eyes and going to her happy place.

We're back on the road and younger son has been reinvigorated by his lunch (and mine). If ever a small child didn't need re-invigorating, it's this one. He has an array of toys, mementos from a dozen other days of keeping busy while daddy works. One of these is a pencil sharpener in the shape of a cannon, which he is pretending to fire under the seats, killing hundreds of tiny massed troops. He is interspersing the sounds of artillery fire with cries of the dying and wounded, clutching his stomach as he mimes vomiting blood and writhes in the foot well. From time to time, he bounces up and sticks the cannon into the sides of our faces, simultaneously shouting 'BANG!' at point-blank auditory range.

It is all undoubtedly inventive and despite being slightly horrified by the gory fixations of this tiny child, Chris and I cluck gently at him, like a pair of reborn Joyce Grenfells:

'No really, George, don't stick the cannon all the way into the ear. Think of the blood!'

'BANG!' shouts the tiny terrorist, 'BANG! BANG!'

'Let's be kind to mummy, George, I think she's going to cry.'

'BANG! BANG! Pencil sharpener is bomb! Explodes! You die!'

Blimey, his English really is very good.

We are all relieved to hear that we are heading for the Botanic Gardens. I am imagining large open spaces where small people can run in circles and large people can hide behind bushes. Screaming like banshees the children disappear in the direction of a river while their mother jogs after them, calling their names in a futile gesture of authority. Chris and I walk out of the sun and under the shade of the giant Pokok Pukul Limas – the five o'clock trees, so called because their leaves fold up at sunset and unfold just after sunrise. The air is filled with woody, earthy smells and our clothes cling to us in the humid embrace of early afternoon. We walk and walk, and would happily stay here the rest of the day but there are workshops to visit and small children to be wrangled into minivans.

As we set off again the smallest son appears between our seats and starts to climb up the side of Chris. He sticks the cannon down Chris's T-shirt: 'Pencil sharpener is bomb! Explodes! You die!'

Chris laughs.

Tiny terrorist is angry: 'No! You die! You die!'

Chris clutches his stomach and groans dramatically, slumping sideward. Tiny terrorist sticks his face into Chris. 'DIE!' he screams, as the drivers' shoulders creep further and further towards his ears, 'DIE! DIE! DIE! DIE! DIE!'

Chris sinks further back into his seat as small boy manages the impressive feat of advancing on him from a position directly behind him. His mother is staring fixedly out of the window. I don't blame her. She has the look of a woman on the edge.

The tiny terrorist is gripping Chris with one small angry hand; his fingers like tensioned steel. His eyes glitter with something: energy, anger, wilful joy. I can't read him. He is wild yet controlled and I can't reconcile those two conditions. There is play and there is menace and in this child the two have come together.

His face presses in on us. 'Pencil sharpener is bomb! Explodes! You die! DIE! DIE! DIE! DIE! DIE! DIE! DIE! DIE! DIE! DIE! DIE! DIE! DIE! DIE! DIE! DIE! DIE! DIE!'

I wonder if he has daddy issues.

By 3.00 p.m. the boys' mother has nothing left. She is wrung out. She sits in the back of the minivan as we make our last visit and her boys climb all over her and jump up and down on the driver's seat.

Our tour completed, Chris and I sink back into the leather seats of the minivan. The doors slide shut and we purr through the dense Malaysian greens, a late afternoon sky sinking low over the van as we move back towards George Town. All is quiet. At least one of the children is asleep against his drowsy mother. Chris squeezes my hand and takes off his glasses. I lean into his shoulder and together we slip into a warm, comfortable doze.

'PENCIL SHARPENER IS BOMB! EXPLODES! YOU DIE!'

The tiny terrorist has launched himself onto Chris's lap and is miming exploding all over us.

He emits a wild cackle:

'PENCIL SHARPENER IS BOMB! EXPLODES! YOU DIE! PENCIL SHARPENER IS BOMB! EXPLODES! YOU DIE! PENCIL SHARPENER IS BOMB! EXPLODES! YOU DIE!'

'F—,' Chris starts to swear but then stops himself. I look back at the mother who is staying resolutely asleep. In fact, you can see her staying asleep with all her will through this stationery-based attack.

The tiny terrorist is now jabbing Chris in his stomach and swatting him on the arms. Chris remains resolutely still. Pinned to the spot by a mixture of fear, human decency and innate Britishness. The tiny terrorist leans in threatening to push said pencil sharper up Chris's hairy nasal passages.

'PENCIL SHARPENER IS BOMB! EXPLODES! YOU DIE!'

Chris's eyes flick briefly towards me. I want to save him. I really do. But I don't know what to do with the small, wild creature. I mean, if his mother doesn't know how to calm him down, where am I going to start?

The walls of George Town glow with a smooth rosy light as the van slides through the quiet streets. The tiny terrorist climbs off Chris's lap and slips down into the well behind us where he proceeds to throw himself against the back of our seats.

'Still want children?' I ask Chris as we rocket together towards the dashboard.

'Our children won't be like this.'

'Course they won't,' I say.

Finally released by our infant hijacker we wander the streets of Little India watching gaggles of Malaysians and tourists queue up for *nasi kandar* and squid biryani: the sweet smell of fried food and roasting shellfish at once comforting and tortuous. On a whitewashed corner a lovely Indian restaurant is covered with painted vines and naive, multi-coloured figures. We squint through the windows. The interior is like a warm, brown cocoon.

'Let's go here.'

The restaurant is small, long and thin, richly decorated with draping fabric down the banisters and across the ceiling. On the wall, painted arbours flicked with gold frame each table and the deep window wells glow buttery yellow with the occasional leaf and vine swirling across the yellow plaster. A lovely young woman shows us to a table down one long side. We order a selection of curries and rice dishes and before they arrive our waitress brings huge, bright green banana leaves and places one before each of us.

'This is plate,' she tells us, smiling.

All over India and Malaysia food is served on chopped and washed banana leaves instead of plates. Purists believe that it imparts a delicate flavour to the food, though many people would question this. I can't say that I notice any subtle enhancements to the taste, but it is certainly a very beautiful way to present your food.

Our baltis and biryanis arrive, fragrant and shiny with *ghee*, in copper bowls like tiny cauldrons. We landscape our banana leaves with curry and rice and so pretty is the resultant diorama that it seems a shame to eat. The restaurant is lit by dim lamps and tea lights and the air itself seems to glow yellow-brown around us. Thick with the air of a warm, Malaysian night, our senses fill with jasmine, cumin, curry leaves and the sharp scents of chilli pepper and lime. We drink tepid white wine and hold hands over the table, laughing about the small boy and his poor, exhausted mother.

Chris is imagining the family table, filled with chatter and food. Him and me surrounded by children and hefty portions of whatever I've chosen to cook that day.

'But we won't ever do this again,' I say. 'We won't sit in restaurants together and drink warm white wine. We won't run away to Malaysia. We won't live out of rucksacks and go wherever we feel like, night or day. What if our future lies in a minivan with a small child shouting, "Die!" at us a thousand times a day?'

'It won't be like that,' Chris says, ever the optimist where families are concerned.

I nod to our surroundings, 'But it won't be like this either. We won't travel. I mean, maybe a weekend camping in the Brecon Beacons. But are you ready to say goodbye to this?'

Chris looks at me surprised. 'Yes,' he says, 'aren't you?'

'I want a baby. And I want to have it at home,' I say. 'I mean, I can't have children and travel the world. If I have to choose, then of course, I choose children. But still,' I say, 'still...'

'I'm sick of travelling.' Chris is matter of fact. 'I want to go back home. I want to have a home. I want a job. You can't mourn leaving here. It isn't the death of anything. It's just the next thing we do.'

We walk slowly back through the streets, bubbling inside with curry and wine and tropical warmth. In this moment, as I stand on the brink of great change – of a new family and a life of commitment – I keep looking back over my shoulder towards the hungry ghosts: those alive and those dead, those human and those abstract. The ghosts of people I've lost; the ghosts of childhood ambition; the ghosts of the billion women and mothers who came before me. I feel a fear of moving on before I am resolved. Of becoming a mother before I am at peace with everything that being a mother means. And yet as I walk through the dark streets turning these thoughts over and over with a fevered hand, I know that no one is ever truly resolved. I am not going to wake up one day and feel at peace with everything that has happened and accepting of everything that might be lost or gained by becoming a mother. This is not a Ladybird book. There are no simple answers. And if I wait for resolution – for certainty – I will remain frozen in time. Sometimes in life you just have to keep on walking even if you don't really know where it is you're going.

Kari kapitan
Captain's curry

This is a *Nyonya* dish from Penang and it really is one of the best and most interesting curries I have ever tasted. The spice paste contains a brilliant mixture of sweetness, sourness and heat: it's like all the flavours of Malaysia have been gathered into one bowl. Here the meat version is made with chicken but pork, beef and prawns can also used. Some cooks recommend that you sprinkle the meat with salt and turmeric and leave it in the fridge overnight to marinate first. If you do this remember to take your meat out of the fridge 30 minutes before you're going to cook with it. This curry is typically served with steamed rice on the side but it would also work well served with roti or another kind of flatbread.

Serves 4
Preparation and cooking time: 45 minutes

Groundnut oil
600 g chicken or 2 large aubergines, either should be cut into large pieces
2 large potatoes, peeled and cut into small chunks
1 tomato, quartered
4 kaffir lime leaves, chopped
350 ml coconut milk
1 tbsp dark soy sauce
1 tbsp palm sugar or brown sugar
2 tbsp lime juice

Spice paste:
8 shallots, peeled and chopped
Half a red onion, peeled and chopped

3 fresh chillies, chopped

2 tsp turmeric

2 cloves garlic

3-cm piece of ginger, peeled

3-cm piece of galangal, peeled

2 stalks lemongrass

3 candlenuts (if not can't find these, use 12 unsalted cashew nuts)

½ tsp *belacan* (Malaysian dried krill paste, available from many Asian supermarkets) or ½ tsp *miso* paste for the vegetarian version

80 ml groundnut or other mild-tasting oil

Pound together all the ingredients for the spice paste with a pestle and mortar or blend in a blender. Set aside.

Heat 4 tbsp oil in a wok and fry chicken or aubergine pieces until browned. Set aside, leaving any excess oil in the wok.

Cook the spice paste in the wok over a medium heat. If it starts to burn add a splash of coconut milk to loosen it. When it is fragrant add the cooked chicken or aubergine, and potato and tomato and stir to coat them in the spice paste. Cook over a medium heat for 5 minutes then add the lime leaves and coconut milk.

Simmer everything for 10 minutes. Taste and adjust seasoning using liberal amounts of soy sauce, sugar and lime juice: the amounts given in the ingredients list are just a starting point.

Chapter 12

The Conversation

I am lying in bed in a hostel room in Kuala Lumpur. The light is filtering through the amber-yellow curtains and the sounds of the market drift up from the street below. Chris is asleep beside me, his yellow hair tousled on the pillow. He breathes deeply, lost in sleep. The day is warm already and a very slight breeze stirs the curtains in front of the open windows.

My heart is full. Full of emotion: good, bad and surprising. I can feel these countries filling me up with colour and fragrance, touch and taste. My senses have been overwhelmed by beauty and strangeness. Memories of the past months tumble through my mind on waking. I feel full of relief and love. Relief at trials past and love for the cornerstones of my life: my family, my friends and Chris. Love for the strangers we have met along the way and the sheer wonder of this extraordinary world that I am lucky enough to travel through. The fear is still here too, but she is not so strong today. Not as strong as love and wonder, anyway. We have only another week left out here and I want to savour every moment.

Far away a market radio chimes out the hour telling me it is 6.00 a.m. One hawker is shouting in Malay, another in Mandarin, a third in Cantonese. Nesting in a line below our window, grey pigeons and mottled doves coo and cry.

One of the things I'm going to miss most about Asia is the markets. Don't get me wrong, I love markets in the UK too. I spent an unreasonable amount of time in my late teens hanging around Camden Lock, when everything was a bit grimy and the smell of weed mixed with the smell of samosas wafted around the tie-dyed, lace-up kaftans; the racks of 1960s miniskirts; handmade candles in the shape of kissing dolphins and boxes of second-hand LPs by The Specials and Jimmy Cliff. These days, street markets – the ones where people actually talk to each other and you can buy cheap batteries and large pastel-coloured knickers and second-hand tea sets – are few and far between. In places of any wealth, markets are now farmers' markets that operate in a state of middle-class hush, filled as they are with people terrified that they might have to buy an unwanted wheel of Camembert out of embarrassment.

A market without sound is a sad, decapitated beast. Markets are where you go to people watch, to get your morning fix of conversational back and forth. They are friend to the old and isolated; the mum or dad who lives in a world of children's babble; the writer who hasn't spoken to anyone in three days; the singleton, the stranger and the newcomer. You can lose yourself in a busy market, buy or not buy. An entire culture is spread before you, on the stalls and in the people. There you will find a culture's food, their household adornments, their religious paraphernalia and their clothes. You will hear their language, watch how they interact; you can learn the habits of a culture from watching how people shop.

Asian markets are loud, bustling, vibrant, smelly, captivating whirls of activity. For our final week in Asia we are booked into a cheap hostel in Kuala Lumpur (or KL as it's almost universally known in Asia) right on top of Chinatown's Jalan Petaling market. I lie on my stomach on the bed in our room and stare happily down into the depths of the market which runs all day and most of the night. By day it has a slightly disconsolate air. Stall upon stall of cheap, copied goods: 'Chanel' perfume, 'Gucci' glasses, 'Hilfiger' polo shirts, 'Rolex' watches and 'D&G' handbags. Wan-faced Westerners troop along in little huddles, clutching their backpacks to their chests and staring at the shiny phalanxes of watches and necklaces and the racks of Rooney shirts.

Behind the stalls, hidden from the zombified tourist groups, are the real shops of Chinatown: the fabric shops; the children's clothes emporium complete with tiny three-piece suits for special occasions; the Chinese tea houses and cafes selling morning *congee* and *dim sum*. And hidden away behind all of this is the other market, the food market, the place where the Chinese restaurant owners shop. A tiny alley is piled high with plastic crates of peppers, cabbage, *bok choi* and water nettle. Birds twitter in the rafters and the cramped space rings with the sound of haggling, bantering voices. Pyramids of flat fish, prawns and frogs lie on piles of ice and live crabs and lobsters wave their claws in white crates. Fishmongers and butchers are at work everywhere, skinning and scaling, cutting and plucking, killing chickens to order.

Malaysia is a country whose history and cuisine have been shaped by her unusual geographical spread. Divided into two land masses, Peninsular Malaysia is found at the southern tip of Thailand while East Malaysia lies to the north of one of Indonesia's many islands.

Malaysia has been inhabited for tens of thousands of years but she owes much of her modern historical progress to her position as a trading post for the great countries of Asia. As early as the first century both China and India had established trading ports on Malay soil and today roughly 40 per cent of the world's trade still travels through the Strait of Malacca. The country's trade position made her enormously attractive to foreign empires. From 1511 Malacca was ruled by the Portuguese; followed by the Dutch from 1641. In 1786 the British Empire took hold of Penang, a crucial island trading post, and by 1824 the Empire had control of Singapore, Malacca and Labuan.

The invasion of Malaya by Japan during World War Two led to the growth of nationalism and the birth of an independence movement. After a number of British experiments in reorganising the Malayan territories, Malaya was granted independence in August 1957. Independent Malaya renamed herself Malaysia, before splitting from Singapore in 1963.

Malaysia's ethnic mix, her culture and her cuisine have all benefited from immigration and global trade. The taste of curry in Malaysia often combines centuries of Asian influence. Indian traders working in the ports of Malaysia in the sixteenth and seventeenth centuries brought with them the ingredients and knowledge of Gujarati and southern Indian cookery: curry pastes based on onion, garlic and ginger, a generous hand with oils and chillies and the use of tomatoes. Traders from Sumatra and Indonesia brought galangal, kaffir lime leaves and cloves. Chinese traders contributed star anise and soy sauce as an alternative to the native fish paste. From Malay's home-grown cuisine came a widespread use of lemongrass and coconut milk.

All three major cuisines now bear the imprint of the others. On the streets of KL and George Town you'll find Chinese food made with coconut milk and fish paste; bowls of Indian noodles topped with tofu, egg, bean sprouts and sliced cabbage; and dishes like the Malay fish stew ikan asam pedas flavoured with tamarind, chilli, tomatoes, okra and Vietnamese coriander.

KL is also famous for its architecture, not least for its iconic twin towers. We visit the Sky Bridge that links the Petronas Towers and gaze across the city, 170 metres above street level. Below the towers lies an expanse of landscaped parkland and beyond that more towers and a huge, sprawling but surprisingly green city, which reaches out to the tree-clad hills beyond. On sunny days the shadows from the towers lie like great grey fingers over several city blocks.

KL is just 160 years old and has only been the country's capital since 1896. Her architecture is a wonderful, if slightly confused, jumble of styles and influences. Her large colonial buildings, such as Central Market or Kuala Lumpur railway station, were concocted from a strange and fanciful combination of Spanish and Moorish influences with the odd Tudor flourish thrown in for good measure. The pastel-coloured shop fronts, which survive from the 1890s, are straight out of an eastern European town square, though the style was probably imported by way of Penang.

Meanwhile, KL has channelled some of her considerable wealth into financing strikingly original modern buildings. The black and white tiles on the roof of the National Library form patterns seen in traditional Malay fabric, but are strangely reminiscent of Scandinavian Fair Isle sweaters. The Istana Budaya – Palace of

Culture – is an entertainment complex with more than a passing resemblance to Sydney Opera House or a particularly ostentatious nun's wimple (depending from which direction you approach it). It is in fact modelled on a moon kite in flight and its multiple turquoise roofs with their white undersides soar above the visitor.

Everyone, but everyone, recommends the Islamic Arts Museum to us, so we make it one of our first calls. We arrive via an unpromising walk through some dimly-lit subways. But then the tangle of A-roads gives way to Kuala Lumpur's Lake Gardens: home to a bird park and a butterfly house, a vast mosque and the huge, blazingly white building which is the Islamic Arts Museum. You enter through a capacious iwan (the entranceway to a sacred place) decorated in deep blue tiles bearing flowers and vines symbolising the tree of life.

Islamic art does not mean art that discusses and illustrates the teachings of Islam. It is the artistic product of all those countries where Islam was a significant force over the past 1,400 years. And as such it's extremely diverse and often secular. There are weapons from India and beds from China, shawls from Malaya and carpets from Persia, wooden chests from Spain and whole rooms – including walls and ceilings – transported from Syria.

Here it is in all its glory: the conversation. This is the thing that has drawn me in ever since we first arrived here. The transfer of ideas, of art, of food, of belief from one part of the world to another.

As you travel you find that the same dishes turn up again and again, transliterated from one country to another, moving backwards and forwards on the waterways and over those shifting borders. The classic Khmer dish *loc lac* (shaking beef) derives from the Vietnamese standard *thit bo luc lac*, yet in Cambodia it is regarded proudly as a home-grown national dish. On our travels we have drunk beer from a German brewery on the banks of the Yellow Sea and walked through a Garden of Allah in central China. The Islamic arabesques on the banisters in the Peranakan Mansion in Penang spent the best part of a millennium travelling along the Silk Road from Persia to India, then west again to England before being fashioned and fitted for a Chinese house in Malaysia. The French mansions of Vietnam and Cambodia are covered now with creeping vines and jungle flowers but working people eat their lunch of curry with freshly baked baguette. These are the wages of colonialism, of cultural exchange, of shared enthusiasm for food, for art, for religion and ideas.

We walk into an exhibition on the influence of Islamic Art on the West. In the first millennium Islamic artefacts were mainly prized for their economic worth but from the medieval period onwards the aesthetic influence of Islam started to reach beyond its borders. The Empress Josephine of France, wife of Napoleon, bought huge quantities of Kashmir shawls and wore them constantly. She set in train a vogue for Kashmir-style shawls that spread across western Europe. In Scotland, the weaving town of Paisley started to create their own imitations. And this is why the famous teardrop motif with its bent tip, which is known as boteh in Kashmir, is better known as paisley in the UK.

In the early twentieth century, collections of Islamic art and artefacts started to be shown in large exhibitions around Europe. Charles Rennie Mackintosh, in his early work as a textile designer, used Javanese batik as his inspiration: creating bold abstract fabric that looked as if it had been block printed. In London, William Morris was busy designing everything from fabric to furniture, merging styles found in British medieval art with decorative tropes from India, China and Persia.

Henri Matisse was heavily influenced by geometric designs from Moorish Spain and his work with cut outs shows how he began to flatten and intensify his colours. The illustrator Hergé owed a great debt to Persian miniatures: his *ligne claire* (clear line) style in The Adventures of Tintin comic strips with its bright colours and lack of shading is based upon the vibrant paintings of Iran in the late middle ages. Léon Bakst used the clothes and colours he saw in Eastern art to create costumes for the Ballets Russes. M. C. Escher leapt upon Islam's celebration of playful and ambitious geometry as inspiration for his tricky tessellations.

The conversation gives me hope. The conversation speaks of progress, change, accommodation. The conversation is not a linear thing. It isn't simple or cohesive. It doesn't have an end point. In part it mirrors the conversations we have with ourselves. These images and fragments that have followed me round Asia – memories of childhood and travel, food and family – have been part of a conversation I've been having with myself. A conversation about settling down and becoming a mother. A conversation about identity. Outside my normal life, I am free to sift through the people I have been and the things that I have done trying to find some sense of who I am now and who I want to be. I want to be a writer and am scared of losing that part of myself. I long for children but fear the changes that motherhood will bring. I want to be with Chris but I have cherished the emotional safety of the single life. I know what scares me and why it scares me. But I cannot stand still. I have to keep walking: on into the unknown. Because I only have this one life, this one shot at human adventure.

By night, Jalan Petaling market really comes to life. As darkness falls the street is lit with yellow and red paper lanterns. The evening market throngs with Westerners and Malaysians; Chinese, Thai and Japanese visitors.

The restaurants do a roaring trade, feeding *ma po tofu*, rice with prawns and bottles of Asahi beer to people crowded round red plastic tables: eating dinner out in the street, in among the throng. Portable fans whir all around us, cooling the cooks and sellers, for the evening is hotter than I ever imagined evening could be. Chinese pop blares from tinny radios on counters; Asian rap pumps from somewhere behind the counterfeit shirts. The whole street is pulsating like water bubbling and flowing over rocks, a rippling sea of bodies dancing around tables, stalls and human obstacles.

There are stalls selling flatbread, ten different kinds. Fruit stalls and fruit shake stalls, which mix any selection of fruit together and deposit the result into a plastic cup. There is open-air hot pot, or steamboat as it's called in this part of the world. Stalls are heaped with ready-made kebabs of meat and vegetables and deep pots of stock bubble and steam on the kerb ready for you to dip your kebab and take a bite. Over wildly flaming cauldrons, chefs cook clay pot chicken in black, lidded vessels. Streaming with sweat, their barely covered hands dip constantly into the fiery rows to check the chicken, wipe the rims of the pots and sprinkle spring onions over whatever is ready to eat. Chinese families gather around Formica tables near a noodle stand eating bowls of noodles in broth topped with sliced beef: a variation on the lovely dish we ate in Guilin and Yangshuo.

Here is the conversation in edible form. Noodles from China in a stock laced with spices from India and garnished with herbs from Thailand. Here is the food of Islam and Buddhism, Imperial China and modern Malaysia: steaming in hot, fragrant lines. Here is the impulse that unites us: the impulse to feed others, to delight with our cooking, to transform the everyday ingredient into something worth savouring and remembering. Here is trade and nurture, the wages of colonialism and the profits of travel: all brought together on one night in one marketplace.

We sit and drink beer and watch the world swim round us. Even at 9.00 p.m. it's easily 25 degrees Celsius. In a few days we'll be on a plane and heading back to Britain. I understand now why people come here and never leave. The temptations of a warmer climate are many. The average Westerner can live high on relatively little. The food is plentiful and exciting. The culture of the night is convivial and celebratory. If we weren't about to try for a family I could see myself staying, maybe for two years or five. But not forever.

It's oddly unfashionable to say that you love Britain. And that depresses me. Because I do love Britain. It's a set of beautiful islands full of verdant hills and gorse-covered moors, slow-moving rivers and quiet mountains, night-blue lakes and pale, endless beaches. It's a land of diversity – much as Malaysia is – built on thousands of years of immigration and intermarriage. We have the benefit of being four nations rather than one. There is a superabundance of history, architecture, design, literature and scientific innovation: enough to inspire and entertain us a hundred lifetimes over. We are a grumpily tolerant bunch for the most part, given to rubbing along with others despite the best attempts of our print media to play divide and rule. Yes, we have flaws but so do all nations. I refuse to hate my homeland. I refuse to say its day is over and it's on the way out. We don't need an empire: we have a world of riches nestled within our shores and the reach and outlook to welcome in still more.

Chris and I are slightly giddy tonight. There's an end of term feeling about this last stay in KL. Our house is ours again, ours to start a family in. These travels that I have loved, have wrung me out all the same. All those trains and boats and cycle rides. Lugging our rucksacks up and down hills and riverbanks and in and out of boats. The constant swirl of other languages. The getting lost three times a day. I have been free and anonymous for nine months now. I have drifted away from Chris and found my way back. I have drifted away from my country and my life but now I'm on my way home.

We are trying to pick and choose, a little from every culture, for our last week in Asia. We head to Brickfields for a final banana leaf meal. Brickfields is the Little India of Kuala Lumpur. The shops here are filled with racks of red and purple saris which glitter at you as you pass; silver and blue bangles stacked 70 deep like little leaning towers of Pisa, giant silver earrings with layer upon layer of silver scales, drops and leaves. As you wander down the streets your senses fill with frying onions, cumin and curry leaf. Many of the buildings and signs are painted brightly in shades of terracotta and burnt earth, sea blue and warm grey.

The smell of incense tells us we're nearing a temple and sure enough a mountain of gods, spirits, trees and flame-topped rainbows await us above the doorway of a Hindu temple. A tower of jewel-bright columns, covered with tableaux of smiling gods and worshippers stands more than a dozen metres high, topped with gold-leafed urns. I am transported back to Angkor, where the grey and brown stone was once painted and leafed in gold, just like this. So much life and passion is channelled in these colours that it's hard to tear your eyes away.

On Jalan Scott we stop for lunch and find ourselves enacting all the old rituals of our courtship. I pick my way through little bowls and basins of food, pointing to the mustard seeds in the dish of okra, finding the prickle of fennel and cumin seed in the dhal. We spoon our banana leaves high with hills of pickled vegetables and dip curling leaves of deep-fried bread into a blood-red curry. We raise a bottle of cold beer to our adventures in Asia and toast to the adventures yet to come.

We are flying home with SriLankan Airlines, via Colombo because they are the only airline tickets we can afford. We joke about our 20-hour stopover and the grimness of budget travel but as it happens we couldn't be more wrong. On arrival in Colombo we discover that we will not be spending a day sitting in a departure lounge because the airline puts up its travellers in all-inclusive beachfront hotels.

At Colombo airport we are loaded onto buses and driven out of the city. After 30 minutes travelling along the coast we arrive at a large and comfortable beach hotel in Negombo and are allocated a double room with an ocean view. Chris looks out the window at the untrammelled stretch of sand.

'Now's the moment. We're at the beach. It isn't raining. Where's the tennis game?'

'In Colombo airport, in our one piece of checked baggage,' I tell him.

We head out onto a great smooth ochre-coloured beach, dotted with palm trees. Young boys fly kites as the afternoon light starts to fade and locals come down after work to sit along the edges of the dunes and smoke.

Surf from the Laccadive Sea pounds hard against the beach and we take our shoes off and run through the white crests. The world is turning pink around us as we splash through the warm waves, thigh-deep in a rosy sea. We don't talk. We laugh. Watch the sky change. Hold hands. And when the world is on the edge of darkness we squelch damply back to the hotel and eat curry and rice gazing out over an electric indigo sea.

Pajeri nenas
Pineapple curry

Don't be put off by how sweet this dish sounds. This curry is actually hot and rich and sour with lots of delicate Indian spicing. The little explosions of sweetness when you bite into the pineapple help to balance the sour notes in the sauce and the resulting curry is truly delicious. Serve with plain rice or flatbread.

Serves 2
Preparation and cooking time: 50 minutes

1 pineapple, washed
250 g uncooked prawns (optional), peeled and washed
3 tbsp *ghee* or butter
1 onion, sliced finely
2 cloves garlic, chopped
1–2-cm piece of ginger, peeled and finely chopped
100 g raisins
4 curry leaves
2 red chillies, deseeded and sliced
2 tomatoes, cut into wedges
1 tbsp sugar
1 tbsp *kerisik* (recipe below or available from some Asian grocery stores)
1 tsp salt (more or less to taste)
350 ml coconut milk

Wet spice mix:
3 shallots, peeled

1 dried chilli
1 fresh red chilli, top removed
3 cloves garlic, peeled
½ tsp *belacan* (see *kari kapitan* recipe in Chapter 11) or
miso paste for vegetarians

Dry spice mix:
1 cinnamon stick
2 star anise
4 cardamom pods

Take the flesh out of your pineapple and cut into bite-size chunks. Put the wet spice mix ingredients in a blender to make a paste.

Heat a large saucepan or wok. Add *ghee* and then fry all the ingredients for the dry spice mix, until fragrant. Now add the wet spice paste and the onion, garlic, ginger, raisins and curry leaves. Cook for 4 minutes. If using prawns, add them halfway through this 4-minute cooking time. You want the prawns to be lightly stir-fried before adding the final ingredients.

Add the pineapple chunks, chilli, tomatoes, sugar, kerisik and a little salt. Cook through for 2–3 minutes and then add the coconut milk. Simmer for 30 minutes or until curry thickens. Taste and season with extra salt and sugar as necessary.

Additions and tips:
For a more authentic and drier curry omit the coconut milk.

If you can't find *kerisik*, you can make it at home. Take 500 g of fresh grated coconut. Heat a dry wok over a low flame and add the coconut. Cook for 15 minutes, stirring constantly. The coconut should go brown and release an aroma. Remove the coconut and grind it (in a spice grinder ideally, otherwise a large pestle and mortar). When it starts to look oily, it's properly ground. Freeze the excess, to be used another day.

Nasi tomato
Tomato rice

This popular Malaysian dish is normally served on the side of curries. It can be eaten topped with fried onions and slices of hard-boiled egg for a light meal, as pictured. Alternatively, you can add raisins and cashew nuts for texture. For an extra-rich version you can substitute half of the water for coconut milk.

Serves 2
Preparation and cooking time: 50 minutes

2 tbsp *ghee* or butter
Half an onion, finely chopped
2 cloves garlic, crushed
1 star anise
1 clove
2–3-cm piece of cinnamon
1 cardamom pod
180 g basmati rice, washed and drained
250 g passata
1 tbsp tomato puree
Pinch of salt
250 ml water
1 spring onion, finely chopped

Heat the *ghee* in a saucepan or wok over a medium heat. Start to cook the onions. After 1 minute add garlic, star anise, clove, cinnamon stick and cardamom pod. Cook until onions are translucent and spices are aromatic.

Add the rice and stir to coat the grains with the ghee mixture. Add the passata, tomato puree, salt and water and bring to the boil. Stir to combine, and then reduce the heat to low and cover the pan or wok. The rice should now be simmered for around 15–20 minutes until almost all the water has been completely absorbed.

Take off the heat, fork through the rice and leave covered for 10–15 minutes to allow the rice to finish absorbing the water. When ready to serve, garnish with spring onion.

Epilogue

We arrive home to a warm Welsh autumn. Walking down our road, firmly strapped to our giant rucksacks, Chris dragging the Lotus bag and Korean tennis game, I feel like a visitor from another planet. We have been away so long and yet everything looks the same. We unlock the door and drop our things in the hall. Hearts in our mouths we go and unlock the basement room. I make Chris do it, I said goodbye to my possessions months ago and am ready for them all to be gone.

Chris fiddles with the lock and levers open the door. It is dark inside, multiple curtains drawn against the light. He goes inside, or at least as far as he can manage. There is silence for more than a minute. I sit miserably at the dining room table.

When he comes to find me his brow is furrowed.

'Well?' I ask.

'I can't remember what it looked like when we left.'

'Is anything gone?'

'I don't think so. Come and look.'

I go inside. Floor to ceiling there are piles of archive boxes. There have been landslips here and there. Boxes have toppled, spilling endless paperbacks over the floor. I ease my way round several towers and peer beneath the desk. There's my Mac. Untouched. The curtains and the windows and the doors look as they were. It's all quite Haversham. But it's all there.

I feel a trickle of relief then a glow of warmth and then a flood of misery that now I have to unpack all this crap. I think I rather liked my alternate reality in which everything disappeared apart from the odd emotional treasure. We buy a bottle of cava from Best One and an Indian takeaway and try to figure out what to do next.

We have survived it all. The stress, the rift, the rivers, the mountains, the earthquakes. We're back home. And we love each other. And we're ready to try for a child. I will go back to my work for Radio 4. Chris has lots of freelance marketing work to keep us going through the pregnancy and beyond. Things are good. We can do this. It's time.

All those months we'd been away in Asia we'd been caught up in our own adventures and hadn't fully appreciated the seismic economic shifts going on back home and in the States. On 13 October the British government bails out five of our major banks. By late October, as corporations across Europe and the US freeze their marketing budgets, Chris's work evaporates taking with it three-quarters of our joint income.

On 6 November, I sit up and watch Barack Obama elected forty-fourth President of the United States. My period is late. I cry. A lot.

On 8 November, we go out. Chris's mother Mary has bought us tickets to see Leonard Cohen in Cardiff as a welcome home present. Chris eats his dinner and most of mine. I still haven't taken a test or told Chris what's happening but I am riding a wild, wet sea of nausea.

'Are you sure you're OK, love?' Chris asks.

Oh, for God's sake. Where's *The Pursuit of Bloody Happyness* when you need it?

We watch Leonard Cohen. He is wonderful. People are still reeling from Obama's election. All night I wait for Cohen to sing 'Democracy'. I need that moment of release. I feel stunned, poleaxed, by the increasingly undeniable fact that I'm going to have a child. The audience is on its feet, clapping, cheering. Cohen plays three songs for encore. And then, there it is, the military drums, the bass and Cohen sings of democracy coming through a hole in the air. His 'Tiananmen Square' recalls the protests of 1989, but I hear the name and a flood of images pass through me. Ding Jitang wiping the ink from his hands; bulldozers resting on the *hutong* neighbourhoods of Beijing; silent families waiting outside a faceless police station and the empty imperial residences of Liugong Village that nature and the farmers are starting to reclaim. And I cry. I sob. I may have actually howled.

Because I am pregnant. Because I don't know what Chris is going to do without a job. Because my baby is going to be born into a world where an Afro-American man can become president. Which means that change is possible. Which means that there is a world of progress waiting for us and for him or her. Which means that democracy will one day break its way out of the popular imagination and become something real and flawed and tangible in China and Vietnam and Cambodia...

I am full of hope and terror.

EPILOGUE

Alice arrives – by emergency caesarean – in the middle of July 2009. The view outside the hospital window in Wales is of a tree-covered mountainside and on days of summer storms mist rolls down the side and lies all around us like a rumpled eiderdown smothering the view. Alice is tall and muscular with long powerful legs; she looks like she spent the pregnancy swimming vigorous laps of my womb.

My mother comes to visit.

'She doesn't really look like a baby at all. She looks like a tiny adult.'

But we agree that she is beautiful. Her kick is so powerful that at only a few weeks of age she will use it to propel herself off the changing table. We had planned to give her a middle name that was delicate and musical but this baby looks like she could shoot thunderbolts from her fingertips. So her middle name becomes Juno. She is a singularly uncompromising little god.

Chris has started work at a hostel for the homeless in Cardiff. He has no paternity leave so Alice and I sit at home together and stare at one another. In between stares I feed her for what feels like 20 hours a day. Motherhood turns out to be much more straightforward than I expected: I love her more than I have ever loved anyone and I am permanently exhausted. These seem to be the main features of parenthood.

Seven weeks after Alice's arrival Chris announces that next Wednesday we're going to hire a car and buy rugs at Ikea. Money is extremely tight so this seems an odd extravagance but I like the idea of a day out. We'll drive down the coast in the afternoon and go and look at something.

The day arrives and we pack Alice into her car seat and set off for the great blue box. Having bought our rugs Chris tells me that there's a brilliant waterfall that we should go and see over in the Vale of Neath. The car makes Alice sleep so I am happy to go pretty much anywhere. We drive west past crooked hills and lines of trees fringed with orange- and ochre-coloured leaves. In a little over an hour we're there. We take Alice out of the car, pack her into her sling and pay our money to the National Trust. Inside there is a cafe and many steps up to a series of falls. As I start to slowly climb these, Chris leaves my side and begins to dash about like a demented wasp.

'What?' I ask him, 'What is it?'

'It's wrong!' he tells me, his voice full of panic, 'We have to leave.'

'But we just got here.'

'It's the wrong waterfall!'

'Chris, I really don't care. The baby's asleep. There's a tearoom.'

'We have to get back in the car.'

We get back in the car. Chris now has a wild look about him. He is muttering under his breath. We drive in circles for a bit and Alice goes back to sleep. We arrive at a car park beside a line of forested hills. We take Alice out of the car and pack her into her sling. She starts to cry so we take her out of the sling and feed her. Then we put her back in the sling and go and speak to the man in the little ticket booth. He hands us a map and points towards a path running beside a river.

'It's a nice walk to the Lady Falls,' he tells us.

We set off with Chris carrying the sling and walk the narrow dirt track along the side of the river. After a while the path gets steeper and we start to climb, scrambling over tree roots and fallen branches. My body is still battered and aching from pregnancy and the caesarean.

'Can we go back now?' I ask. But Chris is far, far ahead of me, striding onwards with Alice – awake and crying – in the sling around his neck. We make a wrong turning and have to go back. Finally we find the right path. It is shaded from the late afternoon sun by the canopy of trees overhead. Chris hurries along, rocking Alice and talking to her as he goes.

At the end of the path we come to a clearing. Water falls in white spears from a shelf of rock above a dark pool rippled with green reflections from the trees and bushes all around. Birds sing in the trees and the sound of the water rippling and churning seems to own the space: as if the waterfall is saying 'this is mine'. Alice has finally gone back to sleep so we stand on the muddy edge of the pool and listen to the quiet. Wobbling gently due to the baby tied around his neck Chris drops down on one knee. I stare at him. He produces a small blue box from his pocket and holds it open. The ring inside glitters and winks at me.

'Miranda, I love you and I want us to spend the rest of our lives together. Will you marry me?'

I stare at him and I stare at the ring. I can't speak. Chris's face becomes just a little more tense and I notice that he is moving very slowly backwards: his whole body sliding through the mud and down the slope towards the pool.

'Yes!' I say, 'Yes. You can get up now. I'd love to marry you!'

Chris grabs a tree root and hauls himself upright. On the walk back along the river he asks me if I know the date.

'9 September.'

'9 September 2009. 999.'

'Because this is an emergency proposal?'

'No! Because when I was working at the Internet company in Beijing I told all my friends there how I wanted to ask you to marry me. And they said that I must choose an auspicious date. In China the number 9 is symbolic of something long lasting – something eternal – so they said we should get married on 9 September 2009. But, you know, then you got pregnant. And we didn't have any money. So I thought I'd propose instead.'

'It was a good proposal.'

'Why, thank you. I gave it some thought.'

It is a long engagement. It doesn't do to rush these things.

Acknowledgements

This book started with a very speculative four-sentence-long email to Jennifer Barclay in the summer of 2011. Without her encouragement and guidance, it would never have been written. So, first and foremost, I must say thank you to Jen.

Thank you to Emma, my long-time reader, unofficial editor, occasional collaborator, gentle critic and constant cheerleader. Every writer should have an Emma.

Thank you to all the people who have lent me encouragement: my parents, my parents-in-law, my friends, all the teachers who cared enough to take an interest.

And finally, I am a writer with two small children who would not be a writer if she didn't have a Chris who was so very good at taking Ali and Ros to the library, doing bedtime and generally keeping them happy and amused while Mummy writes. Thank you. And I love you.

Bibliography

Chapter 1

Library of Chinese Classics, *Selected Poems of Su Shi Xu Yuanchong* (2008–12, Hunan Publishing House).

Chapter 5

Weiwei, Ai, *From Ai Weiwei's Blog: Writings, Interviews and Digital Rants 2006–2009*. Translated by Lee Ambrozy. (The MIT Press).

Chapter 6

Wen Zhengming, *Travelling to Tianping Mountain* (c. 1508). Hanging scroll. Ink on paper.

Chapter 11

Chee, Johny *A Tapestry of Baba Poetry*. Verse translation in English by Lim Poh Keng (2007, Areca Books).

Have you enjoyed this book?
If so, why not write a review on your favourite website?

If you're interested in finding out more about our books,
find us on Facebook at **Summersdale Publishers** and follow
us on Twitter at **@Summersdale**.

Thanks very much for buying this Summersdale book.

www.summersdale.com

**For more information on Miranda's travels, writing
and recipes, visit mirandaemmerson.com.**